EXETER COLLEGE

The First 700 Years

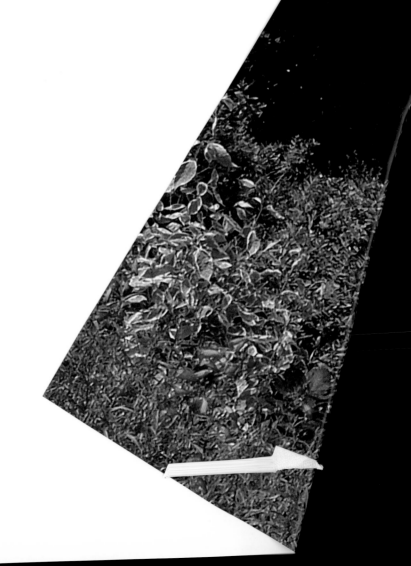

EXETER COLLEGE

The First 700 Years

Edited by **Frances Cairncross**
Co-edited by **Hannah Parham**
With **Dr John Maddicott** and **Christopher Kirwan**

THIRD MILLENNIUM
PUBLISHING, LONDON

Exeter College: The First 700 Years
2013 © Exeter College, Oxford and
Third Millennium Publishing Limited

First published in 2013 by Third Millennium Publishing Limited,
a subsidiary of Third Millennium Information Limited.

2–5 Benjamin Street
London
United Kingdom
EC1M 5QL
www.tmiltd.com

ISBN: 978 1 906507 88 6

British Library Cataloguing in Publication Data
A CIP catalogue record for this book is available from the British Library.

Picture Credits

The principal photographer for this book was Hugh Palmer (1970, Literae
Humaniores). Unless otherwise noted, illustrations have been provided by Exeter
College, drawn from the extensive College Archives, ancient and modern.

Alison Brooks Architects 51; Courtesy of Martin Amis 180; Courtesy of Alan
Bennett 175T+C; Bodleian Library 7B, 29BR, 32–3; Bridgeman Art Library
93B; Bridgeman Art Library/Milwaukee Art Museum 63B; Courtesy of Reeta
Chakrabarti 183; Courtesy of Sir Ronald Cohen 155TR; Mark Dobson, Exeter
University 15; Jill Floyd 17T; Courtesy of Richard Ford 92TL; Gillman & Soame
99; With kind permission of Clare Hastings 164; Henry Ashby and A.H. Fogg
91L; Imperial War Museum 160–1; John Soane Museum 31; Library of Congress,
Washington D.C. 76T; Courtesy London Oratory School 67; Mary Evans 69BR;
National Portrait Gallery 22L, 22R, 70T, 71, 77, 86B, 88; Courtesy of Joseph Nye
176; *Oxford Mail* 97, 181; Oxfordshire History Centre 50; PCF 96; Courtesy of the
President and Fellows of Trinity College, Oxford 108T; Press Association 126T+B,
152TR; Rector and Scholars of Exeter College, Oxford 23T, 24BL, 24TR, 25TR,
26BL, 28T, 29BL, 29BL, 30, 42T, 62, 65TL, 72T, 98, 100, 108B, 134, 139, 111T,
135BR, 136–7, 138T, 154C; John Salmon 17B; Thanks to Sanders of Oxford
23B; © Jean Schormans, Réunion des musées nationaux, France. Reproduced with
pemission 135BL; John Shobbrook 94T, 95, 169TR; Richard Stevens 44T; Courtesy
of Admiral Stansfield Turner 173; Victoria and Albert Museum 75TR; Matthew
Wilson 24TL, 26TR, 28BR 34, 90L+R, 103; Williams College, Massachusetts 151

Project Editor	Clare Howell
Design	Matthew Wilson
Photography	Hugh Palmer (1970, Literae Humaniores)
	Additional photography by Rob Judges,
	Max Mulvany (2009, Fine Art), Fiona Potter (2011,
	Modern Languages and Linguistics), Matthew
	Baldwin, Kinsey Forsdyke and John Rux-Burton
Additional Research	Penelope Baker (Archivist) and Joanna Bowring (Librarian)
Production	Bonnie Murray
Reprographics	Studio Fasoli, Verona, Italy
Printing	Gorenjski Tisk, Slovenia

Contents

Preface 6

Section 1: FOUNDATION AND THE EARLY YEARS

Section 2: ARCHITECTURE AND LANDSCAPE

Section 3: VICTORIAN REVIVAL

Section 4: THE TWENTIETH CENTURY

Section 5: COLLEGE LIFE

Section 6: RECOLLECTIONS

Section 7: *FLOREAT EXON*

Preface

FRANCES CAIRNCROSS, RECTOR

Exeter College is an extraordinary institution. It has existed on the same site for 700 years, undertaking the same task, that of educating the young. Very few other institutions – parliaments, companies, even countries – have been in uninterrupted existence for such a length of time.

Throughout its long life, Exeter has provided a window on a changing world. This book tells of the turmoil of civil war that almost emptied the College of students; of the Victorian rows over religion which split the Fellowship; of the ravages of the First World War on the brightest young men; and of the 20th-century debate over the admission of women that divided students and academics.

Exeter has lived through good centuries and bad. It has had periods of devastation, most dramatically in its first century of existence when plague swept through England. It has had periods of great success, as in the first years of the 17th century when the College grew rapidly, built elegantly, and attracted some of the country's finest scholars. It has taught plenty of impoverished students such as John Prideaux, its finest Rector, who paid his way by working in the buttery. It has also taught the occasional aristocrat, such as Anthony Ashley Cooper, the patron of John Locke, who was later made 1st Earl of Shaftesbury for his work to restore the monarchy after the English Civil War.

But the story of the College is not just an account of 700 years of higher education. Every Oxford college is a marketplace for ideas, and a forum for

influential friendships and connections. What makes Exeter special is its walk-on role in many aspects of the country's religious, political, intellectual and artistic life through seven centuries.

Over the years, the College has produced a great many churchmen, distinguished and undistinguished, reflecting Oxford's long role as a training ground for priests. Their number includes a Catholic martyr and saint, Ralph Sherwin, Fellow from 1568; one of the translators of the King James Bible, Thomas Holland; Samuel Wesley, father of the more famous John and Charles; and Frederick Temple, the Archbishop of Canterbury who crowned Edward VII. However, it is probably fair to say that no Exonian divine achieved as wide a fame as Parson Jack Russell, who bred the line of dogs that carry his name.

In the arts, the College brought together as undergraduates William Morris and Edward Burne-Jones, two key figures in the Pre-Raphaelite movement, from vastly different social backgrounds; its library provided the first stimulus for the young J. R. R. Tolkien to dream up his magical world of hobbits and wizards; and Richard Burton, one of the most successful British actors, combined a short wartime course at Exeter with one of his first performances, in *Measure for Measure* directed by Exeter's English don, Nevill Coghill. In sport, a young Roger Bannister, the first man to run a mile in under four minutes, trained at the College that had, a century earlier, first begun to develop athletics as a competitive sport.

An Exeter historian, Hubert Parry, grew up to become the composer who wrote the music for 'Jerusalem'; an Exeter classicist, Charles Lyell, became one of the earliest geologists and a key influence on Charles Darwin; an Exeter English student of the 1960s called Nick became, as Philip Pullman, the creator of Jordan College and the author of *His Dark Materials*; another Exonian, Alan Bennett, developed the sketches that launched post-war British satire (and his career as a writer) with performances to the College JCR.

In the past century, Exeter – like Britain – has grown more international. It has educated international statesmen, such as Liaquat Ali Khan, who went on to become the first prime minister of Pakistan; writers such as Qian Zhongshu, one of China's most famous novelists; and Sir Sydney Kentridge QC, the South African lawyer who represented the family of Stephen Biko at the inquest into his death.

Through Exeter's Front Quad have passed, over the centuries, not only future writers, scientists, statesmen and dog-breeders, but thousands of young men, many of whom would never have won a place today. The College's stock-in-trade for much of its existence was the education of West Countrymen. Those links have weakened over the past century and a half; more recently, the young men have been joined by young women, in roughly equal proportions; and more recently still, Exeter's graduate students, a rarity half a century ago, have come to account for a third of the student body.

Much that happens today in Exeter College would be unrecognisable to those who passed through the Front Quad or ate in the 1618 Hall in centuries gone by. But some things continue. The College still, like its founder, Walter de Stapeldon, aspires to educate students regardless of their financial resources; like Sir William Petre who revived the College in the late 16th century, it aims for academic excellence; and like Rector John Prideaux, it is drawing on the generosity of its alumni and friends to help build new accommodation.

This book sets out to give a sense of the College's rich heritage. It has benefited considerably from the work of one of Oxford's most distinguished medieval historians, Dr John Maddicott (Tutorial Fellow from 1969 to 2006 and now Emeritus Fellow), whose scholarly book on the College from 1314 to 1592 is forthcoming. It contains new work by my co-editor, Hannah Parham, on the evolution of the College's physical site, and on some of the dramatic changes in the 20th century, including the admission of women. The College *Register*, successively edited in recent years by James Hiddleston, John Maddicott and latterly by Christopher Kirwan, who has also helped with the final stages of this book, has provided an invaluable resource. There are also reminiscences from many of Exeter's Old Members – some happy, some wistful, some scurrilous – which capture the changing tone of undergraduate life in the past 60 years.

This is a book written partly by Exonians, partly about Exonians – and undoubtedly for Exonians. It is the history of a remarkable institution, but also a record of the collective memory of Exonians. Enjoy it.

THE FIRST HALF-MILLENNIUM

FRANCES CAIRNCROSS

Exeter College had a modest start, followed by an equally modest two and a half centuries. Its early years were not auspicious. It began poor, remained poor, and emerged briefly from obscurity in the late 16th and early 17th centuries. Then it relapsed into torpor until its late-Victorian renaissance. It is not a glorious history, but it is one that probably reflects the reality of Oxford life through the ages more realistically than does the story of some grander colleges.

The city in which Exeter College began life in 1314 had started to emerge a century earlier as a centre for scholarship, packed with student life. The infant University had already acquired a chancellor and a modest library. The little streets that criss-crossed the centre of this Midlands market town would have been crammed with students from many parts of England, as well as other 'nations'. The Oxford of 1314, however, was almost unimaginably different from early 21st-century Oxford.

There were probably about 1,000 to 1,500 students. They would have to find money for rent, keep, teaching fees, and incidentals like books. Most of them, unless they were student members of a monastic house or friary, lived in 'halls' (*aulae*). Such a hall was generally a large house, with a central space for eating and lectures, and sets of usually poky rooms for students, hired by an enterprising graduate who would normally be a *magister* – a holder of an MA degree – and a teacher. He would rent the space to students whose behaviour and studies he undertook to the University to oversee. There were at least 123 of them in 1313, often housing students from a particular part of the country. This regional segregation gave the young men some protection from student fights, which usually pitted one part of the country against another.

By 1314, the demand for student accommodation was booming. The citizens of Oxford, then as now, were annoyed. 'The multitude of masters and scholars grows from day to day' grumbled a citizen in 1303.[1] The halls continued to multiply. But they relied on an uncertain source of income: the rents they charged their students. However, by 1314, there were three experiments under way in Oxford which offered greater stability. University, Merton and Balliol were colleges, not halls, and all were endowed – massively, in Merton's case. That allowed them to support their

Previous pages: *Watercolour of the Fellows' Garden by William Turner of Oxford (1789–1862).*

Left: *Medieval teaching.*

Opposite: *The foundation charter drawn up on 4 April 1314 is still in the College Archives. Walter de Stapeldon grants the church of Gwinear, Cornwall, with its tithes, to the chapter of Exeter Cathedral for the benefit of Stapeldon Hall.*

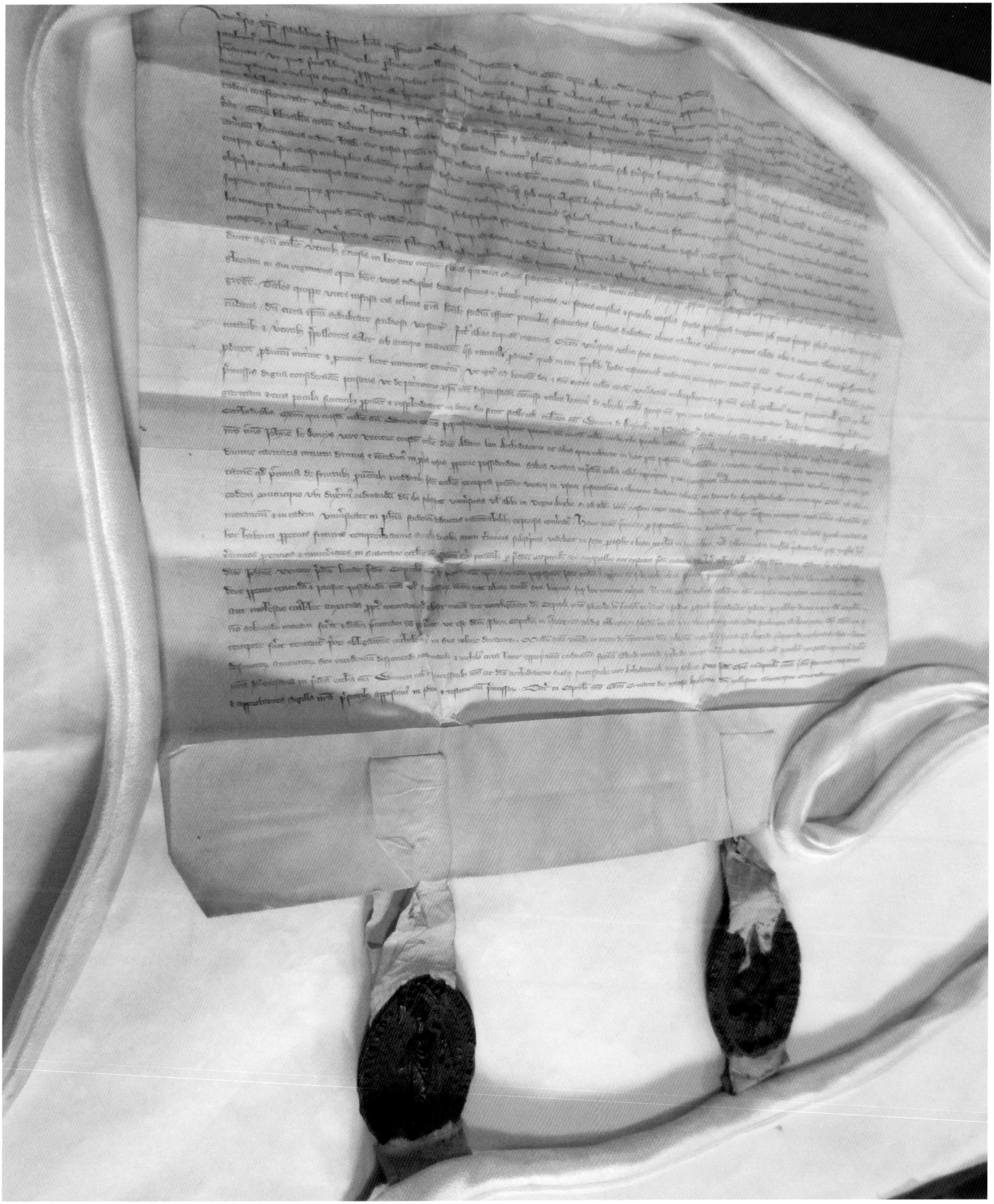

students, rather than the other way around. They owned their sites. This, together with a constitution and a structure that gave them durability and administrative sophistication, provided continuity and stability. Their way of life was regulated by statute in a predictable way, rather than by the whim of a particular principal.

This was the model that Walter de Stapeldon, Bishop of Exeter, followed in founding the body that he named Stapeldon Hall. Stapeldon's own remarkable life is described later in this book *(see pages 14–16)*, but he had come to Oxford as a young man, probably in the 1270s, to take his BA and his MA. He had subsequently prospered as a bishop in his home see of Exeter, managing a difficult and distant territory with impressive energy, business acumen and practical skills. Not surprisingly, he rose to become Treasurer of England and a confidant of Edward II. But his position near the centre of power of a particularly oppressive government eventually cost him his life. In 1326, an infuriated London mob decapitated Stapeldon on the steps of St Paul's Cathedral, thus giving Exeter College the unique and unfortunate distinction of being Oxford's only college to be founded by a man who was subsequently murdered.

The Foundation of the College

A good birth date for the young College is 4 April 1314, the date of Stapeldon's charter making over the tithes of the Cornish church of Gwinear to support the new foundation. Three days later, the Bishop acquired Hart Hall *(see page 17)*, which housed the students for the first year of the College's existence and which generated rental income that continued to make a small contribution to the College's finances for half a millennium. In 1315, the scholars decamped to St Stephen's Hall, running east from Palmer's Tower through what is now the Rector's Garden, parallel with the main building of the Library. On this cramped site, gradually expanded and realigned, the College has remained ever since. Walk past Palmer's Tower into that narrow alleyway that leads to the Rector's Garden, and you walk in the steps of 700 years of Exeter students.

The earliest College statutes were issued in April 1316, just two years after the College had come into being. Stapeldon's statutes are succinct, well thought

out, and practical. The College was to comprise 12 scholars, plus a priest to serve as a chaplain. The scholars were to come from the Bishop's own diocese, eight from Devon and four from Cornwall, and they were to be elected only after they had supported themselves for two years on the BA course. Stapeldon clearly wanted men with some proven staying power.

The scholars were to receive commons of 10d a week (about 4p, or ten times the daily pay of a skilled farm worker), and an additional annual allowance of 10s. (50p). The Rector and Chaplain were to receive double this. The first set of scholars was to be chosen by Stapeldon; thereafter they were to be elected by the other scholars as vacancies arose. Each scholar was to serve for a probationary year; thereafter he might be dismissed if two-thirds of the other scholars so decided. Disputations were to take place twice a week, and there were to be two in Logic to one in Natural Philosophy.

The first Rector was nominated by Stapeldon and to serve for a year; thereafter the scholars were to elect the Rector annually from among their own number.

Letters patent from Edward II permitting Walter de Stapeldon to grant two properties to 12 scholars studying in the University of Oxford, 10 May 1314. The 12 scholars constituted the founding body of Stapeldon Hall.

Right: *A doctoral disputation in a late medieval university.*

His role was to allocate rooms on the basis of seniority (still a dreaded task); to engage servants, administer funds, decide quarrels and enforce obedience. Together with the Chaplain and the Senior Fellow, he held the keys to the chest that contained the College's cash, papers, books and deeds. (This chest, or one very like it, once stood in the Old Bursary and still stands in the hallway outside the Bursar's office.) Finally, on the day of his admission, every scholar must swear to observe the statutes – as every Fellow still does.

Two things are striking about these regulations. First, they make no formal division between the teachers and the taught. Both undergraduates reading for a BA and their seniors reading for an MA or acting as lecturers, who might be teaching the juniors, were all equally members of the College, drawing the same allowances and receiving the same privileges. To put it anachronistically, dons and undergraduates were on a par. Secondly, the statutes give extraordinary power to these scholars, some of them probably 19-year-olds, most of them probably around 25 years old. Once the College had got going, it was to be the scholars who elected the Rector, who elected other scholars, and who decided on removals after the probationary year. The Rector himself was more like a temporary presiding officer and bursar than a ruler. So the scholars gained a training in the exercise of responsibility – and, of course, a good education which was largely paid for.

How was it paid for? Exeter's endowment was modest from the start, and all through the Middle Ages the College was relatively poor. The original endowment of the Gwinear tithes meant in practice that the College gained the sale price of one-tenth of the parish's agricultural produce, which would normally have gone to the parish priest. Stapeldon appointed the Dean and Chapter of Exeter Cathedral to act as middlemen and trustees, presumably collecting the produce and selling it, before handing over the proceeds to the College in two annual instalments. The Gwinear income was worth about £20 a year, and it was the College's main source of funds until 1355, when the College acquired similar control over the income from another church, St Mary's, Long Wittenham, in Oxfordshire. Together, these two churches provided a share of the College's income until the late 19th century.

Below: *Two James I gold coins discovered under the floorboards of the Lodge in the 19th century.*

Below right: *A medieval oak muniment chest, probably 14th-century, which may have housed key College documents and cash, still stands outside the Bursar's office today.*

►

13

WALTER DE STAPELDON *c.*1260–1326, FOUNDER OF EXETER COLLEGE

Walter de Stapeldon, the son of a Devon small farmer, was educated at Oxford. He says so, in the College's foundation charter, drawn up in April 1314 and still in the College archives. 'The University of Oxford', he says, 'which so greatly advanced us in the study of letters when we were young, nourished us, and promoted us, though we were unworthy.' Stapeldon's rise, to become Bishop of Exeter, diplomat and Treasurer of England, turned very much on his Oxford degree.

By the time he was elected Bishop of Exeter in 1307, Stapeldon was probably in his mid- to late-forties and about two-thirds of the way through his life. Three features of his character stand out. Firstly, he was clearly both clever and learned. He had not only become a *magister*, but he went back to Oxford later to study successfully for a higher degree in Civil and Canon law: a mark of exceptional distinction. After his death, about 90 books, mainly on Civil and Canon law, were found in his rooms in Exeter. Secondly, he was clearly a good practical man of business, with a local weight and influence which made his help very much worth having. But, thirdly, there was also a darker side to Stapeldon's character. As we will see, it was marked by a streak of hard acquisitiveness which led him towards the accumulation of wealth and property.

Stapeldon's election as bishop led him in two directions: first, into politics and diplomacy, and, second, into the management and pastoral care of a particularly difficult episcopal see.

Politics meant that he was in London two or three times a year. Edward II's accession in 1307, the year of Stapeldon's election, marked the start of a dismal period in English history. The King was idle and incompetent. Robert Bruce was leading the Scots towards victory in the North, and Bannockburn in 1314 was one of the greatest English military disasters of the Middle Ages. The King's favourites were a constant cause of trouble. And to cap it all, one of the worst famines of the Middle Ages devastated the country between 1314 and 1317, causing hundreds of thousands of deaths. Stapeldon was often present at court, although his role was increasingly that of diplomat and ambassador, deploying his close knowledge of Roman law and skills in advocacy.

As for the diocese of Exeter, it was remote, large, difficult to get round, and poor – the second poorest of all the English dioceses. Stapeldon had to travel almost incessantly. His main business was the business of any bishop: ordinations, confirmations, the dedication of churches, and the visitation of parishes and religious houses. One project particularly dear to Stapeldon was the rebuilding of his cathedral. He pressed forward with the replacement of Exeter's old Norman cathedral by the latest Gothic model. A great deal of the cathedral today is Stapeldon's work, notably the huge wooden episcopal throne, 60 feet high to the top of its spire, built with oak from the episcopal estates, and described by Pevsner as 'a monument of unprecedented grandeur'. Along with the College, Exeter Cathedral is Stapeldon's greatest surviving monument.

The bridge between Stapeldon's local and pastoral concerns and the College is his interest in education and learning. Behind it lay the need to produce an educated parish clergy. Since 1298 priests had been allowed to use the income from their benefices to support them while they took time off to study at university. But to do this they needed a licence from

Below: *The painted and gilded recumbent effigy of Walter de Stapeldon, Bishop of Exeter, adorns his tomb in Exeter Cathedral.*

Opposite: *The monumental bishop's throne in Exeter Cathedral. The 60ft-high, intricately carved oak canopy, conceived by Stapeldon, took a year to build and was completed in 1317. It is the largest and highest episcopal throne ever constructed.*

give, and the College had to compete with his other priorities: the year in which he gave about £55 to the College was also the year when he gave nearly £700 to the Cathedral building fund. But the fact that Exeter had an endowment, however slim, meant that Exeter could make available what was essentially a free education for poor but able students. Stapeldon's own memories of his time as an impoverished student at an unendowed Oxford hall some 40 years earlier may have played some part in his decision to found a college.

The foundation charter of 1314, which digresses at length on the value of learning, gives some idea of Stapeldon's larger aims. He saw the practical value in learning (and that meant serving the state as well as the church), but he also set value on learning almost as a good in itself, as a means of training the rational intellect. He also had one very personal motive. In the original statutes, Stapeldon laid down that for as long as his foundation should exist it should be known as 'Stapeldon Hall' – which only goes to show the vanity of human wishes because, by about 1470, 'Stapeldon Hall' had permanently given way to 'Exeter College'. Stapeldon's foundation was to be a living memorial to himself – and even if its name has changed, so it remains.

In the last phase of his life, between 1320 and 1326, Stapeldon became ever more embedded in the world of politics and government. From 1322 to 1325 he was Treasurer of England and right at the heart of Edward II's regime. But his high place at court was to do for him. Edward II's last years were probably the nearest medieval England came to a tyranny. Political violence, brutality and corruption were the order of the day. By the end of his reign Edward had £62,000 in cash in the treasury – probably a greater sum than any English king had ever amassed. As Treasurer, Stapeldon was responsible for collecting royal debts. In addition, he used his office to pile up a fortune for himself. One chronicle calls him a man 'greedy beyond measure'. He was particularly hated in London. He flaunted his wealth in at least two London town houses, one of them by Temple Bar. But he also apparently initiated financial measures that were tremendously damaging to Londoners.

When the end came it wasn't surprising that it came in London. In 1326 Queen Isabella, who had

their bishop; and Stapeldon granted more of these licences to study than any other bishop for whom we have figures. Here was a bishop who saw educated priests as a basic means of Christianising the laity.

The foundation of Exeter College was, of course, Stapeldon's greatest contribution to education and learning. The original endowment of the young College was pretty thin. It conspicuously lacked land, largely because Stapeldon had very little land to

fled her hated king for France, landed in Suffolk with an army. Stapeldon was denounced as an enemy of the Queen, and his house by Temple Bar was looted and burnt by the London mob. His jewels and silver were stolen and many of his books destroyed. Stapeldon immediately made for the safety of the Tower. But his way was blocked by the crowds and he then turned desperately to St Paul's for sanctuary. Outside the north door of the cathedral he was caught, dragged from his horse, stripped of his armour, and beheaded with a bread knife. A man called Robert of Hatfield later confessed to cutting off his head, and another man to supplying the bread knife.

The body was thrown into a pit, and the head sent to the Queen, but both were later reunited and buried in Exeter Cathedral in March 1327.

Stapeldon's career has the ingredients of a classic tragedy. From an unpromising background in the wilds of North Devon, he had hauled himself up by his own talents and through his Oxford training. He was a good man of business, a good organiser and administrator, a great benefactor to his cathedral, and a man who believed passionately in the need to educate and train a literate priesthood. His social conscience showed in the financial provision that he made for poor scholars and in particular for the poor scholars of Stapeldon Hall. Yet Stapeldon's abilities were his undoing. If he had kept clear of politics and the court, he might have been remembered simply as a generous benefactor to education and a virtuous and vigorous pastor. As it was, his abilities exposed him to the temptations of wealth and power which in the end cost him his life.

Stapeldon's will does not survive, but we do have the inventory and valuation of the goods found in the palace at Exeter. Among the items recorded in the Bishop's room were a pair of spectacles and three magnifying glasses; three sets of chess men; and leashes for hawks and hounds. But look at what else was found in the room: 1,006 French gold florins; 4,000 Florentine gold florins; £801 in English money; silver plate worth £515; and 92 rings. The whole hoard was worth more than £2,000. This old man, with his weak eyes and his fondness for chess, and his dogs and his hawks, was also inordinately rich.

John Maddicott
Emeritus Fellow in History

Left: *The magnificent, palm-like, tierceron vault in Exeter Cathedral is 300ft long – the longest complete stretch of Gothic vaulting in the world. It was paid for by Walter de Stapeldon, who contributed vast sums of money for the rebuilding of his cathedral.*

Below: *Statue of Walter de Stapeldon in the doorway of the College Chapel.*

MEDIEVAL HALLS:
HART HALL, ST STEPHEN'S HALL AND LA LAVANDERIE

Exeter College was founded on 4 April 1314, or at least that is the day on which Bishop Walter de Stapeldon gave the revenue from the rectory of Gwinear in Cornwall to support 12 scholars at Oxford. Three days later the Bishop found a home for his fledgling college: two buildings known as Hart Hall, on the site of the present Hertford College, and Arthur Hall which seems to have stood just to the north of St Peter in the east, on ground now occupied by New College. These he bought from a fellow West Countryman, Richard de Wydeslade, Precentor of Crediton. On 6 October 1315 the College moved to its present site, also purchased from a Westerner, Peter of Skelton, Rector of St Stephen's-by-Saltash in Cornwall. This was no virgin soil, however, but a row of tenements known as St Stephen's Hall and La Lavandrie. In the century that followed, the College acquired further halls and tenements: Hambury, Culverd, Sheld, St William's, Checker, Peter, Castel, Scott, Patrick and Fragnon.

But what did these ancient halls look like, and how did they function? None would have been above two storeys high. The principal space was, as the name implies, a hall with stone walls, an open-truss roof and a central hearth. At one end of the hall was a wood screen, creating a passage which led to the outside door (in the arrangement that came to be common in most dining halls in Oxford). Beyond the screen's passage were chambers for sleeping, perhaps just a room on each floor. Most halls had some timber outbuildings for cooking, animals and ablutions, and a small courtyard or garden.

It is possible to get some sense of the appearance of the halls by exploring behind the shops at 106–107 The High. Here stands Oxford's sole-surviving medieval academic residence, Tackley's Inn, comprising two chambers and a hall just 33ft by 20ft on plan. St Stephen's Hall was no doubt similar and the scholars may have slept six to a room in the early years, dining communally in the hall whose fire provided the only source of warmth.

Hannah Parham
(2001, Modern History)

The tithes of both the church at Gwinear, Cornwall (top) *and St Mary's, Long Wittenham, Oxfordshire* (above) *were bestowed on Exeter by Walter de Stapeldon.*

The College site was also an important resource. In October 1315, Stapeldon paid £40 for St Stephen's Hall, the first building on the present site. By the time of his death in 1326, piecemeal purchases had added another four halls and other tenements on the site; the central block filled the area of the Rector's Garden and the present Library annexe. Other properties were acquired around the city, most of them rented out for about £5 to £10 a year – so the total income (Gwinear tithes plus Oxford rents) was approximately £25 to £30 a year. Such a modest income meant that the College was often in deficit. There was enough to provide for the commons and allowances for Rector, Chaplain and scholars, but the problem lay in the upkeep of buildings (as every Bursar since 1314 has no doubt found). Building repairs could easily cost more than the buildings' rental value. Stapeldon himself stepped in several times in the 1320s to support the College, giving about £55 in 1325–26. But this was cash rather than endowment and it did little to improve the College's long-term position.

One of Stapeldon's intentions in founding Exeter College was clearly to make available a free education for poor but able students. After his death, his executors paid out small sums of money to about 40 poor scholars. Another goal was to create an educated priesthood with the knowledge and intellectual skills to educate the laity in their Christian duties. Most of the men whom Stapeldon and the College supported went on to careers as country priests in Devon and Cornwall, as did their successors for centuries. In addition, Stapeldon's statutes laid down that, for as long as his foundation should exist, it should be known as 'Stapeldon Hall'. Although, by the end of the 15th century, 'Stapeldon Hall' had become 'Exeter College', Stapeldon's foundation remains a lasting memorial to this visionary, flawed, tragic medieval figure.

A Medieval Democracy

For its first quarter-millennium, Stapeldon's college was inconspicuous. The reason was partly its comparative poverty – but also the restrictions that Stapeldon's statutes imposed on the range of subjects that the scholars could study, and the range of degrees that they could aspire to take. These confined Exeter scholars to the basic arts course, requiring only the Chaplain to study Theology or Canon law. So the College's academic ambitions were restricted from the start. The best scholars, when they became masters, had to migrate to other colleges if they were to continue to higher degrees. Among those who left in the early years were four who subsequently became Fellows of Oriel, founded a few years after Exeter.

Through the Middle Ages, Exeter College was tiny. It had a Rector, Chaplain and (after a while) 13 other scholars (or Fellows, as they soon came to call themselves). Their lives would have been spartan. Many walked to College from their West Country homes, returning only at the end of their studies. The youngest would have shared a sparsely furnished room with other youngsters, with an older MA or BA to keep order. They would have studied for three hours in the morning and again in the afternoon. The statutes demanded that they spoke French or Latin at dinner and wore black shoes, presumably as a mark of sobriety and decorum.

This was a surprisingly egalitarian society. Every Fellow received the same allowance as the most recently elected newcomer, who might be an undergraduate ten or 12 years his junior, and would have the same vote in the election of the Rector. So the College was, in a sense, a democracy of young men, jointly choosing their colleagues and (for a year at a time) their leader.

But there must have been some tension between the masters who had gained their MAs (some of whom were Heads of Halls and had pupils of their own), and the younger Fellows who had gained only their BAs. The masters, as members of the University, had some jurisdiction over these younger men outside the College's ambit – but the College statutes made no distinction. One of the masters was generally the Principal of Hart Hall, which belonged to Exeter but had more scholars, giving the role more weight than a Fellowship of the College itself. There is a hint of the tensions in the College in a document drawn up by John French, who was Rector in 1539.

He complains about the insolence of the younger Fellows of the College and attempts to enforce more respectful behaviour towards the masters and the regular attendance of the bachelors and other younger scholars at lectures, disputations and in the Library. But the Rector, with perhaps a year in office and no support from the statutes, must have found such a task almost impossible to sustain.

College Finances

For the first 250 years after its foundation the College's finances were precarious. The consequences for the size and shape of the infant College are the subject of new research by Dr John Maddicott, to be published in *Founders and Fellowship: The Early History of Exeter College, Oxford, 1314–1592*. The 14th century was one of turbulence and plague, killing off Fellows and reducing rental income; and the economic depression of the 15th century lowered income still further, by cutting rents and tithes. As a result, Fellows' allowances were reduced, as was spending on the College's one extravagance, the annual feast. Essential maintenance building work was postponed. The most expensive venture between 1440 and 1470 was the construction of a new lavatory, at a cost of £4 12s. It all sounds glumly familiar. Only in 1479, when the College was given the Cornish rectory of Menheniot, worth £20 a year, was there a return to modest comfort.

As time went by, a further source of income appeared: the College began to rent rooms to students who were not 'on the foundation' – i.e. not Fellows – and provide them with some teaching as well as accommodation. These formed the nucleus of the later body of undergraduate commoners. The College also occasionally began to rent rooms to mature scholars, who wanted somewhere to continue their studies. For instance, William Grocyn, who had been a Fellow at New College, rented rooms in Exeter for two years on his return from Italy in 1491. His lectures stimulated a new interest in learning Greek, which he shared with Cornelius Vitelli, another scholar of Greek, who lived in rooms in Exeter at the same time.

These two are among Exeter's few scholarly names from its first 300 years of existence. The constraints of Stapeldon's statutes and the modesty of the endowment limited its ambitions and its reputation. Halfway through the 16th century, that was all to change. ▶

SIR WILLIAM PETRE 1505/6–1572

Exeter has had two founders, both of them Devon farmers' sons who advanced in national politics on the back of an Oxford education. William Petre navigated his way through the Tudor court, a world almost as perilous as that of Edward II. But unlike Walter de Stapeldon, he avoided losing his head – in spite of serving four Tudor monarchs. He was a bureaucrat of consummate skill, who avoided the high public profile that ultimately led to the murder of Stapeldon.

He was born in 1505 or 1506, and came to Oxford as a law student in 1519 – though whether he studied at Exeter College as an undergraduate is not clear.

He was certainly clever: he became a Fellow of All Souls in 1523, and went on to study and then to practise law. In 1535, Petre began handling administration for Thomas Cromwell, the King's Chief Secretary. For the next five years, Petre was principally occupied with carrying out that great property transfer of the Tudor era, the Dissolution of the Monasteries.

He undertook the task with efficiency and fairness. He also used his position to build a substantial landholding, mainly in his native Devon and in Essex, where he visited the abbey of Barking and, once its lands had been surrendered to the crown, bought its manor of Ingatestone. This transaction might have been construed as the plundering of Church property, but during the reign of Queen Mary the Pope conveniently exonerated Petre from any such charge.

Petre redeveloped his new property, making good use of his contacts with the monasteries, for which all the most able architects worked. Since then Ingatestone Hall has been owned and occupied by 18 generations of the Petre family.

On Cromwell's fall in 1540 Petre's office lapsed. But he was soon appointed to the King's Council, his sharp mind and easy command of paperwork making him an invaluable public servant and administrator. When Henry VIII went on campaign in France, Petre was effectively left in charge of the national bureaucracy. When, a couple of years later, Henry's young son was crowned Edward VI, Petre became Secretary of State, a role he retained until his retirement in 1557.

In 1550 he was one of a group negotiating the return of Boulogne to the French. His diplomatic skills considerably reduced English compensation payments to the French. 'Ah!' said a French diplomat, 'We had gained the last two hundred thousand crowns without hostages, had it not been for that man who said nothing.'

On the death of the boy king, Petre once again showed his skill as a survivor. He was one of those who swore allegiance to Queen Jane in July, three days after Edward's death. Within less than a fortnight the coup had collapsed. Nimbly, Petre changed sides and proclaimed Mary Tudor as Queen. His agility paid off: a few days later, the new monarch spent the night at Ingatestone and reappointed Petre as Secretary of State.

Left: Portrait of Sir William Petre (1505/6–72); unknown artist, 1567.

Below: Sir William Petre's signature on his new College statutes, issued in 1566.

Now under his third Tudor monarch, Petre speedily took charge of restoring religious provisions that Edward had removed from the statutes. He helped to negotiate Mary's marriage to Philip of Spain. When Philip arrived to meet his bride, Petre was in attendance, and after the King's departure he became one of the councillors through whom Philip channelled his directives to England. The civil servant who had advised Protestant Edward was now at the heart of the administration of Catholic Mary and her Spanish husband. In fact, Petre may have been sympathetic to the reunion with Rome. His family remained Catholic for generations after his death.

When Mary died, her sister Elizabeth retained Petre as a councillor, but he does not seem to have held any office of state. In retirement he turned his attention to Exeter. He rewrote the College statutes and munificently endowed eight new Fellowships, mostly with properties he had bought from the Crown. The College also benefited from his passion for books, many doubtless acquired through his frequent requests for English envoys abroad to send him rare books.

And Petre left Oxford one further legacy. Dorothy, his daughter by his first wife, married Nicholas Wadham. On her husband's death in 1609, this generous woman adhered to her husband's (unwritten) wish, and founded another Oxford college. In this case, unlike that of Stapeldon or Petre, the College retained its founders' names, and Dorothy's statue overlooks Wadham's main quad.

FAC

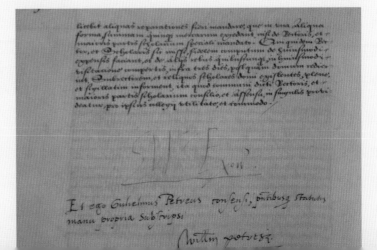

Petre's Refoundation: A Golden Age

The Rector's Account for 1564 includes a charge of 14d (about 6p) 'for wine and sugar at the reception of Mr Woodward with whom we talked over the plan and design of Sir William Petre'. In March 1566 Queen Elizabeth gave authority to the Bishop of Exeter to draw up new statutes, with Petre's advice. Petre's statutes, backed by his generosity, restored the fortunes of the College and gave it the security and structure on which its subsequent growth was based. He not only guaranteed the long-term financial survival of Exeter College, but also transformed its administrative structure, making the College easier to manage and better designed to provide effective teaching.

In particular, he brought three important changes to its corporate life. First, the bulk of his benefaction went to endow eight new Fellowships, to be held by men from counties in which he and his heirs held land. That added Somerset, Dorset, Oxfordshire and Essex to the geographical pool from which the College could recruit its senior members, increasing the opportunity to choose men of academic promise. The posts were principally financed with the gift of four Oxfordshire rectories: Kidlington, Merton, South Newington and Yarnton. With all of these parishes the modern College has continuing ties.

Second, Petre revised Stapeldon's statutes. A hierarchy of College offices was created, including that of Sub-Rector, which remains in existence today. The Rector was now to be at least 30 years old and to hold an MA. By attaching to his office the vicarage of Kidlington, Petre ensured that the Rector should have a secure and substantial income (even if he might be largely absent from the parish). Both the Rector and ▶

THE TITLE OF RECTOR

Few aspects of Oxford's many confusions baffle outsiders more than the range of titles that colleges bestow on their heads – known as Heads of House. There are Wardens, Masters, Presidents, Provosts, many Principals and a single Dean. But only one other college – nearby Lincoln – has a Rector.

Why the title? There are two theories. In his chapter on 'The Early Colleges' in the first volume of *The History of the University of Oxford* (1984), Dr Roger Highfield has argued that the title reflected the fact that the Dean and Chapter took over as corporate Rectors of Gwinear. It was therefore appropriate that the head of the institution which they served with the Gwinear money should also be titled 'Rector'.

An alternative explanation, by Mark Buck, the biographer of Walter de Stapeldon, is that Oxford's Proctors were originally called Rectors, as they were at the University of Paris. Like the Rector, the Proctors were annually elected within the first eight days of Michaelmas Term, and like him, they had to render annual accounts. That analogy may explain the name.

However, it took a while for the title to gain a hold. When Bishop Burghersh of Lincoln in 1321 granted a licence for the erection of a chantry, or small chapel, in the College, he referred to the head of Exeter as 'Master'. Confusingly, when Oriel College was founded a few years after Exeter, its first head, Adam of Brome, was initially called Rector. Within a couple of years, he had become 'Provost' – a title usually used for an official of a collegiate church such as St Martin le Grand in London or St George's Windsor. At least the Provost of Oriel was thereby saved from the frequent fate of the Rector of Exeter College: to receive letters addressed to the Reverend Such-and-Such, on the assumption that she or he is still a cleric.

FAC

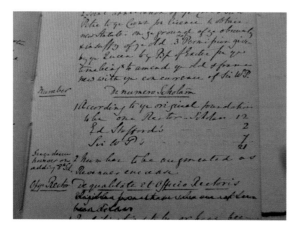

Left: *Entries in the Rector's notebook of duties; late 16th/ early 17th century.*

Above: *Page from the book of Sir William Petre's statutes, with College resolutions, offered under the seal of the Bishop of Exeter, James Turberville; late 16th century.*

The arms principally associated with Exeter are described in the mysterious language of heraldry as follows: *Argent two bendlets nebuly within a bordure Sable charged with eight pairs of keys addorsed the bows interlaced and the wards upwards Or.*

There seems to be no direct evidence that Walter de Stapeldon ever used arms. No coat of arms appears upon his episcopal seal. However, the earliest version of the College seal, which may have been in use during Stapeldon's lifetime, incorporates a shield displaying two *bendlets wavy* (two wavy diagonal stripes), arms that were being used by the founder's brother, Sir Richard de Stapeldon, as early as 1311.

At some point, the basic arms were augmented by the bordure and keys, to create a distinctive shield that could suitably represent Walter de Stapeldon in particular. A pair of addorsed keys is the emblem associated with St Peter, to whom Exeter Cathedral is dedicated, and the two keys (together with the sword of St Paul) appear in the arms of the founder's bishopric of Exeter. This version of Sir Richard's arms seems to have come into existence a century or more after the Bishop's death.

The arms became equally associated with the College (which was of course called Stapeldon Hall in its early years). At all events, the College's use of the arms (with the bendlets clearly nebuly) was officially recognised in 1574.

However, confusingly, there is an alternative version of the shield, which incorporates the arms of Exeter's second founder, Sir William Petre. This alternative version is shown in impaled form: that is to say, with the two sets of arms combined into one shield, separated by a vertical dividing line. In heraldry, this arrangement usually denotes a marriage, the husband's arms being placed on the left of the shield and the wife's on the right. But it can also be used to represent other unions, for example when the arms of a bishopric are combined with the personal arms of the current bishop. In the case of Exeter, it is the founder and re-founder who are heraldically conjoined, de Stapeldon's arms being placed on the left and Petre's on the right.

Petre's arms are fairly complicated. In heraldic language, they are *Gules on a bend Or between two escallops Argent a Cornish chough Sable between two cinquefoils Azure on a chief Or a rose between two demi fleurs-do-lys Gules.* They seem to have been

granted to Sir William during Henry VIII's reign. The Tudors had an unfortunate tendency to clutter up their coats of arms, a practice that continued to bedevil heraldic design until quite recent times.

A simplified form of the Petre arms, used by Sir William's descendants, appears in the arms of Wadham College, which consist of an impaled shield representing the marriage of Nicholas Wadham and Sir William's daughter Dorothy Petre. Rather than have all of Sir William's bits and bobs crowding out the right-hand side of Exeter's shield, our College has on the whole preferred to display the de Stapeldon arms alone.

Patric Dickinson
(1969, Modern History)
Clarenceux King of Arms

Top: *The 1574 recording of the College's arms, incorporating the keys of St Peter, patron saint of Exeter Cathedral.*

Left: *Exeter's full shield (left) derives from Sir William Petre's arms (far left), impaled (combined) with those recorded in 1574 (above).*

the Fellows were henceforward to be appointed not by the year but for life. Once that change occurred, Rectors could and did have a much greater impact on the College's reputation and on the character of the students it educated.

Third, Petre made formal arrangements for the College's undergraduates, appointing a dean and a lector to oversee their teaching, and drawing up a timetable for the day's work. It began – at least in theory – with Logic lessons at 6 am and ended with Logic disputations at 6 pm. But Tudor students seem to have been as easily distracted as those of today. Other clauses in the new statutes forbade the keeping of hunting dogs, ferrets, rabbits, hawks and horses inside College and banned shooting within its boundaries. At 9.15 pm the gates were to be locked and the keys kept in the Rector's custody until morning. Petre, a hard-working bureaucrat all his life, was determined to impose a discipline that would prevent idleness and encourage directed study.

Religious Turbulence

Petre's refounded College began its new existence with a certain amount of turbulence. Through the religious upheavals of the Tudors, Exeter's sympathies remained strongly Catholic, perhaps because of its ties with the conservative counties of the West Country. John Neale, the first 'perpetual' Rector, was initially elected on the old annual basis in 1560 and then for life in 1566. But he was ejected in 1570 for refusing to attend the reformed services in Chapel. And several Fellows whom Petre appointed became prominent defenders of the old religion under Elizabeth I. Two of them died for it: Ralph Sherwin in 1581 and John Cornelius in 1594, both hanged, drawn and quartered. Sherwin is the only saint among Exeter's Fellows, canonised in 1970.

Indeed, Exeter's Catholic sympathies became so notorious that the Crown twice intervened to secure Protestant Rectors from outside the College: Thomas Glasier, elected in 1578, and Thomas Holland in 1592. Holland is buried in the chancel of the University Church. In choosing him, Queen Elizabeth showed her usual good judgment. Holland was Regius Professor of Divinity and one of the translators of the King James Bible. Under his rectorship, the College acquired a new eminence, attracting fine scholars as well as benefactions for both buildings and scholarships. The

Rector of Lincoln College, in his oration at Holland's funeral, recalled that his customary farewell before starting any lengthy journey was: 'I commend you to the love of God, and to the hatred of popery and superstition.' Not surprisingly, from this point on, the College's religious allegiances shifted, so that by the early 17th century it was known for its Puritanism.

Rector John Prideaux

Holland's successor, John Prideaux, continued the College's revival *(see page 25)*. He was Rector for 30 years, from 1612 to 1642, a span exceeded by only one other Rector in the College's history. He was a formidable and distinguished figure, with a sharp mind – and a sharp tongue. His skill as a Rector must have been tested by young men such as Anthony Ashley Cooper, later 1st Lord Shaftesbury and founder of the Whig Party *(see page 28)*.

However, under him, according to Anthony Wood, the 17th-century Oxford diarist, Exeter 'flourished more than any house in the University'. It began to attract undergraduates not just from the West Country but from other parts of England. In 1612 it had 183 students – a number not exceeded until late in the 19th century. Luckily for posterity, Exeter's magnificent Hall, built in 1618 on a scale that testified to the College's growing prosperity, could still just about accommodate that number.

Above left: The martyrdom of Ralph Sherwin, Fellow of Exeter, in 1581.

Above: Thomas Holland, Rector from 1592 to 1612, Regius Professor of Divinity and one of the translators of the King James Bible.

Indeed, the College benefited from three great benefactors at this time in its history. Sir John Peryam, whose portrait hangs in the Old Bursary, was the brother of Sir William Peryam, a Fellow of the College (his portrait is in the Hall). Sir John became alderman and Mayor of the city of Exeter, and is remembered in Peryam Buildings, the handsome row facing the Fellows' Garden. The Hall itself was built largely through the generosity of Sir John Acland, who had inherited lands in Devon and London, made two good marriages which added to his wealth, and died

Top right: *Portrait of Sir John Peryam (1540–1616); unknown artist, 1616.*

Right: *Exeter College Hall. The new Hall was built in 1618; from an engraving, published by Rudolph Ackermann in 1814.*

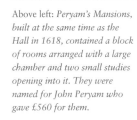

Charles had been its benefactor, endowing a Fellowship for scholars from the Channel Islands (which survives as an undergraduate scholarship); Prideaux had been Chaplain to the King's brother; and its students still came largely from the Royalist southwest. In the College Hall hangs a portrait of William Noy, who had been a student in the 1590s. He had worked with Sir Francis Bacon in the early 17th century; become MP for various Cornish constituencies from 1604 to the late 1620s; opposed the King on many issues, but without being a committed parliamentarian; he then became Attorney-General to Charles I (an apparent volte-face for which he was much criticised). He was partly responsible for the levying of ship money, and associated with some of the most unpopular features of Charles I's personal rule.

During the War, the King commandeered the College's silver plate in spite of the reluctance of the Fellows, who petitioned the King to be allowed to refuse. From earlier days, there remains only a fine silver chalice, given in 1610 by George Hollwaye, and a splendid pair of tall silver tankards presented to the College in 1628 by John, Lord Robartes, who had studied at Exeter shortly before the Civil War and went on to fight on the Parliamentary side. According to College legend it is in protest against his raid on the College's treasures that the portrait of Charles I hanging in the Hall behind High Table remains unilluminated. ▶

childless. He gave £800 of the £1,200 bill; while George Hakewill, of whom more in a moment, paid the lion's share of the cost of building the new Chapel. Exeter in the early years of the 17th century must have been the favourite college of every builder in Oxford.

The Civil War and After

Exonians played prominent roles in the events that led to the Civil War, and indeed in the War itself. Among them was William Strode, whom Charles I tried to arrest in 1642, and John Blackmore, one of the signatories of the King's death warrant. But Exeter almost certainly bred more Royalists than Cromwellians. Oxford as a whole was largely Royalist, but Exeter had particular reasons for loyalty: King

Above left: Peryam's Mansions, built at the same time as the Hall in 1618, contained a block of rooms arranged with a large chamber and two small studies opening into it. They were named for John Peryam who gave £560 for them.

Above: Portrait of Sir William Noy (1577–1634) by Cornelis Janssens van Ceulen.

Below far left: The portrait of Charles I (1600–49), which hangs behind High Table, is a copy after Anthony van Dyck, attributed to Henry Stone.

Below left: James I silver chalice, given by George Hollwaye in 1610.

Below: Pair of Charles I silver flagons presented by John Robartes, 2nd Baron Truro, in 1628.

RECTOR PRIDEAUX 1578–1650

John Prideaux, Exeter's most important Rector, came from a modest background. But his remarkable life shows how far an intelligent and ambitious man might go without a fortune.

He was the fourth son of a Devon farmer whose early death left Prideaux's mother with 12 children to bring up. He could sing, and so competed for a place at his local church at Harford. He failed to get it, but attracted the attention of a wealthy local lady who paid for him to stay a little longer at school.

In 1596, at the age of 18, he walked from Devon to Oxford, and worked his way through his undergraduate years in the buttery of Exeter College. For the rest of his life he kept the old leather breeches he had worn as a young man in order to show his students the social distance that diligence had raised him. Within five years of his walk to Oxford he had become a Fellow, and subsequently he was made Chaplain to King James I's son, Henry, Prince of Wales. The Prince died young, but not before he had secured Prideaux's election as Rector of the College in 1612.

Even before his long rectorship began, the young Prideaux was admired for his scholarship and his teaching skills. But he also combined humanity with his intellectual powers as a theologian. This, together with his moderate Calvinist sympathies, widened the geographical range of students and scholars that the College attracted. Most students still came from the West Country, but some now hailed from other parts of England, from Scotland and even from other parts of Europe.

A contemporary described him as a man of 'plain and downright behaviour', who enjoyed good relations with the young. His skill as a Tutor was captured in his textbooks and his manuscript notes, some of which were later used by John Aubrey, the diarist, to teach logic and moral philosophy. But he also seems to have handled deftly the self-important young Anthony Ashley Cooper, later 1st Earl of Shaftesbury *(see page 28)*, as well as James, Duke of Hamilton, and Richard Spottiswood, a future Secretary of State.

Prideaux had another key attribute of rectorial success: he was an excellent fundraiser. He persuaded Sir John Maynard, his kinsman, to endow readerships in Theology and Hebrew. Sir John Acland funded a new Hall, Sir John Peryam new buildings and George Hakewill a new chapel.

He also played an important role in University life. He was Regius Professor of Divinity, and twice Vice-Chancellor. But he had a sharp tongue which made him plenty of enemies: he imposed a relative of the University's Chancellor as Principal of Jesus College in the teeth of opposition from the Fellows; he tried unsuccessfully to get a candidate elected as Member of Parliament for the University; and he repeatedly got into arguments with William Laud, high churchman and Charles I's Archbishop of Canterbury. His attacks on those with whose theology he disagreed rankled for years afterwards.

With the fall of Archbishop Laud, Prideaux's career revived. The King made him Bishop of Worcester. He left Exeter and Oxford. But the appointment came at a bad time. In the Civil War that followed, Prideaux lost his bishopric when Worcester surrendered to Parliamentary forces in 1646. He was briefly imprisoned, and his son, William, died for the Royalists at Marston Moor.

Prideaux himself died of a fever, an impoverished man, in 1650. But his reputation ensured a magnificent send-off. 'Such was the number and quality of persons attending his funeral', wrote a contemporary, that 'such as deny Bishops to be Peers, would have conceived this Bishop a Prince.'

Testaments to the sadder moments of Prideaux's time at Exeter are three little brass plates in the floor of the Chapel, memorials from the older chapel to Prideaux's small sons. His portrait, the first of any Rector, hangs behind High Table in Hall.

FAC

Top right: *Portrait of John Prideaux (1578–1650), Rector of Exeter from 1612 to 1642; unknown artist.*

Below: *The death of three of Prideaux's young sons is recorded with brass plaques in the Chapel floor.*

A Period of Decline

'The period after the Civil War,' says Dr Maddicott, Exeter's Emeritus Fellow in History, 'was the most dismal in the College's history; its Rectors were incompetent, its Fellows divided, its undergraduates famous only for "drinking and duncing", according to contemporary observers.'

Few Exonians achieved real eminence in these years, but one exception was the marvellously named Narcissus Marsh. Elected a Fellow in 1658, he was later Provost of Trinity College Dublin, Archbishop of Armagh and a benefactor both of the Bodleian and the library of Trinity College, Dublin. He promoted the Irish language as an instrument of religion, and was responsible for the publication of the Old Testament in Irish. He was also a pioneering scientist, with a special interest in sound, and the first scientific writer to use the word 'microphone'. He turned his own notable library into the first public library in Ireland (it is still housed in Dublin); gave £300 to the building of the College's new front gate and the buildings

linking it to the Hall; and, in addition, gave £1,000 for the building now forming the east side of the quad. He was the College's greatest benefactor of the early 18th century.

His philanthropy was not universally admired. 'Marsh has the reputation of the most profound and universal learning,' wrote the satirist Jonathan Swift, 'this is the general opinion; neither can it be easily disproved. An old rusty iron chest in a banker's shop, strongly lock't, and wonderfully heavy, is full of gold; this is the general opinion, neither can it be disproved, provided the key be lost … Doing good is his pleasure, and as no man consults another in his pleasures, neither does he in this.' In spite of Swift's gibes in his essay 'Character of Primate Marsh', the Archbishop's name is commemorated in the College's Benefactors' Prayer, and his vast portrait hangs above the gallery in the Hall.

A quite different religious figure was Samuel Wesley, the father of Charles and John Wesley, who came from a strongly dissenting family in Dorset. Because only Anglicans could attend Oxford University, he got up very early one morning and slipped out of the house to avoid his family's disapproval. He walked to Oxford, where he entered as a poor scholar (the lowliest of the College's four categories, *see page 142*) in 1684 and worked as a servitor. He also, says Robert Southey, his biographer, 'composed exercises for those who had more money than mind and gave instruction to those who wished to profit by his lessons.' Coaching undergraduates is a hand-to-mouth existence familiar to many of today's graduate students. Later in life, he told his brother that he had entered Oxford with just over £2, but left with nearly £11.

During the Civil War the College rents had fallen into arrears, and ten of the Fellows, informed on by their colleagues, were thrown out by the Parliamentary visitors in 1648. John Prideaux's successor, George Hakewill, had paid much of the cost of the new Chapel during his days as a Fellow, but he was already 64 when he was elected Rector, and spent most of the War in his native Devonshire, leaving the College rudderless. The College recovered under his successor, John Conant, a distinguished orientalist and a strict disciplinarian who maintained the College's reputation for scholarship and increased its numbers. But the reputation departed with the Rector. ▶

Above: *The coat of arms of Narcissus Marsh, Archbishop of Armagh, stands above Staircase 2.*

Below left: *Portrait of Narcissus Marsh (1638–1713), Fellow from 1658; unknown artist, 1704.*

COLLEGE TREASURES

Apart from its precious Bohun Psalter *(see pages 130–31)*, the College's greatest treasures are three objects which, on the most important occasions, are always displayed on High Table.

The oldest *(below left)* is the Coconut Cup: a whole coconut set in silver-gilt mounts, dating from about 1500. Oriel and New College also have coconut cups, which are slightly older.

A similar treatment of a curiosity a century later is the College's Ostrich Egg Cup, dating from about 1610 *(below centre)*. Because of their extreme fragility, ostrich egg cups are rarer than coconut cups, and most date to the mid-Tudor period at the earliest. Exeter's specimen is believed to be the gift of James Clere. The egg is set in a beautiful silver-gilt mount supported by three ostrich feet.

The third treasure is a cup and cover *(below right)* made of gold, dated 1661–62 and presented to the College by George Hall together with an estate at Trethewin, Cornwall. Hall, whose portrait hangs in the College Hall, was the son of a bishop of Exeter and one of three brothers who studied at Exeter College. He became a Fellow of the College, Chaplain to Charles II and eventually Bishop of Chester. According to Hall's biographer, David Berwick, this cup and cover is one of only two pieces of pre-18th-century gold to be found in Oxford. It came to the College on the death of Hall's wife Gertrude.

In 1940 the Rector and Fellows presented a replica of the gold cup and cover to the captain and crew of HMS *Exeter*. Within two years that ship was to be sunk by Japanese action in 1942, but when a namesake was commissioned later, the replica was kept in its wardroom until it was decommissioned in 2010. The College's 1940 presentation commemorates the Battle of the River Plate, at which three cruisers, HMS *Exeter*, HMS *Ajax*, and HMS *Achilles* of New Zealand, attacked the German pocket battleship *Admiral Graf Spee* on 13 December 1939. In the following engagement the *Exeter* was severely damaged and could have been sunk; but meanwhile a shell from her own guns had destroyed the *Graf Spee*'s fuel processing plant, demanding urgent repairs. The *Graf Spee* withdrew to Montevideo in the mouth of the Rio de la Plata, her enemy waiting over the horizon outside. Eventually the authorities of neutral Uruguay required her to leave their port. Knowing doom was unavoidable, her captain scuttled her.

FAC

Below left: *Coconut Cup and Cover mounted in silver gilt, c.1500. These objects of curiosity were fashionable in the late 15th and 16th centuries.*

Below centre: *Silver-gilt Ostrich Egg Cup with Cover, dating from c.1610. The base is engraved with ostriches and scrolls with inscriptions. The egg rests on the stem of three ostrich legs; the cover has an ostrich at the top.*

Below right: *Two-handled Gold Cup and Cover, dated 1661–62, presented by George Hall, Bishop of Chester. It is decorated in repoussé with lozenge-shaped gadroons, and engraved with flowers.*

Portrait of Anthony Ashley Cooper (1621–83), 1st Earl of Shaftesbury; copy after John Greenhill.

ANTHONY ASHLEY COOPER

Among the students who passed through Exeter in the golden age of the early 17th century, few were to make more of a splash than Anthony Ashley Cooper, later 1st Earl of Shaftesbury, Lord Chancellor to Charles II and founder of the Whig Party. Both his parents had died before he was eight years old, and he had been brought up by a succession of guardians. He was a gentleman-commoner at Exeter in 1637–38.

'I kept both horses and servants in Oxford,' he recalled in his autobiography, 'and was allowed what expense or recreation I desired.' His good fortune, he said, allowed him to entertain the poorer students when they ran short of food: 'it being no small honour among those sort of men that my name in the buttery book willingly bore twice the expense of any in the University.' His tale of generosity was undermined somewhat by Charles Boase, the College's 19th-century Librarian, who went and looked up the buttery books, and found Ashley Cooper spending, indeed, about twice the usual amount, but less than two other extravagant young men.

With the easy immodesty of the aristocrat Ashley Cooper recorded that he owed his leadership of the undergraduates to 'my quality, proficiency in learning and natural affability'. He boasted of two triumphs of leadership. First, he ended the custom of 'tucking freshmen' – a sort of hazing, in which one of the older students would scrape the skin off the chin of a freshman and then force him to drink a beer glass of water and salt. Freshman Ashley Cooper, accompanied by two hefty cousins and other stalwarts of his year, attacked the older students in the dining hall and drove them down into what sounds like the Undercroft, where they beat them until Rector Prideaux came to intervene.

Ashley Cooper's second triumph involved leading the Jacobean equivalent of a student rent strike: when the Senior Fellows tried to dilute the College beer, then notorious for its strength, the young aristocrat and his friends led the rebellion by threatening to withdraw their names from the College books. This direct threat to their income persuaded the Fellows to beat a retreat, and leave the beer unweakened.

FAC

His successor Rector Maynard, reported Anthony Wood, was 'much given to bibbing; and when there is a music meeting in one of the fellows' chambers, he will sit there, smoke and drink until he is drunk and has to be led to his lodgings by the junior fellows.' Rector Bury, who followed him in 1666, did even worse. He mismanaged the College finances, suspended five of the Fellows from their Fellowships (only to have his decision reversed by the Vice-Chancellor); shut out the Visitor, the Bishop of Exeter, when he tried to enter the College; and published a theological treatise which was condemned as heretical. In 1690, he was expelled and the College Chaplain, who had abetted him, was excommunicated.

Exeter's Rectors in the early 18th century were mainly worthy but undistinguished. One example was Matthew Hole, who emerged as a compromise candidate after a contested election in 1716. Hole was 75, and seems to have had the main advantage of being rumoured to be rich after 30 years as a country parson. He quickly became a liability. He botched negotiations over Hart Hall, in which the College had begun life and which had continued as a hall ever since. In 1710, the Hall acquired a capable and ambitious new Principal, Richard Newton, who was determined to turn his institution into a fully-fledged college. A part of Hart Hall's now expanded buildings was still leased from Exeter. After a legal battle to retain control of the whole of Hart Hall, Hole – to the fury of his Fellows – caved in. But Exeter's rumbling opposition meant that Hart Hall did not become fully

The stone commemorating Matthew Hole, who was elected Rector in 1716 at the age of 75 and remained in post until his death in 1730, aged 90.

incorporated as a college (Hertford) until 1740, two Rectors later. Meanwhile, Hole remained Rector until the age of 90, a powerful argument against rectorial elections swayed by compromise or the hope of riches. A large stone to his memory, transferred from the Jacobean Chapel to the Victorian one, lies immediately in front of the Rector's pew – a warning, perhaps, to subsequent Rectors not to overstay their welcome.

Exeter's rise and decline reflects not just the impact of a succession of inept Rectors, but also the climate of the times. The students still came from a limited geographical area and mainly from the West Country; still studied the antiquated syllabus of Dialectics, Philosophy and Rhetoric; and often returned to a vicar's life in the country parishes of Devon and Cornwall. In this pattern, there was much that Stapeldon would have recognised. Indeed this period was Oxford's most dismal since the Middle Ages. The University's complacency shocked Adam Smith, Scotland's father of political economy, who famously found the teaching at Glasgow University vastly better than that at Oxford, where 'the greater part of the public professors have, for these many years, given up altogether even the pretence of teaching.'

Three more capable Rectors followed. John Conybeare, elected in 1730, was a distinguished preacher and theologian (and took on Dr Newton and his ambitions for Hertford, in true Oxford style, with an excoriating book called *Calumny Refuted*, published in 1735). In less than two and a half years at Exeter – the College's shortest rectorship since the Petre statutes – he tightened discipline, ended emoluments

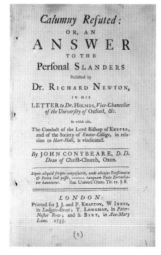

for absentee Fellows, instituted a fair process for appointing College servants and dismissed incompetent ones. Conybeare then moved swiftly on from leading Exeter to become Dean of Christ Church, another Augean stables. The next two Rectors – Joseph Atwell and James Edgcumbe (the latter commemorated with a stone in the floor of the Chapel) – presided over a rather dull college, producing few figures of distinction.

Benjamin Kennicott is one of the few Fellows of that era who survives in the College's memory – thanks less to his academic distinction than to the large fig tree that spreads across the eastern wall of Peryam's Buildings. A Fellow of the College from 1747 to 1771, Kennicott was the greatest Hebrew scholar of the century, and a friend of Samuel Johnson.

From a poor Devon family, like so many of Exeter's distinguished scholars, he began life teaching in a charity school. But he attracted the attention (and the financial support) of the local gentry after the wife of a neighbourhood squire accidentally ate a poisonous herb, fell ill and then recovered. Kennicott wrote a poem to describe the near-fatal meal and to celebrate her recovery:

> *At dusky eve the insidious herb obeys,*
> *Their favourite greens the happy pair surveys:*
> *She eats, nor doubts the fatal Sallad good,*
> *Till the dire Venom rages in her Blood;*
> *The tainted Current thrills in ev'ry Vein*
> *And Tortures all her vital Powers sustain.*

Above right: Dr Benjamin Kennicott's fig tree still flourishes on the east wall of Peryam's Buildings.

Below: Portrait of Benjamin Kennicott (1718–83), the great Hebrew scholar; unknown artist.

Below right: Calumny Refuted, *Rector John Conybeare's response to the 'barbarous aspersions cast on me by Dr Richard Newton', published in 1735.*

This got him to Exeter, where his diligence and assiduous cultivation of appropriate patrons ensured a stellar career as Fellow. William Keatley Stride, author of a College history published in 1900, says slyly: 'He was by no means a genius … But he won his way by a mixture of indomitable pertinacity and never-failing promptitude.' However, the students seem to have treated him with less respect. Resenting their night-time raids on his delicious figs, he protectively labelled one especially fine specimen 'Dr Kennicott's fig' – only to find it gone in the morning and replaced by a cheeky note saying, 'A fig for Dr Kennicott!'

Towards 1800

Among the College's other notable Fellows in the late 18th century was Thomas Broughton. By the time he was elected to a Fellowship at Exeter College at the age of 21, he had joined a group called 'Methodists' led by John Wesley, but he speedily fell out with them, having challenged Wesley's claims of instantaneous conversion. He subsequently resigned his Exeter Fellowship (Oxford Fellows were not allowed to marry) and married a Miss Capel, by whom he had 15 children, five of whom died in infancy. Broughton's later career was as secretary of the Society for Promoting Christian Knowledge, a position he held for 35 years. He died in London on the morning of St Thomas's Day, as he was preparing for a service, and was found by friends on his knees in clerical attire in the Society's house in Hatton Garden.

One of the most extraordinary episodes of the 18th century was Exeter's role in the Oxfordshire county elections of 1754, part of the general election of that year. As perhaps befitted Lord Shaftesbury's college, Exeter in the 18th century was one of only four colleges in Oxford that generally supported the Whigs (the others were Merton, Wadham and Christ Church). Political clashes between Whigs and Tories were often ferocious. The polling booths were set up on the south side of Broad Street, abutting what was then the College's back gate and is now the Back Quad. On the morning the polls opened, the town's Tories set up a guard in front of the booths.

But Exeter used its location cunningly. For the six days that the election lasted, Whig voters poured through the Turl Street gate and were smuggled out

Portrait of Thomas Broughton (1712–77); copy after Nathaniel Dance-Holland.

by the back to cast their votes. Elections being riotous affairs, the Hall was filled with 'a smoking, drinking expectorating crowd', according to the (Tory) Vice-Chancellor, who attacked Exeter in Convocation. To rebuff his accusations, the then Rector, Francis Webber, wrote a pamphlet with the all-encompassing title of 'A defence of the rector and fellows of Exeter College, from the accusations brought against them by the Reverend Dr. Huddesford, Vice-Chancellor of Oxford; in his speech to the convocation, October 8, 1754, on account of the conduct of the said college, at the time of the late election for the county'. Webber asserted, rather improbably, that many of the voters had 'attended chapel at the hours of prayer'.

And ugly though the scene in Hall may have been, even the Senior Common Room was uncivilised by modern standards. Charles Boase, the College's 19th-century Librarian and historian, reported that John David Macbride, who had been a young Fellow at the start of the 19th century, recalled in later life the moment when a carpet replaced the sanded floor dotted with spittoons. The Senior Fellow turned his back and announced, 'Gentlemen, if you will introduce such a monstrous luxury, I will never enter this room again.' He never did.

An Election Entertainment
by Hogarth, the first of four
paintings satirising the Oxford
contest in the General Election
of 1754, depicts the Whigs'
attempts to gain voters through
bribery and corruption.

It seems somehow appropriate that the Rector who saw out the 18th century was Dr Henry Richards. According to a contemporary, George Cox, quoted by Stride, Richards was 'rather a rough, undignified person whose domestic arrangements were not (it may be supposed) of a very refined character, he having married a daughter of a former cook of the College.' Undignified perhaps, but he remembered the College generously in his will. As the College reached the end of its first half-millennium, it had only modest reasons to be proud of its past, and those were mostly confined to the early 17th century. Exeter in 1800 was, says Dr Maddicott, 'an unreformed college in an unreformed university'. It was a popular but unintellectual college, attracting the sons of good West Country families, many of them expecting to go back to inherit and manage their fathers' estates. By the middle of the 19th century, it had changed from backwater to success story, and was leading change rather than ignoring it.

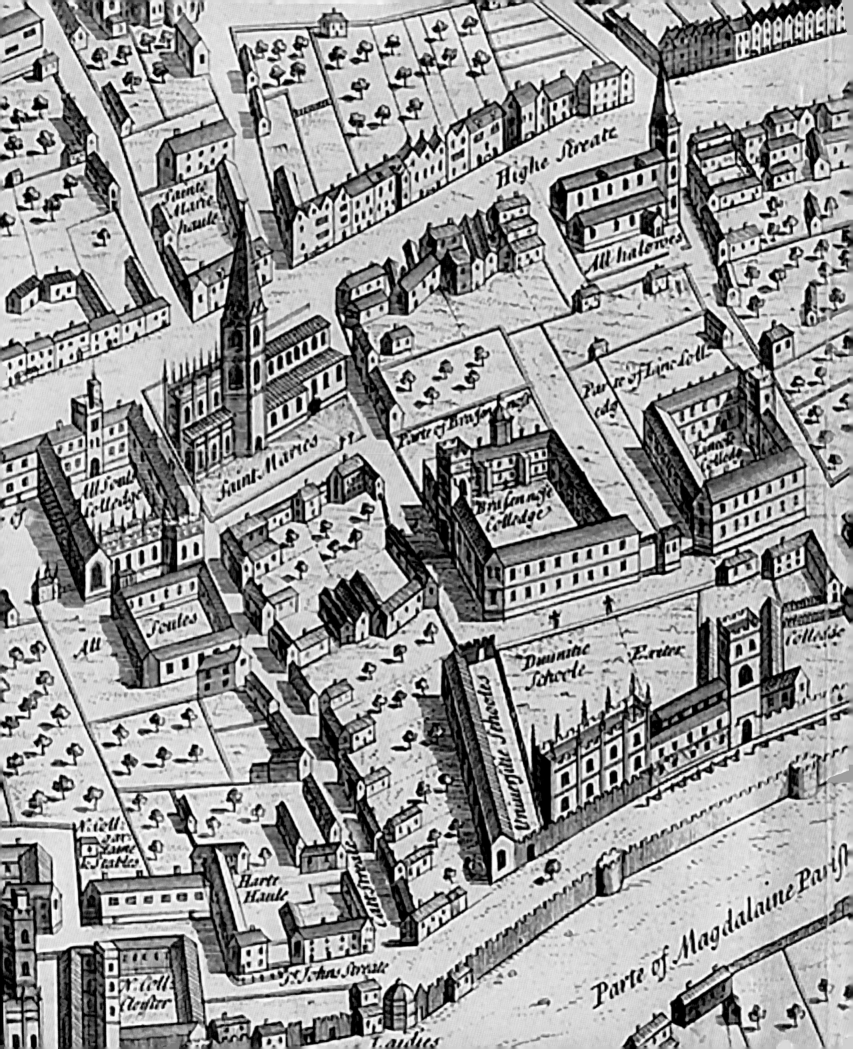

Highe Streate

Saincte
Marie Haule

All halowes

Parte of Lincoll
edg

Parte of Bras

All soule Colledge

Lincoll
Colledge

Saint Maries

Brasen nose
Colledge

Divinitie
Schoole

Exeter

... Colledge

All Soules

Schooles in Common

All

... Lane
& Stables

Harte Haule

... College
Cloyster

St Johns Streate

Parte of Magdalaine Parish

Ladies

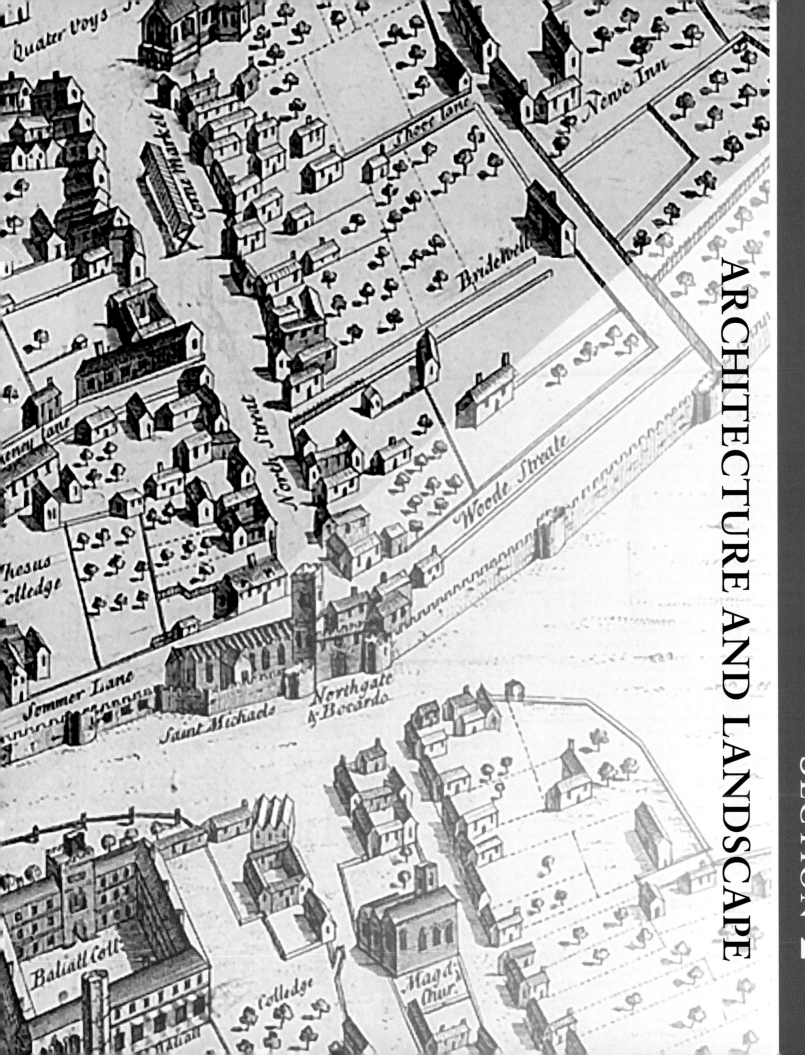

BUILDING THE COLLEGE

HANNAH PARHAM

On 26 April 1859, at the parish church of St Michael-at-the-North-Gate in Oxford, Edward Burne-Jones attended the wedding of his friend, William Morris. At the other end of Ship Street, in the college where the pair had met six years earlier, a massive programme of building works was coming to a close. The rooms that Topsy and Ted (their nicknames for each other) had occupied as undergraduates had been demolished. Indeed the entire quadrangle they knew as Hell Quad was gone. With it went a Jacobean chapel, the Rector's Lodgings, and a diminutive neo-Classical Library in the Fellows' Garden. So thorough was the refashioning of Exeter in the 1850s that the rebuilt College would have been largely unrecognisable to Morris and Burne-Jones.

Yet the ghosts of those ancient buildings still inhabit Exeter's quadrangles. They may be traced in curious dead-ends, such as the gated alley next to Palmer's Tower that once led to Hell Quad. They bring about oddities like the richly carved 17th-century vaulting of the Porters' Lodge that doesn't match its Victorian shell. They determined the location and orientation of the present Chapel, Hall and Library. Some fragments of the old fabric even had a posthumous career beyond the College walls: the carved woodwork from the demolished 1620s chapel ended up in two Oxfordshire parish churches, a pair of private houses and the common room of Radley College.

The buildings of the old College also survive in woodcuts, copperplate engravings, and sepia photographs in the College archives. At first glance,

these images are disorientating to modern eyes accustomed to the architecture of the Victorian Exeter. Interpreted in sequence, however, they provide an accurate survey of the physical evolution of the College from the early 14th century onwards.

The earliest picture of Exeter is a woodcut of 1566 by John Bereblock *(see page 36)*. This shows some of the College's earliest buildings, some 200 years old by the time of Bereblock's drawing.

Bereblock became Dean of Exeter in 1566, the year that Queen Elizabeth visited Oxford accompanied by the University's new Chancellor, the Earl of Leicester. At the University Church, the Queen was shown a set of drawings of the colleges and University buildings made by Bereblock, accompanied by a map. She was later given a personal copy and was said to have regarded the gift as 'the greatest and best she had ever received'. The drawings are the first surviving representation of many of Oxford's colleges, not just Exeter.

In Bereblock's time, Oxford's city wall ran along what would become Ship Street and Exeter's second quadrangle. Palmer's Tower (built in 1432 by the then-Rector William Palmer) stood just within the wall and was the College's front gate and its northernmost boundary. Bereblock's drawing shows Palmer's Tower at the centre of four ranges of buildings: running to east and west is a two-storey row of rooms with chimney stacks in between each window, known as Rector's Row and dating to 1432; beyond it to the east is the Rector's house; extending south from the Tower, a library of the late 14th century; and tucked

Previous pages: *Ralph Agas's bird's-eye map of Oxford, 1578 (first published in 1588). Exeter is still of modest dimensions compared with neighbouring Brasenose and Lincoln.*

Opposite: *Palmer's Tower, 1432, the only surviving medieval part of the College.*

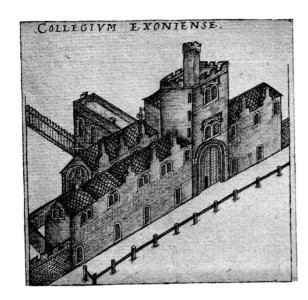

Left: *Illustration of Exeter College from Neal Thomas's and John Bereblock's book on Oxford presented to Queen Elizabeth I on her visit to Oxford in 1566. Palmer's Tower, the original entrance to Exeter, is viewed from the north.*

behind Rector's Row is a chapel, with a traceried east window and a cross finial atop the gable; its three chimneys served the rooms below the Chapel itself, which was on the upper storey.

The 12 scholars whose Fellowships had been endowed by Walter de Stapeldon in 1314 at first made do with existing premises, given to them in 1315 by Peter Skelton, Rector of St Stephen's-by-Saltash in Cornwall. The Chapel was probably the first building erected by the College on its new site, six years later. A licence for its construction was obtained from the Bishop of Lincoln in 1321 (Oxford was then in the Diocese of Lincoln). In 1326 the high altar was consecrated to the Blessed Virgin, St Peter and St Thomas the Martyr. A library followed soon thereafter (straw for its roof appears in the Rector's accounts of 1375), but this is not the building shown on Bereblock's woodcut, which is not thatched. According to the building accounts, this library was constructed in 1383. Its orientation was chosen to make the most of the daylight, with windows facing east and west and thus allowing a full day's study.

When Ralph Agas drew his bird's-eye map of Oxford in 1578, little had changed. There is now another building to the west of the Library, a dining hall, which if it were standing today would project into the middle of Exeter's front quadrangle. Two of the medieval academic halls – Checker Hall and Peter Hall, owned by the College from 1405 and 1478 – face Turl Street and Brasenose Lane. Exeter's position in the cityscape is visible, with the city wall

to its north and the Divinity School to the east. Its poverty in comparison to neighbouring colleges is obvious on Agas's map: Lincoln and Brasenose by this time comprise complete quadrangles of two storeys on each side; Magdalen and Merton have pinnacled stone towers, one soaring, the other wide and low; Jesus, however, has only six or seven barn-like hovels.

There are slight differences of detail in Bereblock and Agas's drawings of Exeter: Palmer's Tower is shown as having a single two-light mullioned window in its upper stage in 1566, two single-light windows in 1578. These are more likely representational conventions or errors of draughtsmanship rather than indications that much had changed in the physical fabric of the College. Where elements correspond, however, they can be assumed to be accurate and it is these points of detail that suddenly bring Tudor Exeter to life: the run of posts and chain creating an area boundary along the street frontage, for instance.

Visitors to Sanders's Print Shop on The High will know the series of prints of Oxford colleges engraved by David Loggan. Published as *Oxonia Illustrata*, the compendium was originally a companion piece to Anthony Wood's history of the University of 1674. Loggan must have made his draft of Exeter after 1672, the year in which the side of the quadrangle between the Lodge tower and the Chapel – shown in the published edition of 1675 – was built.

Loggan's Exeter is both familiar and strange. It depicts the College at a turning point in its history, when most of the medieval buildings of Bereblock and Agas's time are extant, but elements of the modern College are in place too. The orientation of the College has shifted from north to west, and the front gate is now on the Turl. There is a complete quadrangle too. Aspects of the original foundation are still standing, however. The early 14th-century Chapel is identifiable, with its three chimneys and cross finial. It is labelled 'B' on Loggan's plan and the legend reveals that it had become the College Library. It was renovated as such when a new chapel was built in 1624, prefiguring by some 350 years the conversion of two Oxford parish churches to libraries at Lincoln and St Edmund Hall. Running perpendicular to the old chapel-cum-library, along the east side of the front quadrangle, is the Library of 1383, now adapted to create additional student rooms. The number of students at Exeter had doubled between

1572 and 1612 (from 91 to 183) and an extra storey was added to the old Library to accommodate them. This was known as 'Bentley's Nest', named for an enterprising head butler who built it at his own expense and then rented the rooms to students. The practice was common, for in those days each Fellow was expected to provide accommodation for his students and many took to building so-called 'cock-lofts' above their own rooms for the purpose. Richard Carpenter, a Fellow from 1596 until 1606, had a room with two studies to which he added a further eight.

Following the line of buildings along the quadrangle, the next section on Loggan's drawing has barely changed to the present day: these are Peryam's Buildings (Staircase 4), built by John Peryam in 1618. The rooms overlook the Fellows' Garden, which Loggan depicts with a neat row of trees at its far end. The mound isn't depicted, but it was mentioned in Wood's notes on Exeter and so was constructed by the 1670s.

Returning to the front quadrangle, the Hall is on the southern side, with its pyramid of steps (then, as

now, ten in number). In the 17th century it had no fireplaces, but just a louvre in the centre of the roof ridge to ventilate the smoke from the central hearth. The Hall was built in 1618 and largely paid for by Sir John Acland, a Devonshire landowner and probably an alumnus of Exeter.

The quadrangle's south-west corner was a motley collection of buildings when Loggan visited in 1673 or 1674. These ran along the Turl Street frontage up to the Lodge tower, a construction of 1605. Continuing past the Lodge along Turl Street on Loggan's drawing is another building recognisable to modern eyes, Staircases 7 and 8, built in 1672.

The Chapel in Loggan's view, forming the north range of the quadrangle, had been built in 1624 and was mostly paid for by a Fellow, George Hakewill. Remarkably, it was photographed in the 1850s and so we can picture what it looked like from the front quadrangle, as well as from above. Its architectural style, like that of the slightly earlier Hall, is an Oxford speciality: posthumous Gothic. Long after the

Loggan's view of the College from the west, 1675. The main entrance is now in the Turl, with Hakewill's Chapel to the north of the quadrangle and the Hall to the south. The former Chapel, marked B, is now the Library, and 'Bentley's Nest' is to the right. Beyond the chimneys of Peryam's Buildings a line of trees marks the Fellows' Garden.

Far left: *The medieval Chapel, located on the site of the present Rector's Garden, was put to new use as the Library in 1624; copperplate engraving published in 1819.*

Left: *Doorway to the old Chapel, photographed in the 1850s.*

Below left: *Prideaux Buildings, photographed in the 1850s.*

Below: *'Old Gateways', wood engraving by Orlando Jewitt, 1834. By 1680 the College frontage on the Broad extended some distance to the north from Palmer's Tower, and an archway on the Broad gave access.*

monasteries had fallen and long before the medievalist revival of the Victorian period, buildings in Oxford continued to be built with Gothic tracery, buttresses and pinnacles (Brasenose Chapel, still standing, is another example). Exeter's Chapel has four, wide Perpendicular tracery windows overlooking the quadrangle, divided by buttresses. Only the beautiful stone porch with its pilasters and broken pediment and the dainty ogee cupola on the roof hint at the aesthetics of the Renaissance. Inside, the plaster ceiling was painted to resemble the ribs of vaulting.

Returning to Loggan's drawing: the Rector's Lodgings abuts the Chapel at its east end, sandwiched between it and Palmer's Tower. There was a door leading direct from the Rector's dining room to his pew in the aisle, and one on the upper floor of the house leading to a gallery for the Rector's family. Next to the Rector's house on Loggan's print, after Palmer's Tower, is Rector's Row, which we remember from Bereblock and Agas's woodcuts. Behind it, on land acquired by

the College in 1606 when a Royal Charter permitted the old street that ran past Palmer's Tower to be built upon, are the College stables and the Rector's Garden.

Obscured by the Hall in Loggan's view is Prideaux Buildings, an early-17th-century townhouse built by an alderman of Oxford and purchased for the College by Rector Prideaux, who added a third storey in 1620. It too was photographed in the 1850s.

When he later wrote about his rooms in Prideaux Buildings, Edward Burne-Jones perfectly captured the experience of living in a building such as this, constructed for another purpose and then converted to student rooms. He recalled 'they were tumbly old buildings gable roofed and pebble-dashed … little dark passages led from the staircase to the sitting rooms, a couple of steps to go down, a pace or two, and then three steps to go up: your face was banged by the door, and then inside the room a couple of steps up to a seat in the window, and a couple of steps down into the bedroom.' Prideaux Buildings was timber-framed with an almost continuous wave of mullion-and-transom windows projecting along the ground and first floors. These were so striking that when Prideaux Buildings was demolished in 1856 they were reused in the construction of a building on Turl Street. This was known as the Swiss Cottage, presumably for its gable and exposed timber frame.

We can focus on other details of Loggan's bird's-eye view by examining wood engravings of the early 19th century. One by Orlando Jewitt, titled 'Old gateways', shows the small stone archway to Broad Street, with Palmer's Tower behind.

The medieval Chapel, put to new use as the Library in 1624, is recorded too in a copperplate engraving published in 1819. It had disappeared over 40 years previously, so the print must have been based on an earlier illustration. It is pictured in the

OLD GATEWAYS; PALMER'S TOWER, &

middle years of the 18th century, certainly after 1709 when part of the building was damaged by a fire and taken down, and before 1778 when the whole was demolished. The form of the tracery in the east end window matches perfectly that shown in Bereblock's woodcut of 1566, although the cross on the top of the gable has come down by this point. In many respects, the story of Exeter from the Tudors to the Georges is one of continuity; its medieval buildings endured and set the tone for much of what followed.

Elsewhere in Oxford, however, times were changing. In 1700, the Fellows of Queen's College resolved to rebuild the medieval foundation from scratch, adapting a grandly Baroque design by Nicholas Hawksmoor; at Christ Church, the Dean himself, Henry Aldrich, built Peckwater Quadrangle from 1707. Exeter did not have the resources for such boldness, but efforts were made to straighten out the picturesque irregularity of Bereblock and Loggan's time. Medieval buildings were given a Classical face, as the sensibilities of the new era dictated. The gables along the Turl Street front were taken down in the 1680s and a new Lodge tower, with Classical columns, was built in 1702–03 by the famous family of Oxford masons, the Townsends, although the vaulting of the older Lodge tower was preserved.

A third quadrangle (Morris's and Burne-Jones's Hell Quad) was created in 1708–10 by the closing of the gap shown in Loggan's print between Palmer's Tower and Peryam's Buildings. These were Armagh Buildings, named for their benefactor, Narcissus Marsh, the Bishop of Armagh and an Old Member. These extended southwards too and swept away many of the College's medieval buildings, including the 14th-century former library, with its charming 'nest' built by Butler Bentley, along with part of the original chapel.

While Armagh Buildings were under construction, a fire swept through the old chapel-cum-library. To this day there are books in the College collection with charred edges, recalling the devastation. Much was salvaged, however, for the Library served for another 70 years before finally giving up the ghost in 1778 when a new building was constructed. The new Library, built after a design by the Oxford mason William Townsend, had Ionic pilasters between the tall rounded windows, and was later described by a Fellow as 'more resembling a greenhouse than a library'. That may have been the case, but this dainty building certainly suited its garden setting.

The magnificent print of 1739 shows the effects of some of these changes on the architecture of Exeter College. The College is shown devoid of its topographical context, as if it had been transplanted to the Chilterns. Stapeldon, Petre, Charles I, various other benefactors (some busts, some full-height figures) and two cherubs are assembled in the foreground.

Below: George Vertue's 1739 view of the College is something of a capriccio, presenting Exeter as a neo-Classical palace set in a verdant landscape. Ranged before the Classical façade are founder, re-founder and benefactors (including Charles I) attended by cherubs. The new Ionic pillars over the Lodge were to fall victim to H. J. Underwood's Gothicisation of 1834.

Below right: The new Library, built in 1778, so suited its garden setting that it was likened to a greenhouse by a Victorian Fellow. It was pulled down to make way for George Gilbert Scott's Gothic building.

THE NEW LIBRARY.

Despite these caprices, the image was grounded in reality. In the 18th century, the College indeed had a relatively symmetrical and harmonious front quadrangle, for perhaps the only time in its history. An Ionic portico led into a courtyard of uniform height and appearance, with the Jacobean Hall to the south matched by the Jacobean Chapel to the north. The engraver has not included the ramshackle College stables ranged along Broad Street. The oldest part of the College, Palmer's Tower, goes unrecorded. Even the elegant Fellows' Garden, located off-axis behind the main quad, is omitted.

The Rector's Lodgings in the 18th century could be entered direct from Turl Street, via a narrow alley wide enough for a sedan chair, but not a carriage. Its façade was rebuilt *c.*1798 and like the Chapel of nearly two centuries earlier, its architecture was hybrid. But whereas the Chapel was an essentially Gothic building with Classical elements, this was in effect a Classical elevation with Gothic trimmings. The new façade to the three-storey Lodgings was perfectly symmetrical, of five bays with a central porch. Yet the windows had stone mullions, to match Armagh Buildings, and there were crenellations along the parapet. Plans for improvements in 1799 show that inside there was a grand staircase in the Hall, dado rails and fireplaces in all the rooms. College was slowly becoming a more comfortable place to live, for undergraduates as well as the Rector:

fireplaces were introduced into the Hall for the first time in 1811, gas light in 1820.

In 1834, the chameleon-like Turl Street Lodge reverted to Gothic again, taking the form it maintains to this day. The Ionic columns and pediment were removed to make way for a bay window and battlements, designed by H. J. Underwood.

At the same time, Underwood also built new undergraduate rooms on Broad Street, next to the old Ashmolean Museum, in a similarly Gothic-lite manner. This was the kind of superficiality in architecture that John Ruskin railed against. A Ruskin disciple, William Morris wrote to his friend the architect Philip Webb that the College had 'ruined by fakement various' its principal elevations. Yet when in 1847 the rebuilding of the College Chapel was mooted, there was no outcry. For antiquarians, the Chapel wasn't quite old enough to be precious; they had their work cut out in defending genuine medieval buildings from over-restoration by the likes of George Gilbert Scott. For those such as Scott, who sought to recreate the buildings of medieval Christendom, its design symbolised the post-Reformation corruption of Gothic architecture with Classical motifs. Perhaps just one man esteemed the architecture of Exeter Chapel in the 1850s – the architect Richard Phené Spiers, a pluralist who was 'not able to accept the narrowly concentrated point

Below left: *The Rector's Lodgings, rebuilt c.1798, combined Georgian and Regency Gothic features. This early photograph predates the large-scale reconstruction of the 1850s.*

Below: *The Tudor-style 'Swiss Cottage' at the Broad Street end of the Turl reused elements of the 1620 timber-framed Prideaux Buildings, demolished in 1856.*

of view of the Gothic revivalists', according to his pupil W. R. Lethaby. Spiers took a set of photographs of College, including the invaluable images of the old Chapel, before demolition work began.

The decision to demolish Hakewill's 17th-century Chapel was framed as practical – it was structurally unsound and would cost nearly as much to repair as to replace. But ideological considerations played their part as well, for the principles of the Oxford Movement in church teaching and liturgy had filtered across Radcliffe Square from the University Church to be enthusiastically taken up at Exeter. Unlike the unconvincingly Gothic Lodge, the new Chapel would evoke the purity of the medieval church in a full-blooded, authentic way. This was Gothic with a capital G.

The Rector and Fellows commissioned designs for a new Chapel from three prominent Gothicists: Anthony Salvin, James Park Harrison and George Gilbert Scott (William Butterfield, who designed Keble Chapel, was also approached but did not submit a design). Each proposed a building on the exact footprint of the old Chapel, sharing its proportions. The outcome of this contest was to have a profound effect on the College's architecture.

Six years and various deliberations about cost later, Scott was chosen unanimously as architect. A revised design on the site of the College's 'greenhouse' Library in the Fellows' Garden was approved in October 1853, Scott having given up on the attempt to squeeze a new Chapel in place of the old one. Even the new site in the garden was too small: the approved design proposed bisecting the front quadrangle with the west end of the Chapel, which was to have a vast rose window set in a pointed arch. If implemented, this striking building would have been visible across the quadrangle the moment one stepped into the Porters' Lodge. It would have dominated the garden in the same way the east end of Christ Church's Cathedral projects into the garden there, with its west end forming part of the quadrangle. Readers looking out of the windows of Duke Humfrey's Library would have come face to face with the Chapel's stone saints set in niches atop the buttresses; its flèche would have soared over the wall to Brasenose Lane. In the years following his first proposal, which is essentially English Gothic in derivation, Scott had visited France

and his eyes 'at once were open' to the splendour of that country's medieval buildings, most relevantly in this case Amiens Cathedral and Sainte-Chapelle in Paris. Scott abandoned the idea of an aisled, wooden-roofed chapel in favour of a single, tall, stone-vaulted space with an apsidal east end. The Fellowship backed Scott's vision and thus gave Exeter its most distinctive architectural set-piece.

No sooner was the French design approved, however, than a backlash imperilled the whole scheme: the Fellowship got cold feet over the cost of Scott's proposal. The release of some of the College's funds by the Charity Commissioners in 1854 saved the design, although at the last minute it reverted to the original site in the front quadrangle. First impressions of Exeter would never be the same again.

The entire College community got behind the fundraising, with many small donations from alumni, £1,000 from the late Rector, Joseph Richards, and a gift of the ante-chapel screen from the Junior Common Room. A voluntary tax of £100 – roughly equivalent to a year's income – was imposed on the Senior Common Room. This was not just for the Chapel, however. The repositioning in the front quadrangle of a chapel design conceived for a much larger site precipitated a major overhaul of the entire College estate. One after the other, the College's buildings fell like dominoes to accommodate the ▶

HAKEWILL'S CHAPEL

It would not be unreasonable to assume that Exeter's old Chapel disappeared without a trace in 1856. After all, George Gilbert Scott's new building engulfed not only the site of the old one, but also of the Rector's Lodgings next door. The visitor to a pair of Oxfordshire parish churches, however, would know better.

Exeter was granted the right to appoint the priest of St Mary's, Long Wittenham, by Stapeldon in 1322, as it was St Swithin's, Merton, by Petre in 1566, thereby gaining access to the revenues of these churches. Both churches were gifted remnants of its patron's collegiate chapel in the 19th century. St Mary's got a handsome early-17th-century oak screen, formerly in the ante-chapel at Exeter. It has round arches divided by Ionic pilasters and carved cherubs in the spandrels; above the doorway are the arms of George Hakewill, who largely paid for the building of the Chapel, which was consecrated on 28 May 1624. The church's chancel stalls, like those at St Swithun's, are also from Exeter; the bench ends have poppy heads carved with grotesque figures. Other parts went to private dwellings: the Chapel doors to the manor house at Weston-on-the-Green, a screen to Wick Hall, Radley. Parts of the Common Room table at Radley School are made from the base of Exeter's pulpit.

An idea of the quality of this carved woodwork may be gained by inspection of the oak screen in Exeter's Hall, for the strapwork above the screen came from the old Chapel. (The present Chapel lectern and also the bell at the top of the flèche also came from the old Chapel.) The original and the later work match so seamlessly because the Hall and Chapel are almost contemporary, the former constructed in 1618. At that time the College was Calvinist in temperament, though loyal to the Crown (Charles I was later a benefactor). John Prideaux was Rector, the leader of the anti-Arminian group within the Church of England but also Chaplain to James I's son, and later Bishop of Worcester.

The design of Hakewill's Chapel reflected the religious temperament of the College. Its architecture was traditional, with Perpendicular Gothic tracery windows and inside an arcade of clustered shafts separated the nave and south aisle. The aisle was an unusual feature in an Oxford chapel and probably a consequence of the growing undergraduate

Left: *Portrait of George Hakewill (1578–1646), one of Exeter's most generous benefactors, who largely paid for the Chapel of 1624.*

Below: *The beautifully carved 17th-century strapwork above the oak screen in the Hall (seen here) originally came from the old Chapel (see opposite).*

Above: *The houses on the corner of Broad Street and the Turl, purchased before the Second World War, were demolished in the late 1950s to make way for a new College building.*

Above right: *A drawing from the 650th anniversary fund-raising brochure shows the cleared corner site awaiting reconstruction.*

Right: *Drawing of the proposed Broad Street frontage by Lionel Brett, 1955.*

The completed Thomas Wood Building, 1964.

staff, under the direction of College clerk of works T. A. Taylor. Few members of staff can have had a greater impact on the College's buildings.

Bolder plans both preceded and followed this pragmatic and economical refurbishment of the Rector's Lodgings. Before the Second World War, a long-held ambition of many an Exeter Rector and Bursar was at last fulfilled: College purchased the houses on the corner of Broad Street and the Turl. The College's current footprint on its main site was now in place. Grandiose schemes for rebuilding the entire Broad Street frontage were entertained, but abandoned as war beckoned. One, by T. Harold Hughes, shows a palatial frontage to Broad Street, 17 windows-long, with a pedimented, columned centrepiece. Another, unsigned and undated, proposed a low square tower in the centre of an equally vast range with a sweeping concave corner to Turl Street. Given that the New Bodleian Library was to open further along

Broad Street in 1940, and this in a similar interwar historicist-modernist style, there can be few regrets that these schemes came to nothing.

By the time the College was in a position to commission a new building again, in the late 1950s, Hughes was dead and architectural taste had shifted once again. The desire to replace parts of the Victorian College was, however, unabated, although the new system of town planning made it harder to demolish the Broad Street buildings. Instead, the western range of the rear quad was taken down, along with Parker's Bookshop on the Turl Street corner and the Swiss Cottage which had stood next to the Chapel staircase. They were replaced with the Thomas Wood Building, built to designs by Lionel Brett (later Viscount Esher) of Brett & Pollen. Named for the composer Thomas Wood, whose widow St Osyth Wood was the principal benefactor to the building fund, this work was completed in 1964.

Lionel Brett, also the architect-planner of Hatfield New Town and of Portsmouth civic centre, was critical of his Oxford work, pleading (perhaps understandably) that the city 'gave him stage fright'. Geoffrey Tyack, whose research prompted a renewed appreciation of Scott's Exeter Chapel, had nothing positive to say about the College's 20th-century architecture. In Tyack's *Oxford: An Architectural Guide* (1998), Exeter is cited as one of those colleges 'which commissioned buildings of numbing banality' after the war. But Brett is being too hard on himself, and Tyack too harsh. The Thomas Wood Building has genuine qualities – of proportion, materials and detail – that are lacking in some of the more celebrated buildings of 1960s Oxford. The scale of the corner building fits seamlessly into Broad Street and the 1960s tower on Turl Street, next to the Chapel, is neatly proportioned to counterbalance the older Lodge tower. Brett, unlike some of his contemporaries, was attuned to the appeal of organic, varied streetscapes and his building at Exeter is respectful of its setting. The building is well-crafted in stone, yet this is no historicist pastiche. The Thomas Wood Building is thoroughly modern in style, its metal windows set (for probably the first time in Exeter's history) in openings without mouldings or carvings or mullions. Brett's

work is not a feeble successor to Scott's bold Victorian stamp, but its thoughtful counterpart.

Brett's anxiety about the building may be because its design had changed substantially in the drafting stages. Drawings dated November 1955 show a restless, busy composition: to Broad Street, a faceted elevation and over-bearing attic storey; to Turl Street, the windows deflected inwards to the façade at an angle framed by a projecting box (a cliché of 1950s architecture).

By October 1957, the flimsy box had gone, the tower shortened, and the attic had acquired a pitched roof following the line of the Victorian building it abuts. In the final scheme, the Broad Street façade is completely smooth and the idea of faceting the elevation to create depth and shadow has been transferred to the tower feature. The elevational plane of the tower kinks out and back in again, with windows in each angle, giving views up and down the Turl. Such subtle modelling lends this, the most intrusive element of the new building, a strong sculptural quality.

Inside, the new Margary Quadrangle suffered from the same problem as its Victorian predecessor: the Chapel, which forms its southern side, is wholly out of proportion in height to the breadth and length of the courtyard. Nonetheless, it is a mark of the strength of the Thomas Wood Building that when, in the early years of the 21st century, architects were invited by the College to consider its potential replacement or adaptation, few could find fault with the design.

Before it became a home for bikes and bins, the Margary Quad was a fitting backdrop to *Alma Mater*, the sculpture by Joxe Alberdi installed here in 1968. A cheekily doctored photograph of the unveiling ceremony shows the sculptor in beret, and seated, Rector Wheare (on the left) and Dacre Balsdon (far right) pondering its cost. But the only person the satirist assumed was unconcerned by the expense is in fact the one who shouldered it, St Osyth Wood again, seated to the left. The Travertine marble sculpture stands on a grindstone from a spice mill near Putney Bridge, installed as a temporary plinth, but never replaced (the intended plinth was much taller). *Alma Mater* was known colloquially as 'The Object'. The sculptor's principal promoter in the SCR was Dacre Balsdon, who knew that the Fellows would hate his work (which they did).

Satirically amended photograph of Alma Mater, *the sculpture by Joxe Alberdi, unveiled in 1968.*

Ruskin College, Walton Street, Oxford. Founded in 1899, the College aimed to provide university-standard education for working men so that they could act more effectively on behalf of their communities and organisations. Photographed in 1920 by Henry W. Taunt.

The history of the College's buildings can be drawn to a close in 1968, at least for the Turl Street site, and at least for now. Aside from the refurbishment of Staircase 9 (known as 'The Rabbit Warren' in the 1890s), which included the discreet addition of rooms into what was the 'dustbin quadrangle' behind the Rector's Lodgings, there has been no major building work. The attention of College Bursars turned to other parts of Oxford. On the Iffley Road, a group of late-Victorian and Edwardian houses which had been cobbled together to form the Melville Hotel in the 1930s, was purchased by the College in the 1980s and became Stapeldon House and Stapeldon Annex. Another house, once a nunnery, was converted to graduate accommodation and renamed Exeter House.

Half a century of architectural slumber ended, however, in 2008, when the College purchased the buildings of Ruskin College, a college for working men founded in 1899. These include a ponderous Edwardian edifice containing lecture rooms, a 1960s dining hall, and a 1980s library, with student bedrooms from every era. Initially, it looked as if Exeter's architectural history might have ended where it began, with the College adapting a jumble of buildings, constructed for quite different purposes, to meet its needs. But bolder ambition emerged, and the aesthetes will hopefully come to relish the results. In 2011 the College opened its first major architectural competition for a century and a half. The challenge was radically to revitalise the Ruskin College site. The victors were Alison Brooks Architects, fresh from winning the Stirling Prize for architecture for a housing project in Cambridge, who impressed the judges with a bold proposal to build two new quadrangles with great patterned curved roofs

Above: *Saints Peter and Paul, panels attributed to Luca di Tommè, Siena c.1370.*

Right: *Mosaics by the Salviati family of Venice, who were also responsible for the mosaics in Westminster Cathedral.*

Mosaics and Hangings

The mosaics, depicting Christ in glory surrounded by saints and angels, are by the Venetian Salviati family, who worked on the Albert Memorial for Scott, and were responsible for the mosaics in Westminster Cathedral. The company was founded by Antonio Salviati, who had worked on the restoration of the mosaics in San Marco, of which the brilliant gold of the Exeter mosaics is so reminiscent. The tapestry hangings in the apse were added in the 20th century, to a design by William Morris (*Bird*, 1878), and beautifully draw together the Burne-Jones tapestry and the decoration of the apse.

The overall effect is what Geoffrey Tyack calls 'one of the finest *ensembles* of mid-Victorian ecclesiastical art and craftsmanship in England'[7]; a result that warmed the heart of Morris, whose experience of undergraduate life at Exeter had not been inspiring.

A perfect addition to the Chapel has been the four 14th-century Italian paintings on panel. The two earliest panels of unidentified saints in niches hanging on the west wall are attributed to a follower of Sienese artist Pietro Lorenzetti (*c.*1280–1348) and date approximately to the time of the foundation of the College. St Peter holding the keys of the kingdom of heaven, and St Paul bearing the sword of truth under the canopies over the Rector's and Sub-Rector's stalls are also from Siena but this time by the artist and politician Luca di Tommè, dating to *c.*1370. It is rather fitting that they should

hang so close to one another as di Tommè is known to have trained in the Lorenzetti brothers' workshop before going on to establish his own.

The presence in Scott's revival masterpiece of genuine 14th-century art would surely have pleased him; not least because Scott believed firmly that the art of Gothic Revival was no mere pastiche, but rather a taking up into the artistic endeavour of his own age the best of its medieval models. In his *Recollections* he wrote of 'endeavouring to produce an art which … adds [to the best of early Christian art] whatever of better instruction and skill our own age can afford'[8]. The exponents of Gothic revivalism in Britain were not simply recreating a golden age, but seeking those things in the circumstances of medieval craftsmanship that would help to bring about a more just social order, seeing in the common endeavour of creative design and production the overcoming of the alienation of human beings in an industrial age.

The Chapel remains a place of reflection for those who are preparing to take a leading role in the building of the society to which they belong. While we might not share the revivalists' trust in a medieval medicine for the ills of the division of labour, the decoration of the Chapel continues to provoke our reflection on how the beauty which adorns our worship coheres with the Christian vision of a humanity restored to equality.

Stephen Hearn
Chaplain 2011–13

THE ADORATION OF THE MAGI

'I know nothing that's so deliciously half-way,' said Edward Burne-Jones of the art of tapestry-making, which he placed between painting and ornament. He and William Morris had been making stained glass together since their youth but it was 1884 before they collaborated on their first tapestry, *Flora*, the original of which is in Manchester's Whitworth Gallery. Also in Manchester is a copy of the pair's *Adoration of the Magi*, the original commissioned in 1886 for the Chapel of Exeter College by the Rector, John Prideaux Lightfoot. It was Lightfoot who suggested the subject – the visit of the wise men to the infant Jesus, as told in the medieval legend of St Cologne, where they appear as kings Caspar, Melchior and Balthazar. Morris assented to the subject in a letter of 4 September 1886, writing later that the colouring should be 'both harmonious and powerful, so that it would not be overpowered.'

Burne-Jones drew the figures, producing a large watercolour and gouache modello in 1887; the cartoons followed in 1888. Morris added detail and colour, with his craftsman-assistant John Henry Dearle. Two years on the loom at Merton Abbey, the Morris & Co. factory, the tapestry was finally delivered to Exeter in 1890, having first been on display in the company's showroom in London's Oxford Street. Morris and Burne-Jones, who had been made Honorary Fellows of Exeter in 1883, gave the tapestry to the College as a gift.

Nine copies of *The Adoration* were made, the first for the poet and horse-breeder Wilfrid Scawen Blunt, then the lover of Morris's wife Janey. He requested that a camel and an Arab horse be included in the scene, although Morris resisted, pleading 'It would not be easy to get a horse into the original design.' Other versions are at: Eton College; Roker Church, Sunderland; and in the museums at Norwich, Hamburg, Adelaide, St Petersburg (the Hermitage), and Paris (the Musée d'Orsay). The last of these versions formed part of Yves Saint Laurent's remarkable art collection.

Burne-Jones also produced a painting of the same design, but in a blue-green palette with greater detail than could be rendered in wool. From 1891 this was exhibited in the Birmingham Museum & Art Gallery where every 28 August, the artist's birthday, a floral tribute was laid beneath the vast canvas by an admirer of the work. Perhaps only Holman Hunt's *The Light of the World* surpasses *The Adoration of the Magi* in the canon of Victorian religious art.

HP

Adoration of the Magi, *a tapestry from designs by Edward Burne-Jones and William Morris, commissioned by Rector John Prideaux Lightfoot in 1886.*

The College Chapel: Completed in 1859, restored 2007–09.

After two years of painstaking restoration inside and out, George Gilbert Scott's Chapel now stands revealed as a jewel of Victorian neo-Gothic architecture. Drawing on a legacy of craftsmanship, the original detailing was both exuberant and intricate, posing a substantial challenge to Joslin's of Witney, specialists in the restoration, conservation and cleaning of ancient buildings and monuments. Examples of the results can be seen on this page. It was a considerable task to re-hang the original 17th-century bell in the Chapel flèche.

THE FELLOWS' GARDEN

The first surviving picture of Exeter's Fellows' Garden is David Loggan's bird's-eye perspective map of Oxford published in 1675 *(see page 37)*, which shows Exeter with just a short garden, laid out in geometrical patterns of (probably) box hedges. The garden's most striking feature, the mound, seems to have come later. Its origin is unknown, but there is a reference to a mound in the Fellows' Garden in Anthony Wood's notes on the colleges and halls of Oxford written in *c.*1670. Similar works were a fashionable feature from the turn of the 17th century (when Francis Bacon oversaw the construction of the Walks on raised terraces at Gray's Inn in London); Exeter's more modest version may date to the College's heyday under John Prideaux's rectorship from 1612 to 1642.

The garden's aspect was transformed in 1749 when Radcliffe Square was created. By this time the Fellows' Garden extended eastwards in front of the Divinity School and there was a raised terrace at its end from which visitors could survey the staggering Baroque dome of the Radcliffe Camera, completed in 1748. The Fellows' Garden from an engraving of 1786 by 'Michaelangelo' Rooker shows the terrace reached by a set of stone steps at the end of a footpath, shaded by a row of dainty trees. In this peaceful scene, a gardener on a ladder gathers fruit, dons are absorbed in conversation and a lone scholar stands on the mound at the far end of the garden, looking out over Radcliffe Square.

For generations, the view of the Radcliffe Camera at the end of the garden was obscured in summer by two enormous horse-chestnut trees. The larger was known as Bishop Heber's Chestnut because it stood opposite the Brasenose rooms that had been occupied by Reginald Heber when he was an undergraduate at Brasenose in 1800–05. Heber went

Top right: *The Libraries and Divinity School seen from the Fellows' Garden; engraving by Michael Angelo Rooker, 1786.*

Right: *All Souls can be seen beyond the mound, which was in place by c.1670.*

on to become Bishop of Calcutta and a considerable hymn writer. When his tree had to be felled in 1990, a count of its rings by the Oxford Forestry Institute put its possible planting date at around 1771. A second chestnut on the mound was felled in 2006, also a victim of disease.

In the interwar years, part of the mound was removed to prevent damp in the Bodleian Library and Exeter's fishpond was created and with it a habitat for birdlife, including each year (in the early 2000s) a mother duck and her brood of ducklings. Until it was cut back in the second half of the 20th century, ivy threatened to completely obscure and corrupt the stonework of Exeter's 17th-century garden buildings, its Library and the Divinity School. With no ivy, and no chestnut trees, the Fellows' Garden is a lighter place than it once was.

HP

Top: *Seasonal views.*

Left: *Peryam's Buildings and the Library seen from a colourful corner of the Fellows' Garden.*

COLLEGE RENAISSANCE

FRANCES CAIRNCROSS

Few Oxford colleges in the early 19th century took education very seriously, and as Exeter approached the 500th anniversary of its foundation, it was no exception. But the ensuing century saw more dramatic and intrusive reforms of Oxford than at any other time in the University's history, and Exeter played a part in this process which was different from that of most other colleges.

The Exeter of the early 19th century was described by Mark Pattison, Victorian historian of Oxford (and Rector of neighbouring Lincoln College) as a 'genteel but unintellectual' college in which the Tutors did only what was needed to get their students through Schools. The Rector who presided over the end of the College's first half-millennium, John Cole, did little to raise the tone. Among those who came up in 1814 was John Russell, who went on to become a popular and famous West Country clergyman, known widely as Parson Jack. Russell's biographer, E. W. L. Davies, gives an uninspiring picture of the College of 200 years ago:

> An easy going head was Dr Cole, the Rector of
> Exeter, at that period. The tutors, too, taking their
> cue from him ... rarely interfered with the daily
> life of the undergraduates, so long as chapel and
> lectures were attended with tolerable regularity.
> Consequently men did much as they liked at all
> other times: shot, fished and hunted, boated,
> sparred and drove tandem; finishing each day with
> heavy drinking and convivial songs.

The College's Fellows – like their counterparts elsewhere in the University – were often clever young men who had been recently ordained and were waiting until they married or got a church living. In 1814, according to research in the College Library by Matthew Preston (1990, Ancient and Modern History), only five of Exeter's 25 Fellows held teaching or administrative posts in the College. And of the eight students who took a BA in 1809, seven went into the Anglican Church. That may have been unusually high, but in the early years of the century, about half of

Previous pages: *The Turl c.1820.*

Left: *The 'easy-going' John Cole, Rector from 1808 to 1819; portrait by the Cornish painter John Opie.*

PARSON JACK AND HIS TERRIER

The Reverend John Russell gained little academically from his time at Exeter College, where he arrived in 1814. But the time was not wasted. He spent much of it hunting, and some of it fighting rival students from Christ Church.

On one glorious afternoon towards the end of May in his final year, when strolling round Magdalen meadow with a copy of Horace in his hand but more frivolous thoughts in his head, Jack crossed the Cherwell in a punt, and walked towards Marston, 'hoping to devote an hour or two to study in the quiet meads of that hamlet,' according to his biographer, E. W. L. Davies, in 1883. 'But,' the story goes on, 'before he reached Marston a milkman met him with a terrier – such an animal as Russell had as yet only seen in his dreams; he halted, as Acteon might have done when he caught sight of Diana disporting in her bath; but, unlike that ill-fated hunter, he never budged from the spot till he had won the prize and secured it for his own. She was called Trump, and became the progenitress of that famous race of terriers which, from that day to the present, has been associated with Russell's name at home and abroad.' The bitch was 'white, with just a patch of dark tan over each eye and ear; whilst a similar dot, not larger than a penny piece, marks the root of the tail.'

Jack Russell went on to become a popular parson in Devonshire, an enthusiastic huntsman and a skilful breeder of terriers. But of his years at Exeter College, Parson Jack was wont to say that 'It was no marvel Oxford was so learned a place, for men brought up a fair stock of school learning, but carried little away with them.'

Exeter's students followed careers in the church. The College at the start of the new century was still very much an outpost of the West Country, although that had begun to change. In 1760–61, 88 per cent of the students who matriculated had been born in Devon or Cornwall. By 1801–10, that had fallen to an average of 41 per cent. The regional bias of the student body was underpinned by the restriction of many Fellowships and scholarships to the West Country.

'Genteel but unintellectual'

But the University was at last starting to change, and the College inevitably changed too. In the course of the century both would undergo massive expansion, and the University would cease to be a combination of a training school for Anglican clergymen and a finishing school for young squires.

One marked change was in social structure. When Jack Russell arrived at Exeter in 1814, his biographer notes, the College 'teemed with gentlemen-commoners, who as a rule were either the eldest sons of large landed proprietors in the west of England, or men already in possession of their paternal acres.' Those gentlemen-commoners were grandees who had paid higher fees to dine at High Table with the Fellows, and to attend only the lectures they liked. But their day was almost over. In 1816, there were 19 of them (and how they must have crowded the Fellows on High Table); by 1834, they were gone forever. Their memory lingers in the silver tankards that they often bequeathed to the College or left their caution money to purchase.

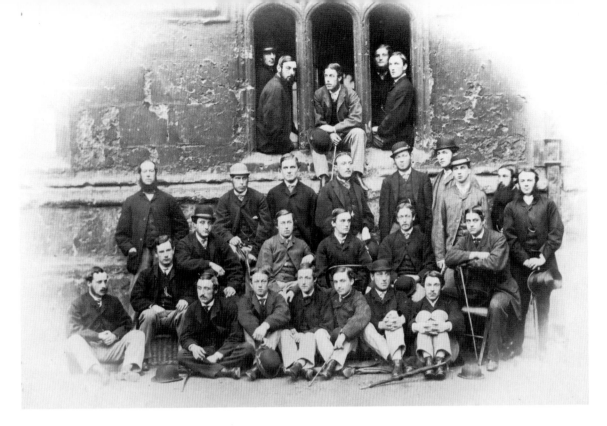

Group of Exeter students, photographed in 1864.

Rising Standards

The departure of the gentlemen-commoners was one of the most visible signs that Oxford was at last starting to take academic life seriously again. For undergraduates, the most dramatic change would have begun in 1807, with the first thorough reform of examinations. Until then, the old University examinations had been conducted orally, on entirely formal and predictable lines, so that they were almost impossible to fail. The historian Charles Boase (College Librarian from 1868 until his death in 1895) described how one Oxford student had been asked just two questions: what is the meaning of Golgotha – and who founded University College?

But in 1807 two Honour Schools were introduced, in Classics and Mathematics, and those taking them were given a class. By the end of the 19th century, these two schools had been joined by Natural Sciences (1850), Law and Modern History (1853, at first joint) and Theology (1870); the less respectable disciplines of English and Modern Languages had to wait, together with many others, until the 20th century for recognition. For much of the 19th century, a majority of students continued to take the easier pass schools, but these reforms provided the basis for the modern examination system.

Exeter was slow to raise its academic tone. Charles Lyell, whose work was to influence Charles Darwin, came to Exeter in 1816–19. He wrote to his father that Dr Cole, the Rector, was so ignorant that if he were shown the title of a book in Greek, he would not recognise the language – but that he knew a lot about

Oxford sausages. The proportion of Exeter students achieving honours degrees was lower than the University average for some time. And it was about ten years after the introduction of class lists that John Spurway of Tiverton became the first Exeter man to get a First. For his success, the College elected him to a Fellowship and later appointed him 'Inspector of the Compositions of Undergraduates', a role that sounds dreary rather than demanding.

Then, as now, getting a First was not necessarily a passport to greatness. Lyell, who took a Second in Classics, wrote to his parents that 'one of the idlest of our gentlemen-commoners, a Winchester man who seems to attend the lectures as a mere lounger … acquits himself better than I do, when I get it up carefully.' No fellow student is more maddening than the one who appears to be lazy and is effortlessly successful.

But Exeter was growing rapidly. This must have been a welcome change after a period of falling rolls, which had culminated in 1767 in a quarter of the College's rooms being unoccupied. In the 1770s the College admitted an average of only 13 students a year. A recovery had begun by about 1790, and by 1818 there were no vacant rooms. By the 1820s admissions were running at double the rate of 50 years earlier, and holding fairly steady from year to year.

College Expansion

Exeter was soon the second largest college in the University after Christ Church. In 1812, there were 72 undergraduates in residence; by 1850 that had

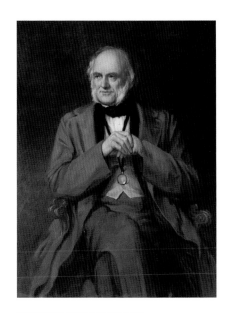

Above: *Sir Charles Lyell (1797–1875) became the foremost geologist of his day. His* Principles of Geology *(3 vols, 1830–33) established his credentials and had a strong influence on Charles Darwin's theory of evolution.*

grown to 139 students and the College was admitting 40 students a year. The numbers declined somewhat in the 1850s but then remained steady until the first years of the 20th century, when they began to climb again on the eve of the First World War. By 1897, the College had 187 students and had thus at last surpassed the success of Holland's and Prideaux's rectorships.

One important aspect of the early 19th-century growth in student numbers was its geographic breadth. Students were drawn increasingly from around the country. At last, the preponderance of West Country men vanished – a change that was reflected in mid-century with the ending of geographical restrictions for scholarships. Many of the newcomers were from London, and were the sons of professionals and businessmen – lawyers, doctors and merchants, as well as – of course – of squires.

The physical appearance of the College also began to change. There had been a lamp in the Front Quad since 1740, but in 1820 gas lights appeared. The following year a servants' hall was built. All those new students required new accommodation, and

in the early 1830s, the College began its expansion in the area that is now the Back Quad. A tortuous negotiation brought full ownership of the Broad Street frontage, some of which had been leased from the city for two centuries, and allowed the construction of the Underwood Building to house the growing numbers of students. In 1855, a large number of students were still forced to live out – at which point, the College embarked upon a frenzy of building. All of this suggests a growing self-confidence and prosperity.

Exeter's success doubtless owed something to its improving academic reputation. The dominant figure in the Senior Common Room of those days was William Sewell, a discursive but electrifying lecturer, regarded by many as one of the three best Tutors in the University. Sewell played a considerable role in raising Exeter's academic standards through the century's middle years. With the introduction of the Honours exams, competent Tutors had become a financial, as well as an academic, attraction: undergraduates were less likely to be forced to buy the services of private coaches.

The quality of college teaching was of particular importance because it was frequently the only teaching a student received (apart, perhaps, from private coaching). For much of the 19th century colleges took pride in doing all the teaching themselves, and never

Above: *Watercolour of Exeter College barge, 1857.*

Right: *Exeter College VIII in 1864, the year they beat rivals Brasenose in Torpids to go Head of the River.*

sent undergraduates to lectures outside their walls. Even the sciences, in early days, were taught largely in colleges. Exeter had its own Laboratory in the 1870s, for students studying Biology. Its equipment included a glass-blower's table, two microscopes, aquariums and a collection of osteological specimens that students could use in their own rooms.

Such inefficient arrangements could not survive the expansion of the curriculum in the later years of the century. Together with the insistence that Fellows be ordained and celibate (and come from a particular county or region), they virtually guaranteed that much undergraduate teaching would be conservative, ill-informed and mediocre.

Indeed, even after Sewell's improvements, an Exeter education was not a particularly academic experience. Arthur Brodribb, a future journalist on *The Times*, who went up in 1869 'after a good many failures', later recalled that:

> *Exeter was not a reading college, though it was courteously supposed to hold its own in the Schools, whatever that vague phrase may be taken to mean. As a matter of fact, the vast majority of its members were only pass-men, who lived healthy outdoor lives, especially on the river, without any great consumption of midnight oil, at any rate for studious purposes; a state of things with which, as I look back upon it, I am convinced that the College authorities were perfectly content. It was a healthy and useful experience; not an education.*

This was hardly surprising, given that many Fellows, right through to the 1880s, had no obligation to teach. (Indeed, as Rector Lewis Farnell later pointed out, their Fellowships carried only the 'negative obligation' of not marrying.) 'The celibate life-fellowship,' commented Farnell in his autobiography, 'encouraged ... the type of amateur, often brilliant and attractive, but unconscious of any educational call and not possessed with any enthusiasm for the increase or communication of knowledge.'

As a result, throughout the century, the business of private coaching flourished, and many young graduates made a living from it. Farnell, between graduating and winning a Fellowship, earned his living by coaching honours students, but later recalled

that 'the most prosperous part of the business was pass-coaching': getting the average undergraduate through a pass degree. Farnell recalled one well-known pass-coach who insisted that his students work eight hours a day. 'If only a college tutor would do this, Morris, there would be no need for you,' said Farnell. 'No,' replied Morris. 'But he can't and I can.'

Looking back, in the 1930s, at the dons he had known when he matriculated at Exeter in 1874, Farnell described how the Reverend Henry Tozer put

Top: *B. G. Nevinson's room at Exeter College, photographed in 1873.*

Above: *Watercolour of Anthony Gibbs's College room, c.1880, with very much the look of a gentlemen's club.*

tremendous effort into his teaching 'but the greater his effort, the more complete was his failure'. Of another: 'As a classical teacher, he was a failure … he never showed any ardent interest in the classics.' There were undoubtedly some remarkable Fellows at Exeter College during the 19th century, including some of great distinction in their academic field. But Charles Lyell would have recognised those criticisms, made more than half a century after his time.

Religion and Reform

With the rise of the Oxford Movement in the late 1830s and the 1840s, Exeter came to be regarded as a stronghold of Tractarian thought. The leading figure in the College, William Sewell, was a follower of John Henry Newman. Sewell's row with James Anthony Froude, another Exeter Fellow, became one of the most famous incidents of the age.

Froude, who deeply resented the necessity of getting ordained in order to keep his Fellowship, published a novel called *The Nemesis of Faith* in 1849. It is the tale of a young man who, under pressure from his father to become ordained, confesses doubts about his vocation, the depiction of God in the Old Testament, and the supposed infallibility of

John Henry Newman (1801–90), portrayed as a cardinal by John Everett Millais in 1889. Newman was a leader of the 1830s Oxford Movement. The intense Christianity of the Tractarians, as they were known, is associated with the Gothic Revival in Oxford by architects such as Scott (Exeter) and Butterfield (Keble). Newman himself became a Roman Catholic in 1845, and was appointed Cardinal in 1879.

the Bible. The hero's adulterous relationship with a married woman added to the uproar that the novel caused. George Eliot greatly admired the book; others, including Oxford's High Churchmen, abhorred it.

Sewell, delivering one of his meandering lectures from his usual position in front of the Hall fire in Exeter, broke off to ask whether anyone had a copy of the offending book. A student called Arthur Blomfield produced one, and in later life recalled how Sewell 'snatched the book … and thrust it into the blazing fire of the College Hall … I see him now, with Hall poker in hand, in delightful indignation poking at this, to him, obnoxious book.' With Oxford's usual gift for hyperbole, the incident soon became a public bonfire of Froude's books in the quad. Froude immediately resigned his Fellowship, to become Carlyle's chief disciple and a great literary figure, writing a *History of England* and a life of his master. He did not return to Oxford until 1892, when he was appointed Regius Professor of History.

The religious prejudices of another Exeter don, J. B. Morris, also achieved notoriety. His rooms were at the top of the tower over the Lodge – possibly those occupied in recent years by Professor Helen Watanabe – and he lived a life of extreme asceticism. He had an obsession with the virtues of fasting, and would eat nothing during Lent until after sundown, when he would boil a couple of handfuls of dried peas in a pan until they were soft enough to chew. On one occasion, he was allowed to deliver the University sermon, an important occasion attended by the Vice-Chancellor and many University dignitaries. To the horror of Newman, he preached on the need for animals to fast during Lent. 'May he have a fasting horse the next time he goes steeplechasing', said Newman crossly. The following week, to even greater dismay, Morris preached the Catholic doctrine of the mass, insisting that anyone who did not accept it was an unbeliever. For this, the Vice-Chancellor carpeted him. Not surprisingly, Morris soon found that his beliefs were incompatible with his Fellowship, and resigned.

In general, the relationship between Fellows and students in the first half of the century seems to have been marked by a growing sense of pastoral care, encouraged by the tutorial system. When Frederick Denison Maurice looked back on his financially troubled College days, he recalled two dons, William

Jacobson (a future Bishop of Chester) and Joseph Loscombe Richards (a future Rector, who paid a large share of the cost of rebuilding the Chapel), both offering him generous support. 'I hope you will allow me to do for you what I have done before now for other pupils, which is, advance any money you require for your immediate use.' Maurice went on to work with Charles Kingsley, as a proponent of the new doctrine of Christian Socialism and a leading figure in efforts to improve the lives of London's poor.

By the end of the 1840s, with Newman's conversion to Catholicism, the religious debate had waned, and political issues assumed greater importance. But the interplay of religious tradition and political reform would be reflected in the first set of new statutes since those of William Petre.

The most lasting impact of this period on the religious life of the College was perhaps the introduction of sermons on Sunday evenings. The Sub-Rector and Sewell divided the preaching between them. With all Fellows then in Holy Orders, it would not have been hard to find a preacher, even if some candidates had extreme or eccentric theological views. Later in the century came the introduction of music on Sundays and Saints' Days, and of an Organ Scholarship to coordinate and provide it.

Sunday evensong was part of a larger social change in College life – and indeed, in national life – in the middle of the 19th century. The usual hour for dinner moved from 5 to 7 pm, creating the opportunity not just for an evening service before dinner but for afternoon tea. Boase recalled another change: bowls used to be played in the College gardens on summer evenings between 7 and 9 pm, but the change in the time of dinner meant that it became too late to play, 'as it got dark and the dew began to fall'. Out too, mourned Boase, went the custom of taking an after-dinner walk on a summer evening.

The more serious academic atmosphere changed the approach to study – powerfully assisted by the advent of gas and then electric light. The Commoners no longer looked down on the Scholars as dreary swots, and both groups jointly began to make up reading parties, taking advantage of the arrival of the railways by the middle of the century.

Student Activities

Artificial light and the new seriousness also encouraged the growth of College clubs. There had been a debating society at Exeter in 1793, but clubs expanded faster from around 1840. At that point, there was an Essay Club, whose members wrote pieces on Greek banquets or the supernatural beings of the Middle Ages. And Sewell founded a Moral Philosophy Club, which flourished for a while. In the 1850s – or perhaps earlier – came the Adelphi, said to be one of the three oldest wine clubs in Oxford. It had a fine collection of plate (the gift of former presidents), its own snuff box and a drinking song, '*post multa saecula pocula nulla*' ('in the distant future there won't be any cups' i.e. carousing).[9]

The Stapeldon Club came later, in 1869, when 26 members of the College met in a Fellow's rooms to consider the formation of a debating society. Starting life as the 'college folk moot'[10], in William Keatley Stride's phrase, it then evolved into the committee of the Junior Common Room. But as late as the 1870s, when Lewis Farnell was an undergraduate, there was no purpose-built undergraduate common room. 'We met each other in Hall and the lecture room,' Farnell recalled, 'at breakfast parties and wine parties.'

By the end of the 19th century, Exeter had a profusion of clubs: a Musical Society, a Dialectical

A College Wine, Oxford.
A popular print of a Victorian Oxford undergraduate society carousing as the clock approaches midnight.

from Trinity College fell into the bonfire, broke his leg and knocked himself out. He was rescued, but the upshot was a disciplinary clamp-down of the sort that Sub-Rectors still from time to time try to impose. 'No intellectual distinction … was ever celebrated by this sort of triumphant outburst,' said Farnell sadly – and that remains the case today.

Farnell was a key figure in raising the College's, and indeed the University's, academic performance. He was elected to the newly created post of Senior Tutor in 1893 and held it for a decade. From that position in College he worked on the introduction of research degrees; on the creation of the English School, which involved a long battle with the forces of conservatism; and towards making the University more than 'an aggregate of rival or isolated colleges'. He also helped to fight off the admission of women to University membership.

In 1914, having been elected Rector the previous year, Farnell presided over the celebrations of the College's 600th anniversary. On 25 June, there was

a commemorative service in the Chapel at which the Bishop of Exeter preached on the moral and spiritual purpose of the College; and a lunch in a marquee at which the Chancellor, Lord Curzon, proposed the toast of 'Floreat Exon' and spoke of the many distinguished men the College had produced in the course of its history.

But outside sunny Oxford, the clouds were gathering over Europe. In the *Stapeldon Magazine* the following December, Farnell wrote:

All our festivities were enhanced by charming weather and our atmosphere was unclouded by any foreboding of the war-storm that has burst upon us. And now the memories of last Term are as a golden vista seen across a dark and perilous flood. The spring has gone from our year … our youth has gone forth. But they have gone forth bearing good seed, and we who must remain abide steadfast in the hope that they will return bringing the sheaves of a triumphant peace and a better life for the land.

Opposite: *Lewis Farnell, Fellow from 1880, Rector from 1913 to 1928, was a dominant figure in the evolution of the College from Victorian and Edwardian days into the interwar era.*

Below: *The 1914 600th Anniversary Ball and other College celebrations took place in glorious weather, though the clouds were gathering over Europe.*

VICTORIAN WORTHIES

The willingness with which Exeter welcomed the University reforms of 1854 demonstrates a new spirit: although Fellows still had to vacate their Fellowships on marriage, many remained in Oxford and were employed as Tutors, to be re-elected when the statutes were changed in 1882. Exeter became one of the most intellectually stimulating Common Rooms of the late 19th century, famous for its twice-weekly guest nights. There were tensions of course, symbolised by William Sewell's public burning in a student lecture in 1849 of his colleague J. A. Froude's *Nemesis of Faith (see page 67)*.

Exeter pioneered new subjects. In science its most distinguished Fellow was Sir Ray Lankester, Tutor in Biology from 1872 to 1875. From 1874 to 1890 he was Professor of Zoology and Comparative Anatomy at University College London, before returning to Oxford as professor from 1891 to 1898. Elected an Honorary Fellow of Exeter in 1889, he was one of the most distinguished biologists of the period, and wrote nearly 200 scientific books and papers.

But Classics and especially Ancient History remained central to Oxford education. During this period Exeter provided two Camden Professors. The first was George Rawlinson: elected to a Fellowship in 1840, he resigned on his marriage in 1846, but remained close to Oxford. He was active in the Tutors' Association, and was an important influence in promoting reform in 1854, when he came to the notice of Gladstone. As Camden Professor of Ancient History from 1861 to 1889 he wrote a four-volume translation and commentary of Herodotus and a prolific series of books on ancient Near Eastern history, much aided by his more famous brother Henry, the man who published the Behistun inscription of Darius and deciphered the cuneiform script (an achievement even more important than the deciphering of the Rosetta stone). But after his appointment as Canon of Canterbury, Rawlinson became an absentee professor: he would descend once a term from London and take a room in the King's Arms, from which he could see whether anyone was entering his lecture hall; each year when no one appeared he would take the next train back to London. By the time of his resignation in 1889 he had outlived his age and was despised as the last of the old-style absentee professors.

Rawlinson's successor as Camden Professor, Henry Francis Pelham, is the most undeservedly forgotten of these Victorian Tutors. Elected to an Exeter Fellowship in 1869, he resigned on marriage in 1873 but remained a brilliant College Tutor, and was re-elected when the statutes were changed in 1882. He became Reader and then Camden Professor aged 43, and President of Trinity from 1897 until his premature death in 1907. During this period his leadership was said to have 'founded a living and productive school of ancient-history studies at Oxford', which is still the largest in the world. He organised his colleagues into providing commentaries on most of the ancient historians, textbooks and collections of inscriptions.

Pelham also helped his school friend, the distinguished archaeologist Arthur Evans, to develop the new Ashmolean Museum, and was a prime mover in the creation of the Society of Hellenic Studies (1879) and the British Schools at Athens (1895) and Rome (1901), with their associated journals. Failing eyesight increasingly limited his own research, and he turned to administration: he was a great liberal, and leader of the reforming group known as 'the Club'. He was responsible for the organisation of subjects into Faculties, and was the champion of Modern Languages, Science, English and Geography; he was a founder member of the committee for Somerville College in 1879, and its President from 1894: 'no-one carried more weight in the counsels of the University, whether as a member of Hebdomadal Council or of Congregation than he.' In one famous debate, responding to a reactionary, he proclaimed to loud liberal cheers, 'Better a leap in the dark than to stand still.'

Other Exonians were great travellers. The geographer, the Reverend H. F. Tozer, was the last of the romantic travellers: elected in 1850, he 'travelled *en grand seigneur* with an armed escort where this was desirable; and on one occasion the wild peasants fled before him as from a brigand-chief, a natural mistake for the simple barbarian who saw a grim significance in his "Piccadilly" whiskers.' According to his pupil, the future Rector Farnell, he was a hopeless Tutor: 'His scholarship was without imagination or light or warmth of literary feeling, respectable,

Above: *Professor Sir Edwin Ray Lankester (1847–1929) by 'Spy' Leslie Ward for* Vanity Fair, *1905. Lankester, Fellow of Exeter (1872–75), was a British zoologist who established clear morphological distinctions in different orders of invertebrates, demonstrating that they had different origins.*

Below: *Henry Francis Pelham's coat of arms and date of birth are immortalised in stained glass in the Hall.*

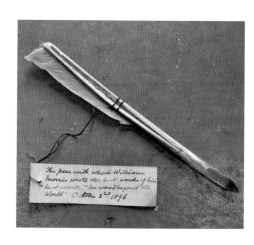

Right: *Edward Burne-Jones (left) and William Morris met at Exeter in 1853, where they lived in the ramshackle Prideaux Building nicknamed 'Hell Quad'. Their artistic legacy to Exeter is to be seen in the Chapel and the William Morris Room: items of Morris's own personal memorabilia are held in the Library.*

Morris's pen (top), button box (above), pipe (below) and spectacles (below right).

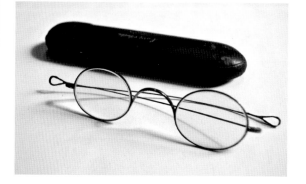

ALFRED NOYES 1880–1958

The poet Alfred Noyes completed his first published collection of poems The Loom of Years *while at Exeter. His most famous poem is 'The Highwayman'. In this extract from his* Two Worlds for Memory *(1953), he recalls his years at Exeter.*

In 1898, when I went up to Exeter College, I was a year younger than the average undergraduate of that time. The many changes that in the twentieth century have come upon that 'dreaming city' had not yet begun to operate....

I was very fortunate in having R. R. Marett as my tutor ... Marett told me that of course all my real work would have to be done during vacations; this was partly because in my first year I got into the College 'torpids' and the following summer into the College Eight. For a time rowing became the most important thing in life....

But I did an immense amount of reading, and in my fourth year completed my first volume of poems. The publisher to whom I sent it wrote a very cordial letter in reply, asking me to come and see him in London. The letter arrived just before my final examinations. His words were so alluring, and questions about Gothic so unalluring, that I went up to London in a state of glorious excitement, cut the examinations altogether and produced a volume of poems instead of getting a degree.

Somewhat to my surprise, I incurred no blame from the University authorities. In my final year I had been taking the newly formed English Literature school in which my tutor had been Ernest de

Selincourt (the editor of Keats and Wordsworth). When I showed him my poems (one of which ... had been published in *Literature*) and told him what I had done, there was a long silence, while I nervously awaited his comments. Then to my utter amazement, he remarked, looking at a letter I had shown him from the editor of *Literature* inviting further contributions: 'This is much more important.' Few young writers have been more fortunate.... It was in the last year of the rectorship of Dr W. W. Jackson (editor of Dante's *Convivio*), when I was revisiting the College. He asked me to lunch, and afterwards, with the amiable twinkle of one who is hiding a pleasant surprise, he said: 'Have you been to see the windows in the College Hall yet?'

I went to the Dining Hall as he suggested. The tall windows commemorate members of the College who are alleged to have acquired merit in various ways, from Elizabethan times downwards. A pane carries the initials of each with the date of birth. One of these windows is devoted to literature and the arts, beginning with John Ford and coming down to William Morris and Burne-Jones. The last pane in this window I discovered had been given to me, and I felt that my Alma Mater had laid a very gentle and generous hand upon my unworthy head.

Above: *Alfred Noyes's monogram and date of birth in the stained-glass window commemorating distinguished men of literature and fine arts in the Hall.*

accurate within narrow limits, but wholly arid.' Certainly his books bear this out, even if they were chosen to be part of the official curriculum in the new kingdom of Italy and the Republic of Argentina. He also achieved a geographical commentary on Byron's *Childe Harold*, and a similarly misconceived edition of Dante.

The epigraphist Sir William Mitchell Ramsay began his career as a traveller under the patronage of Sir Charles Wilson, the consul-general in Anatolia, and explored the area for most of his life

with the support of the Asia Minor Exploration Fund; he did more than anyone else to demonstrate the continuity of the cities of Asia Minor from the Hellenistic period through the Roman to the Byzantine era. Elected a Fellow of Exeter in 1882, he was unfortunately lost to Oxford when he was appointed in 1885 as the first Professor of Archaeology by a University which failed to provide him with a salary. He resigned after a year and spent the rest of his life as Professor in Aberdeen. As his friend Arthur Evans remarked:

Oxford to glorify its Lapidarium
Made a Professor minus honorarium.
The new Professor finding stones and bread
Were not convertible – discreetly fled …
So having trespassed thus on our urbanity,
Let Ramsay go, and teach the Scots humanity.

The most learned classical scholar of the age was Ingram Bywater; elected in 1863 he became a close friend of Mark Pattison, the austere Rector of Lincoln. He declined to be considered for the post of Bodley's Librarian, following Pattison's dictum 'a librarian who reads is lost', but was appointed Reader in Greek in 1883. In 1885 he married the widow of an old Exonian colleague Hans Sotheby (hence Exeter's oldest literary professorial post, the Bywater and Sotheby Professorship of Byzantine and Modern Greek). In 1887 he refused the rectorship. He was appointed Regius Professor of Greek in 1893 by Gladstone on the death of Benjamin Jowett; with this appointment the old conflict between Jowett and Pattison, teaching and research, was finally resolved.

Bywater was a great Aristotelian scholar and founder of the Oxford Aristotelian Society. He resigned the professorship in 1909, having been a Delegate of the Press for 35 years, and connected with the Bodleian Library for even longer. Unlike Pattison, he had a gift for friendship with scholars, as well as such aesthetic figures as William Morris, Edward Burne-Jones and Walter Pater. He was the chief contact of Oxford with continental scholarship. He died in 1914, in time to avoid witnessing the collapse of the European Republic of Letters as a result of his successor, Gilbert Murray, organising a public declaration of eternal enmity towards German culture. His most lasting legacy was to the Bodleian, to which he bequeathed his library of some 4,000 books illustrating the history of classical scholarship.

Oswyn Murray
(1957, Literae Humaniores)

Above left: *Stained-glass pane showing the armorial bearings of Ingram Bywater in the window commemorating men of letters and scholars in the Hall.*

SIR HUBERT PARRY 1848–1918

One of Exeter's most celebrated alumni, Sir Hubert Parry, wrote some of the choral music most deeply woven into Britain's cultural identity: 'I Was Glad', 'Blest Pair of Sirens', and most famous of all, 'Jerusalem'. Together with Elgar, Parry is the giant of Britain's great turn-of-the-century musical Renaissance. The solemnity and pomp of the occasions at which his work is so frequently performed, at Royal weddings, funerals, and coronations, has embedded him in the national consciousness – much like Elgar – as an Establishment figure and a man of religion. This legacy continues at Exeter in the splendid Freshers' and Leavers' services in Chapel, which feature feasts of his music. However, the famous late 'Songs of Farewell', written against the backdrop of the First World War, carry the cry of man in a deep tussle with the ultimate meaning of his faith.

Religion and tradition were important pillars in Parry's upbringing, his father having married twice into clerical families, and his older brother having been disinherited in the wake of losing his faith. Parry's early attempts at composition were pious Victorian pedagogical exercises, setting hymns, chants and Old Testament anthems. But when he arrived at Exeter, the Chapel choir was in a poor state, not approaching its current quality (it is doubtful whether a performance of 'Blest Pair' would have been possible then!), and so Parry's interests broadened to take in chamber and instrumental music, interests he was able to indulge as President of the College Music Society.

At Oxford, Parry read not Music (he had already taken his B.Mus while still at Eton, the youngest person ever to do so) but Law and Modern History. He was a keen sportsman and a member of the Adelphi, the College's elite dining club. He went on to become Director of the Royal College of Music, Professor of Music at Oxford and a baronet. 'Jerusalem', written two years before his death from Spanish flu in the epidemic of 1918, became a battle hymn of the suffragette movement, which Parry supported, and subsequently of the Women's Institute.

George de Voil (2011, Music)
Organ Scholar

A TURBULENT CENTURY

HANNAH PARHAM

On three occasions in the 20th century, the way of life at Exeter College was in peril. On the first, Exeter embraced an unforeseen war with youthful and patriotic fervour. As the tragedy unfolded, the College became older by the day, emptied of its undergraduates; only two matriculated in the years 1916 and 1917. By the Great War's end, Exeter counted 143 of its members among the Fallen including two Fellows. More than lives were lost: gone too was the bravado of confident, privileged, hierarchical Edwardian England. Despite heroic attempts to revive College customs after the Armistice, Exeter had changed. For one thing, its undergraduates were increasingly likely to be up on a scholarship from a grammar or county school. The new generation was serious-minded (bringing better exam results), but more worldly too.

When war beckoned for a second time, barely a generation later, a sombre College braced itself for the worst. The devastation was not, however, as far-reaching as in the First World War. The death toll was lower, at 81 men, though each fallen Exonian was no less deeply mourned. Day-to-day life at Exeter was preserved by the servicemen and cadets who enrolled on short degree courses. These wartime Exonians were from a broad range of social backgrounds, and the trend towards a larger, more meritocratic Exeter continued apace after 1945 and vivified College life.

The third period of unrest began within Exeter's own walls when, in the late 1960s, a new generation demanded liberation from the old rules. Junior Common Room railed against Senior. Students flew the flag for individual liberty, while dons rallied under the banner of the College's communal life and values. The question of admitting women to Exeter provoked a long war of attrition. The student onslaught over guest hours and the time at which the College gate should be locked each

Above: *Exeter College Beagles, September 1904; from an album of photographs belonging to C. E. Palmer, who matriculated in 1903. (Gift of Kate Doyle.)*

Previous pages: *Group photograph of Exeter's students, June 1914.*

80

A postcard view of the Turl and Exeter's Lodge in the early 20th century.

Governing Body removed a single clause in the statutes – that no woman may become a member of the College.

The traditionalists sincerely feared that Exeter's communal life would be irrevocably diminished when the College gates were opened to women, whether as guests after midnight or as full junior members. The opposite proved to be true. After 1979, there was no need for Exonians to join University societies solely to meet female undergraduates, so sociability within College thrived. It was not long before undergraduates were attending the weddings of their contemporaries at Exeter. In the final five years of the 20th century, there were nine Exonian-Exonian marriages, four of which were celebrated in the College Chapel.

Edwardian Exeter

The First World War was so unexpected and so brutal that the years leading up to it quickly acquired a mythical quality once the conflict was over. Edwardian Oxford was a world of moustachioed, upper-class undergraduates, bachelor dons, and deferential servants. The long summer days, the dining clubs, the river, the rugger, punting, hunting and grand balls which ended at dawn: these became the stuff of national memory. Many Oxford undergraduates have striven to recreate that world ever since.

At the turn of the 20th century around 50 freshmen came up each year. The College was small and male, an extension of the public schools from which four-fifths of Oxford undergraduates at that time came. Of the 482 undergraduates who matriculated at Exeter in the decade from 1901, there were 30 from Marlborough, 21 from Charterhouse, 18 from Rugby, 17 from Winchester, and three men apiece from Eton, Harrow, Radley and Exeter School. The College matriculation books recorded the place of birth, father's profession and schooling of every freshman. One or two men a year came to Exeter from grammar schools (about a tenth of the home students), but the vast majority came from a public or independent school. Exeter was not an aristocratic college, however, and most of its undergraduates were sons of affluent business men or professionals: civil servants, mill owners, solicitors, engineers, merchants, teachers,

night divided the Governing Body; it may even have hastened the retirement of the Rector. The students ultimately triumphed. 'Climbing in' became history on 28 November 1970, when a night porter was authorised to admit undergraduates to College at any hour. From 1973, keys were issued and the Turl Street Lodge gave up its long-standing defence of undergraduate morality. In 1977 the College's

bank managers and clergymen. Old Etonian Peter Broughton-Adderley of Tunstall Hall, Market Drayton, whose father was a gentleman of leisure and who matriculated in 1909, was as atypical in his own way as Clarence Cox, the son of a draper of 7 Alexandra Road, Manchester, who came up in 1913 from Manchester Grammar School.

The purpose of an Oxford education was to cultivate leadership and character. Clubs and societies – in particular sports clubs – were not 'extra-curricular activities', but a means of developing practical wisdom. Rowing in an Eight, for example, taught that technique was useless without physical exertion. Exeter's celebrated rowing don, A. B. How

(a Fellow from 1889 and known to undergraduates as 'The Beefer'), wrote in 1909:

> *The crew which maintains its form through a punishing race does so because each man has, by real hard work, toughened and trained his muscles in such a way ... to do this requires a high measure of self-denial, endurance, and pluck, and it is precisely because it demands and develops these qualities that rowing is such a splendid sport.*

Emphatically, the purpose of an Oxford education was not to qualify for a career. The men who came to Exeter had positions of employment waiting for

Exeter College Band, 1902; from William Somerset's (1899, Literae Humaniores) album of photographs, lent by Roy Somerset (1945, Modern History).

to 1 pm. By 1904 they were admitted to read in the afternoon as well, upon application to the Librarian, but junior members could borrow only four books at any one time and permission was required to take a book out of Oxford. The consequences of this policy may be observed in the *Stapeldon Magazine*, which reported in 1905 that: 'The class lists in Honour Moderations were scarcely inspiriting reading … the best we can say is, that the standard of excellence among our representatives was very even … we got seven Thirds and one Fourth.'

'Swotting' was not the done thing at Edwardian Exeter, but that is not to say that the mind went uncultivated. Intellectual enquiry was encouraged through sociable institutions like the Dialectical Society ('the Dialekker'), a philosophical debating club. At one meeting, Bertrand Russell addressed a hundred-strong throng in Hall and similar numbers gathered to hear G. K. Chesterton's 'whimsical attack on anthropologists as a class for being too sympathetic towards the heathen', as Robert Ranulph Marett (a Fellow from 1891, Rector 1928–43, and an anthropologist) recorded. Marett was unusual: he spent his vacations engaged in fieldwork, delivered University lectures, and made a contribution to the newly formed discipline of Anthropology. The majority of his colleagues, half of whom were Classics or Philosophy dons, devoted their time to teaching. College business took up any

Above: *The field takes a ditch at the College Grind, the annual cross-country steeplechase, c. 1904; from an album of photographs belonging to C. E. Palmer (1903). (Gift of Kate Doyle.)*

Below right: *College sporting ephemera from the Edwardian era.*

them when they went down, some in their father's profession, and did not need a degree to succeed. In the Edwardian period, around a fifth of Oxford Finalists were 'passmen', that is candidates for degrees without honours; another fifth took no examination at all. Most Exeter undergraduates read History, Law or Greats, but study played a peripheral role in their lives. Exeter's Library was reserved for the use of Fellows alone until 1902, and then undergraduates were allowed only to enter on weekdays from 10 am

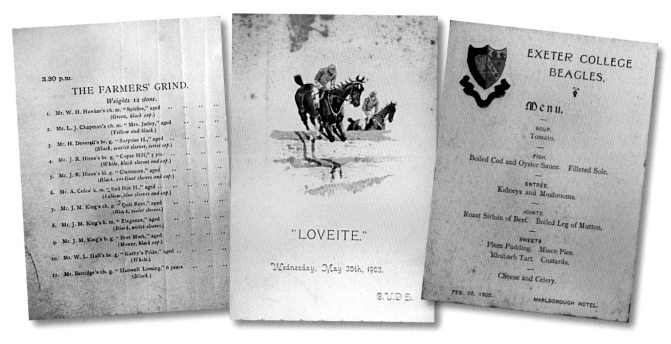

spare hours, for there was no bureaucratic staff in the Edwardian period and the tiny Fellowship shouldered a significant administrative burden.

Dons ate three meals a day in College and devoted their evenings to collegiate activities too, attending the meetings of College clubs and societies, all of which had a senior member. Indeed the relationship between senior and junior members of Exeter was intensely paternal. Marett wrote of the undergraduates he taught before the Great War: 'In our individual and private no less than in our official capacities we had regarded these men almost as sons.' Many of Exeter's Fellows were bachelors and lived in College. Exeter was for them both family and home.

It was a spartan life in the early 1900s, with coal fires, chamber pots, and lukewarm tin baths. These were lit, emptied and filled by College servants. Staircase scouts polished boots, washed clothes, laid fires, and served breakfast and lunch to men in their rooms. These typically comprised a bedroom and a sitting room, the latter with dark-wood furniture, chintz curtains, wallpaper and Turkish rugs. A decanter and glasses on a silver tray would usually be to hand, ready to be poured by the scout when the inhabitant hosted a private lunch party, as many often did.

Exeter's Junior Common Room (the President of which was, until 1910, selected by his predecessor rather than elected) resembled the billiards room of a minor country house. In 1913 the Stapeldon Society raised subscriptions to panel the JCR throughout in oak and insert 'a fireplace in keeping', designed by architect Sir Reginald Blomfield, an old Exonian. A poem was composed for fundraising:

> *Oh! J.C.R., thou Home from Home!*
> *Abode of Toast and Tea!*
> *When shall these glories come to pass?*
> *These joys when shall I see?*
>
> *When shall these eyes thy panelled walls*
> *Of fumèd oak admire,*
> *Thine arms-becoated, carving crowned*
> *And marble-fronted fire?*

The College looked like a country house because to some extent it functioned like one. Exeter College held the living of several parishes and owned a sizable

The Exeter College detachment of the Oxford University Officers Training Camp at Aldershot, 1910; from William Somerset's (1899, Literae Humaniores) album of photographs, lent by Roy Somerset (1945, Modern History).

landed estate. Lewis Farnell (a Fellow from 1880 and Rector from 1913 to 1928) rode out each term to inspect the College's tenanted farms in Oxfordshire and hosted an annual tenants' dinner in Hall where 'we gave our rubicund farmers good old port and they drank our health as easy-going landlords.' The JCR kept a pack of beagles and regular hunts, such as the Exeter College Drag, were arranged for its members. A steeplechase – the College Grind – was held each year.

In June 1914, the College celebrated its sexcentenary with customary aplomb, delighting in a ten-course meal and marvelling at the newly restored Hall. Only a postscript in the *Stapeldon Magazine* for June 1914 had a sense of foreboding, with a poem entitled 'When you are dead'.

Just as its undergraduates swapped their commoner's gowns for greatcoats, Oxford's colleges took on a new guise in wartime. Exeter housed the Oxon and Bucks Light Infantry at the start of the War, then three batteries of heavy artillery, and finally the cadets of the Royal Flying Corps. The College gardener was laid off and the maintenance of the

College's buildings reduced to a minimum, for Oxford was as short of labour as its colleges were of money. The Senior Common Room ceased to serve alcohol for the duration of the War. Not that there were thirsty mouths to quench: by Michaelmas 1915 five of Exeter's nine Fellows were away on service. The Tuition Fund Committee Minutes describe how 'In Mr Balleine's absence on military service his pass work was divided between Mr How and Dr Henderson. Dr Marett undertook the Tacitus lectures in Hilary Term 1915, Mr How the Herodotus and Dr Henderson the Pass unseens.' There were few to teach: Marett recorded that at one point during the War only seven undergraduates were in residence at Exeter.

The Interwar College

The sacrifice of their peers placed a heavy burden on the survivors who returned to Exeter in 1919. The response of many Exonians was to pick up where the soldiers had left off, reviving the traditions of pre-war Exeter. Marett described how 'it was quite pathetic to watch the few survivors who came back to complete their courses as they tried to impress on the freshmen, only too ready to obey, that College custom must be honoured in all its thirty-nine articles.' Lewis Farnell (who, while Rector of Exeter, served for three years from 1920 as the University's Vice-Chancellor) deplored 'the demoralisation of the "jazz-spirit"'. He would have been at home in Cromwell's Protectorate, ▶

THE FIRST WORLD WAR MEMORIAL

Of the 771 Exonians who served in the Great War, the College lost 143 men, including two Fellows. This was a huge toll at a time when only around 50 matriculated each year. Of the 59 who came up in 1911, 23 were killed, the highest casualty rate of any year.

The names of the Fallen are recorded on the War memorial in the antechapel, designed by Sir Reginald Blomfield, an Old Member and one of the official architects to the Imperial War Graves Commission. Blomfield designed the 'Cross of Sacrifice' that stands in every British war cemetery, but for Exeter

Sir Reginald Blomfield's brass memorial recording the names of the College Fallen.

he suggested 'a brass ... with the arms of the college, a border, and the names in Roman letters incised ... set in a black marble border against the wall'.

In a moving ceremony, the memorial was unveiled on 28 May 1921. One of those present, who had lost his eldest son on the first day of the Somme, subsequently wrote to the Rector:

I hope that I did not appear brusque on Saturday when we were speaking about the mistake in my son's initials as engraved on the tablet just unveiled. I assure you I did not intend to be so, (as no one realises more than I the difficulty in these details); the fact was that neither my wife nor myself had sufficient command of ourselves to speak much just then.

The mistake was quickly corrected, in the June of 1921. A further name was added in 1924 – that of Clarence Rupert Cox – but the century had drawn to a close before the College could make a full reckoning of its loss. Robert Malpass, a member of the College staff, discovered three further Exeter casualties in 2009; their names are among those commemorated, together with biographies and places of burial, in Malpass's *Exeter College Roll of Honour 1914–1918* (online at: www.exeter.ox.ac.uk/sites/exeter/files/publications/roll-of-honour), but they are not yet recorded on a College memorial.

HP

for he banned theatre productions which 'gratified the emotions of blood-lust or sex-lust or both combined' and made futile moves to scupper the founding of a new playhouse in Oxford in 1923. Not for the first time (or the last), an older generation condemned the young for carefree pleasure-seeking on the one hand, and serious-minded political agitation on the other. Farnell recalled of the 1920s: 'we were exposed to even worse dangers than mere idleness and frivolity ... Russia sent its evil angels abroad and some of them may have visited Oxford.'

At Exeter, however, both coffee and Communism were given a wide berth. Farnell did not count Exeter men among either the 'lazy and self-indulgent boys' or the perpetrators of the 'Red Terror' that he saw in the University at large. He remarked that 'it was my college-pride to know that none of the troublers of our peace were of my own household.'

Votes in debates in the JCR illuminate the character of undergraduates' political views in the interwar period. In Trinity 1919 two 'hotly contested' moots were held: in the first the 'Aristocratic Principle in Modern Life' was successfully defended, and in the second 'neo-Feminism' roundly condemned. The British Empire was hailed as a permanent institution (by two votes) in 1924; the 'interest now taken in politics' was deemed excessive (by one vote) in 1925. A single vote was again decisive in 1926 when the JCR resolved that 'this house deplores the entry of Fascism into politics'. The JCR's attention in 1934 turned to 'political rights and duties', which elicited an extended discussion, as did 'the religious situation in Germany'. But as international relations became increasingly strained, undergraduates shunned political questions. There were fewer debates in the JCR at large (the collective achievements of which in 1938 were to purchase a bicycle pump and discuss the colour of College ties). The Essay Club debates were, perhaps, more engaging. In Michaelmas 1937 it considered Virginia Woolf's attitude towards character. 'A Lawyer looks at Surrealism' followed in Hilary of 1938 and a talk about music was enlivened by gramophone records. In 1939 'the worth of jazz' was interrogated.

By 1937 there was a wireless in the JCR, but it sometimes seemed as if little had changed since Edwardian days. A young medic on his way to the laboratories one morning in 1938 spotted a fellow

undergraduate 'clad in riding boots, white riding breeches and a white shirt, exclaiming into the telephone, in a loud voice, "Dammit, man, how's the going?".' The huntsman was Old Etonian Walter Luttrell, a PPEist who rode to hounds three days a fortnight in winter, and spent the summer term trout-fishing or playing golf. For him, academic activities came a poor second to sport.

Even those Exonians who didn't hunt were from a privileged background (the medic, Leslie Le Quesne,

Top: *A new generation of College members at the end of the War in 1918.*

Above: *A youthful John Percy Vyvian Dacre Balsdon, whose legendary Fellowship extended from 1927 to 1969.*

who went on to be a distinguished surgeon, was the son of a barrister and educated at Rugby School). The cost of living at Exeter was around £200 per annum in the 1930s (*c.* £30,000 today, converted with respect to average earnings). Fees meant that there were rarely more applicants than places in the interwar period and it was unusual for a qualified candidate to be turned away from Exeter; in fact, there was sometimes concern in the Senior Common Room that there were insufficient applicants. Admissions were dealt with initially by the Rector, who spent many hours responding, often in the affirmative, to letters from Old Members seeking places for their sons.

But expense notwithstanding, there was a new type of undergraduate at Exeter in the interwar years: the county or grammar school boys, who came up to Oxford in increasing numbers after the First World War. By 1938 pupils from state or maintained schools made up a third of the University's undergraduate body. At Exeter, there were nine grammar school boys in the class of 1938 (around 15 per cent of home students). The number of sons of landowners and gentlemen at Oxford tailed off in the interwar years, to be replaced (in some measure) by those of blue-collar workers, clerks, small shopkeepers. In

1939 ten per cent of Oxford undergraduates had such backgrounds, double the number on the eve of the First World War.

The new boys had something to teach the hearties: success in examinations. By 1935 only a tenth of Oxford finalists were passmen and those taking no degree at all had shrunk to no more than 15 per cent. At Exeter, for the first time, in 1921, the *Stapeldon Magazine* writes of JCR members being 'in for the Schools'. The word 'tutorial' came into common parlance in the 1920s too, and was quickly abbreviated to 'tute'. Some of the old-fashioned dons insisted on the older term 'private hour'; Exeter's History Tutor C. T. Atkinson, a Fellow from 1898, maintained this form into his years of retirement in the 1950s.

Some of the more ribald of the ancient customs died in the interwar years. Sconcing (whereby drinking penalties were handed out for lapses of manners, such as talking about work or girls) was unknown to the undergraduate of 1923, reported the *Stapeldon Magazine*. A College initiation ceremony known as 'Uski-wow-wow' (which involved dragging a heavy rail, purloined from a horse-drawn tram, around the College and singing at various points) was abolished in the same year. Some attempts at exclusivity foundered too. A dining society comprising just 13 members, the Thirteen Club, was founded in 1921, but within a couple of years it was finished.

The surviving boisterousness of the good old days was tempered by a more amicable atmosphere in College. The shift is manifest in the mixed fortunes of the patrician Adelphi Club, a dining society in full vigour before 1914 but on shakier ground in the interwar years. When undergraduates returned to College after the First World War, the Rector suggested that the Adelphi be abandoned. The club secretary resisted strongly, pleading 'The Adelphi Club is not a binge club' and claiming that abolition was impractical because of 'the impossibility of disposing of the silver'. The blank pages that follow his record in the minute book suggest that the Rector got his way. An attempt to revive the Adelphi Club was made in 1923, but on strict terms: Exhibitioners were barred from membership; Fellows audited the accounts; diners had to adjourn for coffee by 9.30 pm; and the club would be shut down if conduct was less than satisfactory.

The Adelphi Club dinner of 1949.

Spectacular dinners were held in the 1920s and 1930s, but on an infrequent basis. The club maintained no minutes in these years and had disappeared by the Second World War (though it later re-emerged).

Other clubs and societies were more formally constituted and fared better, although again and again their presidents and secretaries had to plead for more members. 'It is probably of little use to appeal to the hardened picture-goers of the second and third years, but we do at least appeal to the Freshers,' implored the Musical Society in 1934. In First Week, the interwar freshman could expect a stream of callers to his rooms, impressing upon him the liveliness of debate at the Dialectical, the Church Society or the Essay Club. For sportsmen, there were College teams for rugby, association football, hockey, athletics, cricket, lawn tennis and of course, the Boat Club. Scientists could join the Lankester Society, historians the Froude Society, both named after 19th-century Fellows distinguished in each discipline. If the freshman happened to be out when the rugger captain or secretary to the Dialekker called in his rooms, then a visiting card was left – some Edwardian niceties were yet to die out.

This was a serious generation; indeed, the world was a more serious place and politics occasionally intruded on daily life in College. The General Strike in 1926 reduced Summer Eights to four days and caused the cancellation of the annual cricket match and the commemoration ball. There was no question of which side Exeter undergraduates were on in the upheaval: they volunteered to do the work of dockers, shunters, printers and policemen, or 'were called upon for the use of their own cars for transport services'. Exeter men were not deaf to the plight of the poor, however. From 1938 the JCR lent support to a Boys' Club 'both financially and through the voluntary contributions of the time of willing members'. For some, vacation social work modified the default conservatism of their middle- or upper-class backgrounds. Eric Kemp, later Fellow and Chaplain at Exeter, remembered that in 1934:

a number of us became involved with an unemployment centre which had been set up in a disused colliery office in Tredegar and went down in the vacations to help, as well as raising money. It was an appalling state of things in South Wales

… altogether the conditions were such as I have never seen since, and the government seemed to do nothing about it, which moved many men of my time in the direction of the Labour party.

In the General Election of 1929 there were four Exonian candidates (two red, two blue) although only one (blue) was elected. Three Exeter Conservatives were elected in 1931, as well as the daughter of an Exonian, Mary Ada Pickford.

In the Senior Common Room too, change was afoot. Before the First World War, dons were forbidden from marrying for seven years after election to a Fellowship, but this rule had died out by the 1920s. In 1938 the marriage of Exeter Tutor William Kneale to Miss Martha Hurst was announced. Things really had moved on, for Miss Hurst was herself a don, a Tutor in Philosophy at Lady Margaret Hall. For defenders of tradition, married dons were a travesty; how could a Fellow fulfil his pastoral role towards undergraduates from a red-brick villa in North Oxford? Even young dons such as Nevill Coghill (Fellow in English from 1924) and Dacre Balsdon (Fellow in Ancient History from 1927) were adamant that residence in College was an essential part of Fellowship. Inevitably, before long, dons had children too.

The rules governing life in College for undergraduates remained strict. A roll call was taken each morning at 7.45 am and proper attendance was a condition of graduation. The Sub-Rector's permission

Nevill Coghill in 1944. An influential Fellow and Tutor in English Literature (subsequently Merton Professor of English Literature), he was renowned for his production of plays, and his modern translation of Geoffrey Chaucer's The Canterbury Tales *(1951).*

was required to leave College before breakfast, ride a motorcycle, drive a car, acquire a gramophone, or a piano, or any other musical instrument, and to sleep away from Oxford in term-time or in Oxford during the vacation. The College gate was locked at 9.30 each evening. Vulnerable sections of the College boundary wall, such as the length overlooking Brasenose Lane, might be breached by nimble latecomers.

More commonly, undergraduates leapt in through a Broad Street bedroom window; such were the frustrations of being allocated a ground-floor room there. Undergraduate members of the University were forbidden from entering pubs during term time and gamblers ran the risk of rustication. To be apprehended by the Proctors (to be 'progged') resulted in a fine at best. More severe penalties were reserved for men who travelled to London in search of prostitutes, as if the ribbing from one's contemporaries wasn't punishment enough (the late night train from Paddington was known as the Fornicator).

The rules were beginning to rankle a little, but there were still huge advantages to living in College. Undergraduates continued to be served meals in their rooms, for example, and could host personal parties. 'I remember particularly salmon mayonnaise in summer, and gloriously hot anchovy toast in winter,' wrote David Serpell of Exeter's food in 1930. Once wartime conditions returned and rationing took hold of the buttery, these luxuries began to disappear. The rules and regulations, however, prevailed for many years to come. ▶

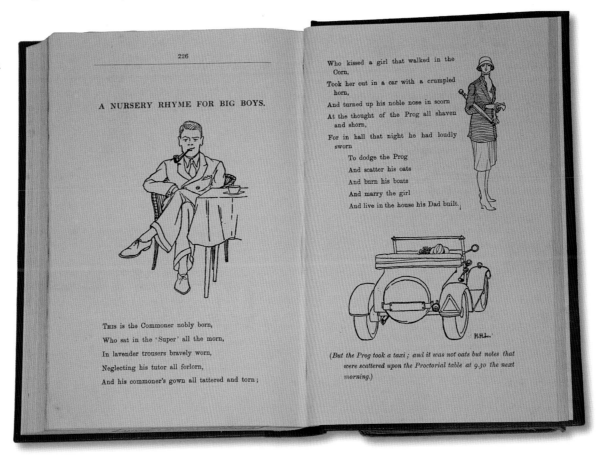

226

A NURSERY RHYME FOR BIG BOYS.

THIS is the Commoner nobly born,
Who sat in the 'Super' all the morn,
In lavender trousers bravely worn,
Neglecting his tutor all forlorn,
And his commoner's gown all tattered and torn;

Who kissed a girl that walked in the Corn,
Took her out in a car with a crumpled horn,
And turned up his noble nose in scorn
At the thought of the Prog all shaven and shorn,
For in hall that night he had loudly sworn
  To dodge the Prog
  And scatter his oats
  And burn his boats
  And marry the girl
  And live in the house his Dad built.

(But the Prog took a taxi; and it was not oats but notes that were scattered upon the Proctorial table at 9.30 the next morning.)

THE SECOND WORLD WAR MEMORIAL

Exeter's losses in the Second World War were especially high – 81 men were killed. The Classics don Dacre Balsdon wrote to the family of each serviceman to express the College's condolences, recalling particular details of the man's time at Exeter. He explained the College's intention to honour the men with a 'visible war memorial' as well as by founding a memorial scholarship for which any surviving sons of the lost men would be eligible to apply. Some 14 boys eventually came up under this scheme, starting with Paul Atyeo in 1947 *(see page 162)*. It was eventually wound up in the middle of the 1960s.

Among the replies to Balsdon's letter is one from the brother of a soldier:

Members of Alistair's old college may be interested to know that his scholarship stood him in good stead during his 2 ½ years in Japanese prison camps. He studied & taught astronomy, Dutch & Japanese, composed a Chinese (Cantonese) grammar, & translated, for the benefit of his fellow prisoners (& at mortal danger) Chinese newspapers smuggled in by friendly natives … after he was released from work on the Burma-

Siam railway in April '43, until his death in Oct '44 (of pneumonia resulting from malaria) he seems to have had more time for study than he had at any other period since he left Oxford & I think his mental activity served to keep him normal & enabled him to contribute substantially towards the general morale of the camp.

Alistair Hayes's name features on the second College memorial, unveiled at the base of Palmer's Tower in September 1946. So does that of a lone German Exonian, Rolf Alf Mühlinghaus.

The memorial, designed by the architect T. Harold Hughes, has a slender crack in the lintel which occurred in transit from the Liverpool studio of the engraver, H. Tyson Smith RIBS, to Oxford. The two stained-glass windows depicting downturned swords which flank the roll of honour were the work of Margaret Chilton of the two-woman Edinburgh stained-glass partnership, Chilton and Kemp. The 15th-century bosses in the Tower were painted at the same time and a bronze lamp installed at the centre of the rib vaulting, all part of the College's commemoration.

HP

90

Exeter in Wartime

'Trench digging is proceeding in the Fellows' Garden. Any volunteers will be welcomed.'

So began at Exeter, with the Bursar's notice on 2 September 1939, the second global war of the 20th century. At first, the contrast with peacetime was not as stark as it had been during the First World War, but the Bursar's plea for volunteers did not go unheeded. Trenches and an air raid shelter were dug in the Fellows' Garden, and a water tank was constructed in the front quadrangle too. A University fire brigade was formed in 1940 and volunteer undergraduates spent their nights on Exeter's parapets, armed with buckets of water and stirrup pumps, watching for fires from incendiary bombs. The blackout made for a spectacular show of stars on a clear night. Gerald Coombe, who came up in 1943, remembers:

> As part of our RAF training we were required to learn the location of the principal stars, and in order to do this I used to climb through my bedroom window on to the ledge overlooking Brasenose Lane and gaze into the night sky … very often as I did this I listened to a barrel organ which was frequently being played in the Turl. Whether or not at that time one heard Oxford's church bells I cannot recall, but I suspect not, as earlier in the war their use had been banned save as a warning if enemy parachutists were sighted.

Like many of his contemporaries, Coombe came to Oxford to read for a special six-month War degree for servicemen. While in Oxford, the young soldiers lived in College, matriculated as members of the University and were subject to University, not military, discipline. They joined College sports teams, attended lectures, and – having handed in their ration books at the beginning of term – ate in Hall. Normal life at Exeter, or something resembling it, thus continued for a time. The Organ Scholar from 1943, Alec Wyton, worked heroically to maintain the Chapel choir in the War years. A choir photograph of 1944 shows nine undergraduates and 16 boys, one in Naval uniform and clearly about to depart on service. At the end of Michaelmas Term, Bach's *Christmas Oratorio* was performed with Balliol. Other colleges suffered much greater disruption. Lincoln became a nurses' hostel and its Fellows and undergraduates took refuge at Exeter.

Despite the extra men and the semblance of everyday life, wartime at Exeter was dreary. Bedrooms were cold; jam, butter, tea and sugar were rationed and cigarettes were scarce; and coal shortages closed the baths under Staircase 9 on Sundays, Mondays and Thursdays each week from 1942. The privations were not solely practical: Burne-Jones's *Adoration of the Magi* was in storage at the Ashmolean and other

Right: *Instructions about coal rationing issued by the Bursar, G. C. Cheshire, on 6 October 1941.*

Below: *In the 1940s, a concrete-lined water tank occupied the centre of the lawn in the Front Quad as an Air Raid Precaution. It inevitably attracted student pranks. Here, 'HMS Ashby', launched by Henry Ashby and A. H. Fogg, c. 1941, sets bravely forth.*

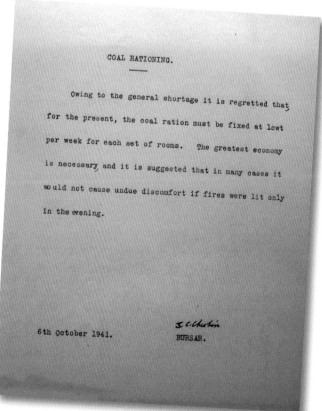

COAL RATIONING.

Owing to the general shortage it is regretted that, for the present, the coal ration must be fixed at 1cwt per week for each set of rooms. The greatest economy is necessary and it is suggested that in many cases it would not cause undue discomfort if fires were lit only in the evening.

6th October 1941.

G. C. Cheshire
BURSAR.

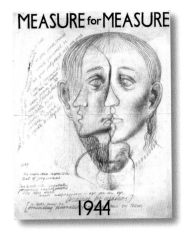

MEASURE for MEASURE

1944

College treasures were sent to the National Library of Wales for safekeeping.

But to Exeter from Wales came in 1944 a 22-year-old RAF cadet, Richard Burton, who read a six-month degree course in English. Burton was cast by Nevill Coghill in an OUDS production of *Measure for Measure*, only the second performance of Burton's career. Coghill's reaction to his Angelo was: 'This boy is a genius and will be a great actor.' Burton was a miner's son from the Valleys and, like many a poor boy, his prospects were broadened by the War.

The biggest boon of wartime was increased political support for University funding. From 1943 the government offered full grants for a university education to servicemen and women whose schooling had been interrupted by the War. Suddenly the opportunity to study at Oxford was open to anyone who could meet its entry requirements, and the soldiers seized the chance in their hundreds. By 1949, nearly half of Exeter's British undergraduates came from county or grammar schools.

Soldiers to Students

Exeter in 1946 was teeming with undergraduates, a heady mix of boys and men. There had been 4,391 undergraduates in Oxford in 1938; a decade later there were 6,159. For the first time in Exeter's history, junior members numbered over 300. The 1944 Education Act had increased the pool of school leavers who could apply for a government grant for university; hence came the boys. The men were demobbed soldiers. Around a quarter of Finalists at Oxford in the period to 1950 were ex-servicemen reading for the shortened Honour Schools.

These former soldiers were held in awe. Nicholas Thomas, who came up in 1947, remembers: 'At least one Exonian had been decorated for gallantry. Another had suffered severe facial injury.'

The Fellowship was still small, just 13 Fellows and the Rector, Eric Barber. There was only one science don, known as 'the Science Fellow', but numbers began to grow as government funding for teaching flowed to the universities. A don's life was becoming increasingly professionalised, as academic research made inroads on teaching time, but in the late 1940s there was still a strong sense of collegiate duty in the Fellowship: 'However agnostic they went to Chapel, however unmusical to concerts, however chilled to the touchlines, and, most certainly, however bored to the Barge in Eights Week,' remembered Greig Barr, Fellow in Modern History from 1945.

Undergraduates crammed into sets of rooms which before the War had accommodated a single man. W. S. Beattie recalls the 'joint sitting room, of reasonable size, even if the floor sagged in the middle, with two little bedrooms leading off it' that formed his living quarters in 1947. This was a bitterly cold winter, remembered by all who experienced it, when there was little coal, little electricity and only one Fellow had a gas fire in his room. Food was still rationed and Barr noticed 'the apparent importance of the nearby Taj Mahal restaurant in keeping Exeter body together with Exeter soul'.

Unlike after the First World War, there was little talk of 'getting back to pre-war conditions'. In 1948 the *Stapeldon Magazine* observed 'everybody realizes now that whatever happens in the future it will be most unlike what has happened in the past.' But the past proved a compelling source of inspiration for the next generation of young men, many from grammar and secondary schools, who relished Oxford's traditions, albeit with very little seriousness. In 1956, the 'suggestions books' of the 1890s Junior Common Room were discovered and republished with delight; 'we and they are uncannily (and encouragingly) alike,' noted Brian Brindley, the JCR President.

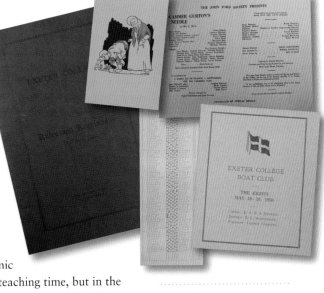

Above left: *A rare poster for Nevill Coghill's OUDS production of* Measure for Measure, 1944, *which included Exeter's young Richard Burton as Angelo.*

Above: *Post-war student life gradually regained momentum.*

Below: *The JCR Suggestion Book, once the repository of solemn handwritten requests by fogeyish junior members, reached new heights of creativity in the 1950s.*

FLORA

POMONA

Above: Flora *and* Pomona, *donated by Nevill Coghill, were the first pair of tapestries designed by Edward Burne-Jones for Morris & Co. in 1884.*

Below: *Burne-Jones's* The Passing of Venus (c.1875), *acquired in 1958, was the subject of much undergraduate ribaldry.*

Indeed, despite the greater number and broader social profile of undergraduates in the 1950s, the long-standing subculture of in-jokes and slang in Exeter's Junior Common Room was undiluted. Each year, undergraduates elected a representative for the 'Fourth Quad' (the baths and lavatories) and a Millerian Professor, whose role it was to pass on gossip and dirty jokes. Since the 1920s, the former had been chosen for the aptness of his surname (Messrs Croucher and Cock had little chance of avoiding office). Brian Brindley took the job in 1958, augmenting the titles of his office thus: 'Lord High Commissioner for Public Easement, Rear-Admiral, Privy-Flushing, Honorary Freeman of the Boroughs of Love Pennycomequick and Piddle-in-the-Hole.' There was an outcry in 1958 when the second door on each set of undergraduate rooms was removed by the Bursar. A closed door – 'sporting one's oak' – was the time-honoured sign that disturbances were not welcome (officially, it meant the undergraduate was studying; more likely, he was entertaining his girlfriend).

The force of tradition in Oxford was irresistible. In 1947 the Adelphi was revived, albeit with ration-restricted menus and mere annual dinners (but 'half an anchovy is better than no hors d'oeuvres', reasoned its President). In 1958 it was back on form, hosting an extravagant centenary dinner. By 1976 it was in peril again, banned from meeting to dine in College after the Sub-Rector's windows were smashed and the Morris Room vandalised. The Adelphi did not long survive this incident.

The Morris Room was the domain of undergraduates in the 1950s and the setting for many a club dinner. It was decorated with Pre-Raphaelite wallpaper and fabrics, forming an appropriate backdrop to *Flora* and *Pomona*, two Morris & Co. tapestries donated to the College by Nevill Coghill on his retirement. Its aesthetic was derided and defended in turn by undergraduates. A new chintz carpet in 1957 'would make a jolly good bathmat,' quipped one. Alan Bennett was not a fan either: 'the Morris Room is hideous. I know Gothic is smart but O! those curtains!'

From 1949 a subscription was raised to buy paintings for the Junior Common Room. Works by Duncan Grant, John Minton, Augustus John, Michael Ayrton and Alan Reynolds were acquired. In 1958, the JCR purchased *The Passing of Venus* by Edward Burne-Jones which set the Morris Room's detractors off again. 'Venus's Passage? … could it, please, be relegated to the Morris Room? If we have to have such obscene nonsense in the college please let's keep it together and stop the JCR being ruined,' suggested J. M. Ashworth. The painting's purchaser, J. H. Morley, replied, 'The Morris Room is too dark for the picture to be seen. This is NOT, despite dissentients, an advantage.' Alan Bennett took up the argument:

There is every reason why the picture Venus Passing should be hung in the Morris Room. Morley, with his essentially superficial appreciation of the nature of pre-Raphaelite art, has not realised that its central idea is one of wholeness. The memory of Morris, Burne-Jones, Madox Ford, Rossetti, the lot, is not served by scattering their works abroad …

Suggest as a possible site for Venus Passing where the blackboard is now – then you could drill

a tremendous screw in the door and fit it on there. All very appropriate. Mind you, it would have to be hung sideways but would be none the worse for that. Venus (passing) might take on new delights, newer from this new position.

The Old Merchant Taylor Haberdasher Askeians who are having their annual beano in the Morris Room this very moment (the sound of hearty Haberdasheraskeian merriment comes faintly through the wall as I write this) would, I think, be hardly displeased were we to add Venus Passing to the lascivious titbits (sic) which we all associate with Old Boy's Dinners.

The art collection was rarely taken seriously, and was certainly not viewed as a monetary investment (although the Burne-Jones was eventually sold at a huge profit). Undergraduate Phillip Whitehead was adamant that 'capital accumulation is not the function of the Art Fund. We ought to buy pictures we shall enjoy.' John Meakin agreed: 'let's have lots and lots of lovely mediocre paintings … I might suggest i) ducks flying over marshes ii) Spanish dancers in red frocks iii) the odd ballet dancer iv) a negress of greenish hue.'

This was an extraordinarily precocious generation that relished arguments about art, but there was bawdy banter too. A large bronze sculpture entitled 'Business', presented to the JCR by Mrs John Mowbray Clarke in 1957, was quickly renamed 'Big Business', inspired by the bull in Stella Gibbons's *Cold Comfort Farm*. The Adelphi Club ritually threatened to hurl it from the College roof and it was occasionally hauled into undergraduate beds (there were no keys on bedroom doors in those days), including that of Alan Bennett. 'A bull, sir, is the perfect embodiment of the Exeter Junior Common Room,' wrote Z. Price Zimmerman in the Suggestion Book of 1957. 'Not, sir, because of the product he so copiously exudes, oh no, sir, oh no! But rather for his incomparable *sexual prowess*. For it is a well-known fact, sir, that Exeter's Bulls are wont to romp the pastures of St. Hugh's and Lady Margaret Hall.'

For all the irreverence of the JCR Suggestion Books, this was not a generation of radicals. If clothes are a manifestation of attitude (as they began to be in the 1950s), then these Exonians – in their sports jackets and flannel trousers (known as 'Oxford bags')

– were decidedly old-fashioned. One undergraduate recalls his father's outrage when he donned a duffel coat; he was told to take it off, and he did. The closest to rebellion it got was a petition from the JCR to Governing Body for permission to drink wine in Hall. This was beautifully scribed in the style of a medieval illuminated manuscript, complete with a tiny picture of a wine-swigging undergraduate in the gilded first letter, and wax seals next to the signatures. The signatories styled themselves appropriately and included Brianus Brindley, Colinus Clowes and Cedricus ap Hugh.

In 1957 the College wall collapsed at a notorious climbing-in point, and by 1959 the long-established rule forbidding ladies in College after 7.30 pm was amended to 9.30 pm. But this was not, for the JCR of the day, the harbinger of change. While both the College walls and strictures concerning lady visitors were routinely transgressed, the regulations were rarely challenged. Indeed, the rules provided just the right level of official control for undergraduate high jinks and humour to thrive.

Above: *Exeter's John Shobbrook recorded the 1956 Oxford–Cambridge Punt Race, in which the Cherwell claimed many victims.*

Below: *Post-war undergraduates – many ex-National Service or recently demobilised veterans – found the University disciplinary structure an irksome burden.*

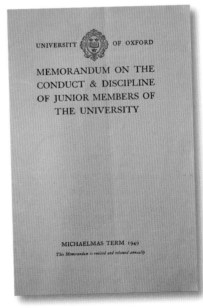

UNIVERSITY OF OXFORD

MEMORANDUM ON THE CONDUCT & DISCIPLINE OF JUNIOR MEMBERS OF THE UNIVERSITY

MICHAELMAS TERM 1949
This Memorandum is revised and reissued annually

In the 1980s, Oxford's funding pact with the welfare state began to fracture. An inevitable plateau in student diversity resulted. Oxford was made up of roughly equal numbers of state and independent or public school pupils in 1982 when Rector Crowther-Hunt reported the College was having 'urgent discussions on how to broaden our field of entry … we want more people from state schools'. In the three years from 2010 to 2012, 54 per cent of undergraduates accepted came from state schools – and 16 per cent from abroad. Exonians today come from a wider range of backgrounds than they did in 1913 or 1930, but probably have a narrower class profile than those who came up in the period after the Second World War.

The 20th century has undeniably been a story of progress. The Edwardian Fellowship would be agog at the choice of degrees, including joint Honour Schools, open to the modern student and at the international renown enjoyed by some of Exeter's dons for research. Those school boys and girls who make it past the Oxford interview today enjoy a breadth of opportunity unrivalled in Exeter's past. These privileges have been hard won. And it will take no less an abundance of imagination, resilience and generosity to defend them in the century to come.

HP

Right: *Antony Gormley's 7ft-tall iron statue is part of his 'Another Time II' series of figures. It was installed overlooking The Broad in 2009, and has been embraced as a College member.*

Below: *The relatively new ritual of 'trashing' candidates on the last day of Schools.*

creating a system of dual University and college appointments. Most of Exeter's Tutorial Fellows, like their opposite numbers in other colleges, now have a dual allegiance, and are paid partly by the College and partly by their University department.

Secondly, sources of research grants multiplied through the century, from Research Councils, from government departments, and from bodies such as the Wellcome Trust, Rolls-Royce, and (to pick one at random from the hundreds in a recent list) the Geological Survey of Denmark and Greenland. Many of the new legion of full-time researchers found college Fellowships.

A third source of state money has been student grants, which made it possible for colleges to admit as undergraduates every well-qualified UK applicant for whom room could be found, not just those dependent on parents or the College's scholarship funds. They reached their apogee under the 1944 and 1962 Education Acts, but dwindled from the 1980s. State support for students continued, although it eventually took the form of a so-called student loan (really a deferred tax on graduates).

New Classes of Fellowship

Another 20th-century change was the arrival of new classes of Fellowship. The first was the absorption of the professoriate into college Fellowships. It was said that in Victorian times a hostess once apologised to a newly elected college Fellow for sitting him at dinner beside a Professor. But the 1923 Oxford and Cambridge Act changed all that, imposing college statutes that created the status of Professorial Fellow and led to the assignment of three chairs to Exeter: Dr Lee's Professor of Chemistry, the King Alfonso XIII Professor of Spanish Studies, and the splendidly named Bywater and Sotheby Professor of Byzantine and Modern Greek Language and Literature. The equally splendid Field-Marshal Alexander Professor of Cardiovascular Medicine joined them in 1973. The holders were and are full members of the Governing Body, but unpaid by the College.

Research Fellows came along too. The statutes in force in 1914 required that at least three members of the Fellowship must be 'Ordinary Fellows', holding posts tenable for seven years with no tutorial duties; but the College's poverty had obliged it to suspend

RECTORS AND FELLOWS

When Exeter celebrated its sixth centenary in June 1914, the Governing Body consisted of Rector Farnell and nine Fellows. By October 2012, nearly a century later, eight Rectors had succeeded Farnell, 46 Fellows were in post, and 180 other Fellows had passed through. Their role had changed over the century. What were the changes, and who had been the most notable individuals?

State Grants Come to Oxford

The most striking change in the Fellowship over the period was its size. From ten in 1913–14, the Governing Body grew to 15 in 1934–35, 34 in 1974–75, and 47 in 2012–13. The growth was fostered largely by the influx of state aid, which reached Oxford's colleges via three indirect routes.

First, after the creation of the University Grants Committee in 1918, public money flowed increasingly to universities in the form of direct grants. Oxford applied some to increase the number of Tutorial Fellows who also held University lecturerships, thus

Fellow 1907–15), the other was **John Jenkinson** (Fellow 1909–15), killed in action at Gallipoli. Oxford's first Lecturer in Embryology, he is commemorated in the University's annual Jenkinson Lecture.

Among those who fought and survived were **Eric Barber, FBA** (Fellow 1913–43, Rector 1943–56), who joined the King's Shropshire Light Infantry and was later in Macedonia with the recently formed Intelligence Corps. His service to Exeter as Classics Tutor and then Rector was to continue through nearly 40 further years. **C. T. Atkinson** (Fellow 1898–1941), a military historian, was rejected for active service on account of poor eyesight. He was a Captain at the War Office from 1914 to 1918 and, nothing daunted, a Corporal in the North Oxford Company of the Home Guard from 1940 to 1944.

In the Second World War **Greig Barr** (Fellow in Modern History 1945–72; Rector 1972–82), undergraduate at Magdalen, served with distinction. By the age of 28 he had become Lieutenant-Colonel in command of an operation in Malaya that was happily overtaken by the Japanese surrender. His friendly but firm authority served him well when as Rector he had to face unruly students in the 1970s. Other academics were deployed more scientifically in wartime. **William Kneale, FBA** (Fellow 1933–60) interrupted his tutorial role in Philosophy to join the Ministry of Shipping. During later hard-won leave he wrote a definitive book about the history of Logic, before going on to be White's Professor of Moral Philosophy between 1960 and 1966. **Joseph Hatton** (Fellow 1956–90) worked as a young conscript on the British Nuclear Project in Canada, before becoming Tutor in Physics.

After 1945 few Oxford Governing Bodies failed to harbour, then unknown to themselves, at least one contributor to the intelligence work at Bletchley Park. Exeter's was **Mervyn Jones** (Fellow 1951–61), who came to the College from Cambridge. Like Hinshelwood, he was a gifted linguist, and after his spell as Exeter Classics Tutor he went on to the Hungarian desk in the Information Research Department of the Foreign Office.

* * * * *

A Fellow who attended the celebrations in 1914 would find Exeter in 2014 hard to comprehend. He (it would of course be a 'he') might be unsurprised at the effects of some changes then already afoot: marriage and family life, pressure to publish, wider recruitment of undergraduates – and would almost certainly welcome them. He would not marvel that the College permitted Fellows to be absent from time to time during term – on special leave or attending conferences – while they remained, all in all, as busy as ever. Growth in the University's student numbers and the state subsidy that had made it possible would surely astonish him, and he would be equally astonished (if not dismayed) by the presence of women in the very confines of his ancient foundation. He might rejoice that far fewer undergraduates (and none among the new growth of graduate students) came to Oxford to waste their time. Above all he would of course like continuity – and he would find enough of it: a Governing Body still formally autonomous under Act of Parliament, freedom of inquiry, a substantially unchanged system of tutorial teaching, and a friendly community of scholars young and old.

CAK

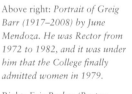

Above right: Portrait of Greig Barr (1917–2008) by June Mendoza. He was Rector from 1972 to 1982, and it was under him that the College finally admitted women in 1979.

Right: Eric Barber (Rector 1943–56) in the Lodgings, 1943.

DACRE BALSDON

When my generation arrived at Exeter College in 1957, Dacre was already busy describing us in his best novel, *The Day They Burned Miss Termag* (1961):

> The students of St George's were grey-complexioned, like their College walls, and their angry green eyes surveyed the world with a certain disparagement, as if it smelt slightly, and they with it. Fear and frustration combined to create their look of anger. Would the Ministry, would their Local Authority remain solvent? Would their grants come at the proper time? And what would happen at the end of it all, when Oxford gave them a degree and kicked them out? The world owed them a living – but, when the time came, would the world honour its debt? … They did not take Firsts, these men; but they did not take Fourths either. They did not act for O.U.D.S. or perform on instruments of music; they did not debate skilfully at the Union or play games at University or indeed at any other respectable standard. They thought, like Romans, that games should be watched, not played; and as a general rule they devoted their afternoons to the enervating pleasures of the cinema and the warm bath.

Dacre's novel is prophetic as well as accurate; for it concerns the fate of a men's college which is chosen by lot to become a women's college in order to redress the social balance. One by one the dons disappear to provincial universities, until only the most congenial are left: these lock the gates against the assembled women and with the help of the students proceed to drink the college dry before the new female Rector can take office.

The world was indeed a male world, and somewhat puzzling to those of us who had endured the realities of National Service, even if our own schooling had been in all-male boarding schools. But Dacre was obviously completely at home in this antiquated environment, where he taught Ancient History from 1927 until his retirement in 1969. He deplored the fact that the younger dons were married and lived out of College: only he and a couple of others so young that they were not yet married shared

the College with Rector Wheare and his unruly household. He clearly knew that he belonged to a passing generation, and enjoyed playing the part. At a nine o'clock Monday morning tutorial, after an SCR guest night, he would lean back in his chair and yawn: 'Stimulate me!' he would pronounce with exaggerated emphasis. And we seldom did.

Yet we loved him for his idiosyncrasies; we treated him like some rare fossil, we mimicked him and even played squash with him. If his book *Oxford Life* was rather depressing to those who hankered after some sort of change, it did at least teach us the rituals of the place. And we enjoyed his mastery of academic politics and his ability to infuriate his colleagues. I remember, one long vacation, seeing two gardeners in shorts, himself and Sir Cyril Hinshelwood, the great Professor of Chemistry, working in the College garden side by side in stony silence, each apparently pulling up the other's plants. He wrote a story about that too, in which two mutual enemies sit in adjacent rooms

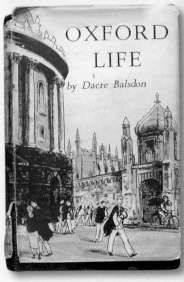

A selection of Balsdon's witty, sometimes barbed novels set in Oxford.

This drawing is being sent at Dacre's request to all subscribers to the Dacre Balsdon Fund

K. C. WHEARE
Rector, Exeter College, Oxford

This portrait sketch of Dacre Balsdon was one of his favourites.

in *Ancient Rome* (1969). The trouble with these books is that they are *too* readable and therefore out of touch with the grim march of social statistics that was just beginning.

Dacre was proud to have come up to Exeter in the days of Rectors Farnell and Marett, though little of their anthropological influence showed. The truth is that the 1920s was a period of doldrums after the pain of the Great War; intellectual life did not pick up until the arrival of the German Jewish refugees from 1934 onwards. Dacre was well aware of German scholarship: it was he who created for Stefan Weinstock a University post in Roman religion, and obtained for him an attachment (later a Fellowship) at Exeter. He was also the man who introduced us to the 'good Germans' after the Second World War – Matthias Gelzer and his pupil Hermann Strasburger.

Dacre had surprising sides: in the Second World War he had been Assistant Secretary in the Ministry of Labour, and developed a great admiration for Ernest Bevin (another novel – *Bedlam House* (1947) about the Ministry of Anticipation). He grew morning glory on his balcony, but he never talked about his origins. He acted the part of an old-fashioned bachelor don, pompous yet quizzical, opinionated and avuncular, infuriating to colleagues but an excellent dinner companion, and a kindly and engaged Tutor. He left College in high dudgeon, because the Fellows would not appoint a successor or let him continue to live in the College after his retirement as previous generations had done. He refused a retirement dinner except one privately arranged by his pupils, who filled Exeter Hall. He retired to Great Haseley, and lived a country life with daily visits to the pub, where he was known affectionately as 'the Prof'. It was not indeed until he died in 1977 that I felt I understood him truly, for at his funeral the church was suddenly filled with little Dacres of all ages – the same round face and the same rolling gait, all dressed in tweed or Sunday best, come up from deepest Devon. Dacre was suddenly revealed as the last of the country scholarship boys, a farming lad from Exeter School, who had arrived from the West Country and made it, like so many Exonians before him in previous centuries, into the rarefied world of Oxford academic life.

in Palmer's Tower, revising each other's obituaries for *The Times* ('A certain aptitude, combined with a feverish desire to better himself'... 'The carelessness which disfigured his first published work was no more commendable than the effrontery which prompted his second'), when the tower suddenly collapses, killing them both, and a brief obituary is published the next day by the editor, recording 'the close association of two such prominent scholars'.

Dacre was a first-rate novelist in the style of P. G. Wodehouse; but he was also, as J. P. V. D. Balsdon, an excellent historian in his day and a Fellow of the British Academy. It was not on the whole a good period for Ancient History: only Ronald Syme's genius has stood the test of time, and almost everyone else is forgotten. Yet Dacre was better than most of his contemporaries: he wrote excellent articles on Roman constitutional history of the sort that everyone had to read. And long before social history was fashionable, he also wrote two books in that vein that are still worth reading. There was *Roman Women: Their History and Habits* (1962) – a surprising topic for a lifelong bachelor; but he showed that he understood the psychology of women from the traditional *femina univira* to the dominatrix Messalina; and his immensely readable and informative *Life and Leisure*

Oswyn Murray
(1957, Literae Humaniores)

113

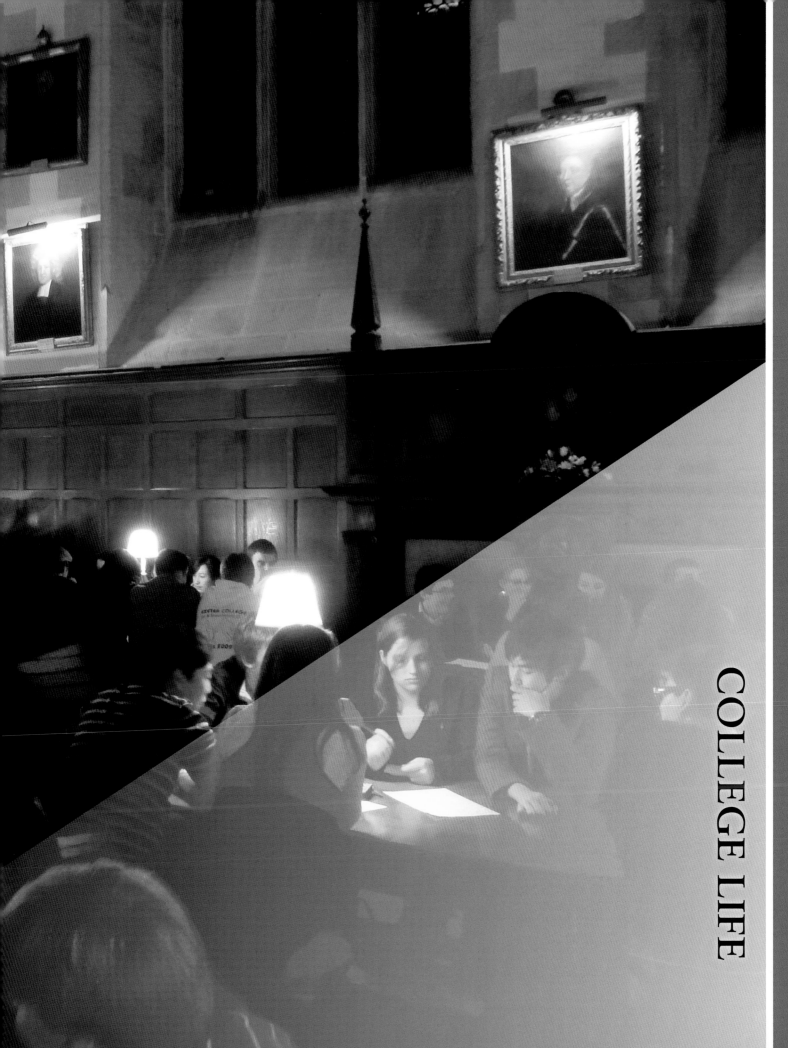

SECTION 5

COLLEGE LIFE

SEMPER EADEM

HANNAH PARHAM

Exeter has long played its part in Oxford's mass-production of nostalgia. Each batch of new undergraduates arrives in the Lodge on Turl Street with an idea, however vague, of the lives of Exonians who have gone before them. Before the year is out, they will have discovered the rhythm and customs of College life; next year, they will be explaining their intricacies to a new class of students.

So it is that aspects of College life never change. Every Michaelmas Term, the second-years urge the first-years to attend JCR meetings, join the debating society, enter drama cuppers, try for the novices' Eight. 'It can never be reiterated too often that gentlemen of the first year in residence are expected, as well as invited, to take part in its discussions,' pleaded the JCR president in 1920. His successor echoed in 1948: 'a few people … seem to think that the clubs and societies – on which the collegiate life hangs – run themselves.' Yet somehow the clubs and societies do seem to run themselves and communal life is sustained. At the close of the 20th century as at the beginning of the 21st, Michaelmas Term ends with a Christmas carol service and a College revue. The latter was known as a 'Smoker' for much of the 20th century and featured sketches, songs and (of course) cigarette smoking. In the early 2000s undergraduates were still sending up Exeter's dons, but smoking had long been banned in Hall; the undergraduate impersonating a chain-smoking politics Fellow savoured his risqué moment.

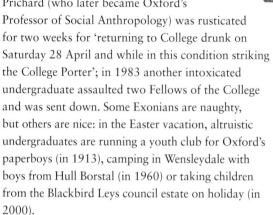

Previous pages: *Evening in Hall.*

Below and right: *Winter and summer in College.*

Hilary Term follows with the traditional Torpids, rain and Prelims. The Rugby Club holds a dinner, ending with a bagpipe tour of the quadrangle (in 1950) and the setting off of 18 fire extinguishers and the fire alarm (in 1974). Entries are made into the Sub-Rector's disciplinary book. In 1923, for example, Mr E. E. Evans-Prichard (who later became Oxford's Professor of Social Anthropology) was rusticated for two weeks for 'returning to College drunk on Saturday 28 April and while in this condition striking the College Porter'; in 1983 another intoxicated undergraduate assaulted two Fellows of the College and was sent down. Some Exonians are naughty, but others are nice: in the Easter vacation, altruistic undergraduates are running a youth club for Oxford's paperboys (in 1913), camping in Wensleydale with boys from Hull Borstal (in 1960) or taking children from the Blackbird Leys council estate on holiday (in 2000).

Then Trinity Term, starting with a ball; May week, and before long the College is in for Schools (except the second-years who are punting and picnicking at the river). Bicycles are stolen (1,539 in Oxford in 1958; 1,785 in 2008). Vehicles line up along Turl Street and suitcases, pictures and lamps are carted round the quad to be driven home. The dons work through the piles of examination scripts; their term ends somewhat later. Class lists are – or were, until electronics superseded paper – posted outside the Examination Schools.

So it was for the Exonians who served in the Great War, remembered by Rector Marett as: 'keen young men … who were just at the metaphysical age, so to speak, when one is ready to toss up the Universe and catch it on the tip of one's nose.' The Exonians of 2014 are doubtless the same. They will not suffer the devastation of the trenches, or aerial bombardment, or rationing, or be stifled by an old-fashioned establishment (we fervently hope); instead they face a future where jobs and natural resources look to be in short supply. Yet Exeter College survived the bloody and dramatic 20th century and it will survive the 21st too. As long as Exonians are ready to toss up the Universe and catch it on the tips of their noses, Exeter College will flourish.

IMAGES FROM THE COLLEGE YEAR

Clockwise: *Through the Lodge just before the start of the academic year; a snow Rector; a recital in the Rector's Lodgings; the College choir; a tutorial with Jeri Johnson; quiet study in the Library; a boisterous Boat Club Dinner; summer in the Fellows' Garden; a summer Ball.*

SPORT

Writing in the *Exeter College Association Register* in 1981, the President of the JCR said 'sport always has been and always will be one of the focal points of College life', and for many, if not all, student members this remains true. While Exeter has never been a self-consciously 'sporting' college (and it seems there have been few, if any, times where animosity between 'aesthetes' and 'hearties' has been evident) sport has played an important role in its life since the mid-19th century. Before that time the word 'sport' in the University of Oxford signified one activity above all: fox-hunting. Clearly derived from the world of the landed gentry, its organisation was centred on the Bullingdon Club. Nationally cricket also emerged from this background and in the University it, too, was organised from that club.

All other sporting activities were termed 'athletic pursuits' and were almost certainly brought into University life during the 19th century from those public and other schools from which undergraduates came and where such activities were deemed to be character-forming. As these pursuits proliferated and became centred on the colleges, and particularly when inter-collegiate competitions grew in popularity (greatly facilitated in Exeter College, according to one writer, by the installation of a telephone in the Porters' Lodge in 1904 as 'a practical solution of the problem of a quick method of communication between college and college'), Exeter was often in the forefront of new developments. As the century wore on, undergraduates were frequently remembered as much for their sporting prowess as for their scholarly endeavours. Thus 'An Old Exeter Man' writing in the *Stapeldon Magazine* in 1906 of his undergraduate time some 35 years earlier recalled Sir Hubert Parry as 'cricketer, football-player, and musician'.

Exeter was, for instance, an early competitor in racing on the Thames which had begun in 1815. Its VIII was Head of the River in 1824 in its famous White Boat *(see page 69)*, and when the first race against Cambridge was rowed in 1829 there was an Exeter man in the crew. The College was Head of the River

again in 1839, from 1857 to 1859 (when it pioneered a keelless eight, a prototype of which it had experimented with ten years earlier) and from 1882 to 1885. In 1857 two of its members, R. W. Risley and R. I. Salmon, won the Ladies' Plate at Henley, and 25 years later the College VIII won the Grand Challenge Cup with, in the crew, the legendary R. S. Kindersley who rowed in three Oxford winning crews against Cambridge in 1880–82, and played rugby for England in 1884 and 1885. Exeter's rowing has never reached such exalted heights since. Indeed, at times in the early years of the 20th century it plummeted

Above: Exeter College VIII at Henley Regatta, 1882, with the Grand Challenge Cup.

Below: Aboard the Exeter College barge, a winning VIII display their trophy (and their dogs, one of which – appropriately for Exeter – is a Jack Russell).

After the races, in a rainsoaked Torpids week (and a brimming Isis), 1901; from William Somerset's (1899, Literae Humaniores) album of photographs, lent by Roy Somerset (1945, Modern History).

to levels deemed by the *Stapeldon Magazine* in 1908 to be 'a positive disgrace for a college of our size' – a situation brought about, it claimed, because rowing had by then to compete with many other pastimes for the athlete of moderate means so that 'the river does not now habitually attract the most athletic men.' These were contributing to Exeter's high standing in that year in athletics, cricket, hockey, lacrosse, rugby, soccer, marching and shooting. At other times, especially in

the mid-1930s and at the turn of the 20th and 21st centuries, Exeter oarsmen have achieved notable success, while enthusiasm for rowing has increased considerably since the arrival of female undergraduates and greater numbers of graduate students. From the 1990s onwards bump suppers have been not unusual events both in Torpids and Eights Week and as in the University generally participation rates on the river, particularly among freshers, are high.

From the mid-19th century the Boat Club's headquarters were in the College barge. The original barge, one of the earliest on the river, was built for the Stationers' Company in 1826 and acquired by Exeter in 1856. In 1873 it was replaced by a new one, built by Salters, which survived until 1959. By then, it was reckoned to be the oldest on the river and in a seriously dilapidated state. In spite of some opposition, it was taken out of the river and scrapped. Its successor was the present boathouse, a facility much appreciated by oarsmen and oarswomen, but deemed by some at the time to mark the advance of ugliness at the expense of beauty.

Originally anyone who wished to row paid a subscription and joined the Boat Club. As other sporting activities grew in number, variety and popularity, undergraduates formed new clubs and levied a subscription and as a consequence the call on an athletic undergraduate's pocket became great. In 1851, therefore, Exeter was the first college to follow Balliol which a year earlier had amalgamated its clubs under one committee, with a don as senior treasurer, charging a single subscription that entitled every undergraduate to membership of all the clubs. The clubs in question at Exeter in the early days were the Boat Club and those for cricket, athletics, and lawn tennis, together with the Musical Club. These were joined in 1885 by clubs for rugby union and association football, and later by a separate Busters cricket club (in 1892) and by hockey (in 1901).

By 1921 clubs represented on the committee by their presidents or captains were rowing, cricket, rugby, soccer, hockey, lawn tennis, athletics, boxing, fencing and music, while two representatives from the Stapeldon Society spoke for minor sports. In 1928 music was disaffiliated and later, swimming and squash gained representation. Over the years the financial responsibility of the committee for other sports has been continually debated, some being accepted and some rejected even in cases where intercollegiate ('Cuppers') competitions took place or blues were awarded. Should the committee fund competition fees for a golfer, or a water-skier, or a canoeist? Is chess a sport, or bridge, or darts, or shove-ha'penny? By the mid-1960s badminton, squash and table tennis had direct representation on the committee while, at that stage, those who turned out

for the more light-hearted cricket teams, the Busters or the Paralytics, or who played darts or shove-ha'penny were deemed to be indulging in social activities rather than true sports.

The committee did not, on the evidence of its surviving minute books, contribute to the upkeep of the Exeter College Beagles whose activities were a feature of College life in the first 20 years of the 20th century.

Above: The College barge, Eights Week, 1901; from William Somerset's (1899, Literae Humaniores) album of photographs, lent by Roy Somerset (1945, Modern History).

Below: Blades from victorious Exeter crews in the 1880s and 1890s.

Before dying out as a named College sporting activity, the pack had become the Exeter and Balliol, and then the Exeter and Brasenose, Beagles. By 1957 the committee was declining to support financially those who wished to hunt with the New College Beagles. Colonel Sir Walter Luttrell was not the typical Exeter student in recalling in the 2005 *College Association Register* his one and a half years at the College before the outbreak of the Second World War:

> *During the winter terms I kept my horse at Grendon Underwood and hunted three days a fortnight with the Bicester. I drove home to Dunster every Saturday to hunt my own pack of beagles (returning to College on time!) and followed the Christ Church beagles on Wednesdays. The summer term was mostly spent trout-fishing on the Windrush, playing golf or sketching.*

The financing of sporting activities was not the only concern of the committee. Sport also has its social and sartorial side. Exeter, for instance, is often credited with having originated the idea of the college tie when in 1880 its oarsmen took the coloured ribbons from their black straw boaters and wore them as neckties. Later, following traditions doubtless brought from school, colours were awarded for achievements in other sports, and this led to frequent discussions in the committee over the design of ties to be worn by the recipients, the colour of team blazers, and even the metallic content of blazer buttons. These matters largely lost their importance in the later 20th century as the fashion for wearing ties declined and the cost of bespoke clothing rose. Some sports, notably rugby, still award to those

Exeter College hockey team, 1907. Geoffrey Francis Fisher, later Archbishop of Canterbury, can be seen top left.

THE BUSTERS CRICKET TEAM

I played in the Busters cricket team. We usually played teams in the villages around Oxford such as Hook Norton, Sutton Courtenay and Begbroke but once had a match against the Balliol Erratics. There was usually a barrel of beer on the field and we had a drink every time a wicket was taken or a boundary scored. The wicket keeper dangerously kept his glass behind the stumps.

Robert Smith
(1948, Modern History)

Busters cricket team 1949.

who represent the College on a regular basis the right to wear a badged blue blazer, but for those who row the traditional distinctive blazer has given way to the more practical fleece or 'hoodie'.

The committee was also faced from time to time with unanticipated social dilemmas. The popularity of lawn tennis among both male and female undergraduates, for example, in the 1930s, together with the construction of the College's own hard and grass courts on its playing field in the first years of that decade, caused problems for an all-male institution over playing matches against the women's colleges and raised the question whether ladies could with propriety use the College courts and pavilion. An experimental measure of declaring one day a week (Sunday) as a Ladies' Day seems to have solved the problem in 1937, and by the end of the Second World War the matter was no longer of concern.

From the early years of the 20th century onwards the committee had to face the inexorable need to increase the subscription. This need was created not only by the increased number of sports being played by College members but also by two other factors. The first was the burgeoning popularity of rowing (always the most expensive of the College's sporting activities because of the cost of its equipment, its headquarters and the need to employ a waterman) and the second was the acquisition of the playing field at Marston, which brought with it the need to employ a groundsman. The readiness of the Governing Body to make interest-free loans for major capital costs on occasion saved the committee from bankruptcy, and in the case of the Boat Club only appeals for funds to Old Members and the increased availability of sponsorship towards the end of the century have enabled the Club to continue to purchase new boats.

By the end of the 20th century the Amalgamated Clubs Committee system, created in the 19th, and operating at arm's length from the College's general financial arrangements, could not properly support or administer the increased sporting activities. Change therefore took place: the Committee ceased to exist, and many of its financial responsibilities were more closely tied in to the bursarial business of the College. Meanwhile the student body now elects an officer to administer sport's day-to-day finances who, interestingly, is not called the Sports Officer, as in many other colleges, but the Amalgas Officer.

From 1844 until the 1920s the College playing field was at Cowley – so far away as to be considered by some as 'antipodean' – but following the construction of the footbridge over the Cherwell from the University Parks, Exeter bought a field in Marston from the University and, in 1924, laid it out for rugby, cricket, hockey, soccer, and eventually tennis. It was opened on 2 May 1925 with a cricket match between past and present College members, won by the undergraduates despite G. J. C. Harrison (an Exonian who had become a Conservative Member of Parliament) taking 7 for 49 for the opposition. A pavilion was needed but a fund opened by the Amalgamated Clubs Committee to build one lurched only slowly along until a gift of over £2,000 by Robert Cluet III, who had come to Exeter from Williams College, Mass., in 1921, enabled what the

Exeter Athletic Club, 1985.

College Association Register called 'the finest pavilion in Oxford' to be built to the design of T. H. Hughes. 'If Waterloos are won on playing-fields,' trumpeted the *Stapeldon Magazine*, 'the British Empire may now feel tolerably secure.' In 1960–61 a squash court was built on the field to replace one on Manor Road which, since the 1930s, Exeter had rented from Merton College but which was pulled down in 1961 to facilitate access to St Catherine's College, then in course of construction.

Like the British Empire, however, neither pavilion nor squash court survived the second half of the 20th century unscathed. By the century's end neither was equal to its task, while the use of the playing field too had changed. Rugby and soccer continue to flourish there, but cricket is a sport far less popular in the College than it once was. Hockey enjoys great popularity and success as a mixed sport but is now played on artificial surfaces rented elsewhere and the tennis courts no longer exist, while squash and other sports for which there is now much greater enthusiasm (such as basketball) are served on a University-wide basis at the Iffley Road sports centre.

The activities for which these playing fields provided facilities have, over the years, however, produced cup-winning teams and outstanding individual sportsmen and women, and the general feeling has always chimed with the *Stapeldon Magazine*'s comment in June 1914 that 'though we do not, like some Colleges, specialise in "blues" we have no reason to be dissatisfied with our athletic performances.' The writer of that piece mentioned particularly J. R. P. Sandford, a double rugby and hockey blue who had played rugby for England earlier in the century, and W. C. Moore who won a bronze medal in the 3000 metres at the 1912 Olympics. But perhaps Exeter's greatest sporting era was in the 21 years after the Second World War, when most undergraduates arrived having fought in it or having completed, and been toughened up by, two years' National Service. It was also before the era when, nationally, most sports became the province of full-time professionals. Talented and supremely fit undergraduate sportsmen, particularly in rugby and cricket, could aspire to represent their countries. This was the period when Alan Helm won the English Amateur Golf Championship at Little Aston and played for England, when Denis Saunders captained the Pegasus football team which won the Amateur

Cup, when Chris Winn, a double cricket and soccer blue, played cricket for Sussex and the MCC and had a rugby trial for England, when Lachlan Maclachlan played rugby for Scotland, and when Sydney Newman and John Kendall-Carpenter played for England – the latter going on to captain the team and, later, to lead the way in establishing the Rugby World Cup.

This was also the period when Raymond Barkway ran as a hurdler for Great Britain in the 1948 Olympics, as did Bob Shaw in those of 1956, and when Roger Bannister established himself as an outstanding runner by winning the mile race against Cambridge four times and competing in the 1500 metres at the 1952 Olympics. It was on 6 May 1954, after he had left Exeter and was running for the Amateur Athletics Association against Oxford University on the Iffley Road track, that Bannister broke the four-minute barrier for the mile. The event was witnessed by few if any Exeter dons, since most were at that time dutifully attending the Marett Memorial Lecture being given by the philosopher Professor Leon Roth in the College Hall. Roger Bannister was not the first Exeter College man to hold the world record for the mile. A previous medical student, Jack Lovelock, a Rhodes Scholar from New Zealand who had run in the 1932 Olympics, broke the world record at a meeting at Princeton in 1933, and then went on to win the 1500 metres gold medal in the Berlin Olympics of 1936.

Both Lovelock and Bannister held the office of President of Exeter's Athletic Club, which lays claim, with justification, to being the oldest such club in the world, having been founded in 1850 by a group who, disgruntled at the expense and discomfort of the annual College point-to-point steeplechases (known as the Grind), instituted in that year a series of foot

The "mile of the century" thrilled spectators at the 1954 Empire Games as Roger Bannister and John Landy– up to then the only two runners who had broken the four-minute barrier– competed against each other for the first time. Amazingly, both again broke the barrier, with Bannister surging ahead to win after Landy made the mistake of looking back.

Roger Bannister in Oxford University Athletic Club strip, 1952.

races deemed in recent times to have been the first ever organised athletics meet.

Over a century and a half since that time the picture of College sport is vastly different. In the course of the second half of the 20th century the whole make-up of the College community changed. Now a college for both male and female undergraduates, it attracts a greatly increased number of graduate students, many from overseas. This latter change led to the formation in 1965, alongside the Junior Common Room, of a Middle Common Room which in some sports fields has teams of its own. Some saw the increased emphasis on academic excellence from the 1960s onwards (as measured by the Norrington Table) as being inimical to sport. But, on the contrary, the last 20 years of the 20th century brought another flourishing of sporting prowess at Exeter, greatly encouraged by three successive Rectors from 1972 to 1993: Greig Barr, for many years Senior Treasurer of OURFC and subsequently its President; Lord Crowther-Hunt, ex-Cambridge soccer blue and a dedicated squash player; and Sir Richard Norman, a keen cricket enthusiast. In 1983 the College had, in Steve Higgins, its first rowing blue for 50 years, and two years later (when Exeter reached second place in the Norrington Table) it also won Athletics Cuppers.

The 1990s saw the College admitting two Bradman Scholars from Australia and both (Geoff Lovell and Andy Ridley) scored centuries against Cambridge. In 1992 both the men's first VIII and the women's Torpid VIII earned bump suppers, and the women's cricket team reached the semi-final in Cuppers. In 1996 the women also reached the Cuppers final at soccer. By 1996, too, half the men's first VIII were members of the MCR. In 1999 the first VIII reached third position in the Summer Eights, and in 2004 Exeter had more boats in Torpids than any other college. In 2011 Exeter had a man in the Blue and *Isis* boats, and a woman in the Woman's Blue Boat – all three of which were victorious. By 2005 Exeter women's rugby team was said to be dominating the game in Oxford, later Exeter teams proved extremely successful in basketball, mixed hockey, and croquet and by then the range of sporting activity had widened so that weightlifting, dancesport, and darts were also providing blues for Exeter competitors.

Above left: *Eights Week, 2011.*

Above and below: *Exeter students were in the victorious Blue and* Isis *boats in 2011. An Exonian also rowed to victory in the Women's Boat Race at Henley in that year.*

In the second decade of the 21st century the Amalgas Officer estimates that over 60 per cent of the student body takes part regularly in some sporting activity. Such activity is seen now by society in general as less to do with the moulding of character and more to do with physical health and fitness. In the Oxford setting, it is also seen as serving a social purpose, encouraging contacts between colleges and across the boundaries of gender, academic disciplines, and years of matriculation. Sporting success continues to bring with it both personal and collegiate prestige, and Exeter College, while never setting out specifically to recruit sportsmen and women, can take a modest pride in its record of fostering and sometimes pioneering such activities within an academic community over the past two centuries, and of encouraging those who wish to pursue excellence in the field to achieve it.

David Vaisey CBE
(1956, Modern History; Honorary Fellow)

Above right: *College rugby match between current members and alumni.*

Right: *Football against Brasenose, 2013.*

Below and below right: *Exeter sports ground and 'the finest pavilion in Oxford'.*

THE COLLEGE LIBRARY

Anthony Wood, the 17th-century Oxford antiquary, was of the opinion that the first College Library at Exeter College had been established by Walter de Stapeldon: 'As for the library it was at first, as I suppose, built by the Founder … he gave several books thereunto and would if his life had been spared by the giddy multitude, have enriched it with the rarities of his time.'

As Exeter was not a college with rich endowments, that first Library was probably a rather modest room. However, books were a valuable commodity, and the most valuable were kept in locked chests while other volumes were chained to the Library desks. The Rector's Accounts for 1374 record payment for chains and bars to secure a donation of 25 manuscripts by William Rede, Fellow of Merton and later Bishop of Chichester, and there is evidence that some of Exeter's Library remained 'chained' until the early 18th century as College continued to pay for the purchase and alteration of chains for the Library until that time. Periodically in times of hardship, the College raised money by pawning some of the most valuable books (often Bibles) to one of the University loan chests.

The College had some unchained books which Fellows could borrow, but 'men were glad to read in the library, where there were many books, though chained to the desks, rather than in their stuffy little studies …'[11] Fellows were fined both for losing books and for losing their keys to the Library.

Exeter acquired its books by purchase, commission and donation. Some early purchases were two works by Boethius, *De disciplina scholarum* and *De consolatione philosophiae*, and works by Burley on ethics and logic. Donations came, to a large degree, from West Countrymen, particularly members

Burning the midnight oil in the College Library, designed by George Gilbert Scott in 1857.

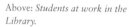
Above: *Students at work in the Library.*

Above right: *Neo-Gothic detailing in the Library interior.*

of the higher clergy such as Bishops Grandisson, Brantingham, Stafford and Lacy. The commissioning of books for the Library further highlighted College ties to the West Country – records show that parchment bought in Abingdon was sent to Plympton in Devon for the copying of works.

By 1374 the Library was said to be in need of expansion and repair and nine years later a new, substantial building was under way, funded by Thomas Brantingham, Bishop of Exeter, and John More, Rector. The new building ran north/south to catch the best light. Gifts of books and increasing numbers of readers put pressure on this building in turn, and in 1404 the Library was expanded yet again and the number of studies for readers was increased to seven.

After the extension of the Library, several rich collections were donated. In 1470, Roger Keyes, precentor of Exeter Cathedral, gave the works of Hugo of St Caro, 18 volumes of biblical commentaries, which bear at the front a curse on any who take the books out without permission of the Rector and Fellows. Further donations came from Henry Laurence, who became Rector in 1541, and John Moreman, Dean of Exeter Cathedral. Philip Bale, Rector 1521–26, left the College in his will: 'The works of S.Augystyn, S.Ambrose, Origyn, S.Jerom,

and certyn books of Byd [Bede], and the works of S.Gregorye, with other such books as my overseer shall think meyt.' In 1559 John Dotyn, a Fellow and Rector, bequeathed all his medical books to the College Library: 'All my books of fisick and naturall philosophie that be in magno volumine and in quatro to be chained in the librarie within three months after my death.' Exeter's Library still has 32 of Dotyn's books today.

Shortly after Dotyn's bequest, in 1567, Sir William Petre gave the College a number of early printed theological works as well as the magnificent manuscript known as the Bohun Psalter *(see pages 130–31)*. The psalter was made for Humphrey de Bohun (1342–73), grandson of Edward I, and had served as the prayer book of two English queens, Elizabeth of York and Catherine of Aragon. Petre acquired the book through his post as civil servant to the Tudor court. It remains one of the College's greatest treasures.

The College Library has always been an important aspect of College life. In 1539, a set of rules called the 'Customs of the College' urged bachelors to refrain from noise, bad manners and unsuitable dress and 'to frequent the public museum or library, and after the octaves of S. Dennis stay there each night from 6 to 8 ... unless the Rector thinks good to intermit it owing to excessive cold ...' ▶

THE BOHUN PSALTER

Psalters, or books of psalms, are among the most impressively decorated books of the medieval period. The central importance of the psalms in litany meant that churches and other religious houses commissioned or acquired examples for use in performance, with magnificent versions often displayed at the altar. The books, which might include other religious additions such as songs or offices, were also used for more private forms of religious observance, initially by monks and clergy but increasingly (from around the 12th century) by the laity. Secular delight and instruction were not excluded from psalters, particularly the lavish examples commissioned by wealthy patrons; these might include, for example, enticing calendar pages bearing signs of the zodiac and occupations of the month together with a wealth of decoration in the borders of their pages or in their elaborate initials. Psalters were sometimes used as primers for children to read and all members of the household might enjoy scintillating illuminations depicting everything from the most fanciful inventions of the artist's mind to intricate renderings of the natural world.

The Bohun Psalter is one of the greatest treasures owned by Exeter College (MS. 47) and one of the finest examples of English illuminated manuscripts of the second half of the 14th century. It was initially made for the Bohun family, evidently for Humphrey de Bohun (1342–73), the 7th Earl of Hereford and grandson of Edward I. His Christian name and family coat of arms occur several times throughout the volume, which was later owned by two English queens, each of whom wrote their names at the front of the book: Elizabeth, wife of Henry VII (d. 1503), and Catherine of Aragon,

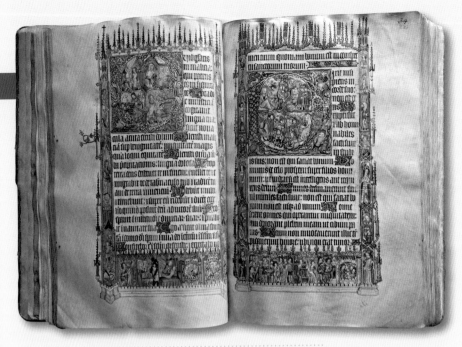

Above: *The Bohun Psalter: one of the finest examples of English illuminated manuscripts, presented to Exeter College c.1567 by Sir William Petre.*

Below left: *Inscriptions of Elizabeth, Queen of Henry VII, and of Catherine of Aragon, Queen of Henry VIII.*

Below: *Detail of Noah and the Ark, fol.8r.*

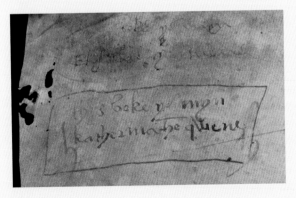

Detail from Psalm 51, fol.31v.

Scholars have recently suggested that it was worked on by a number of artists and scribes, beginning in around 1360 with a team headed by the Augustinian friar John de Tye, and completed by others at London some 30 years later for an unknown patron. Tye was associated with the Bohun family seat, Pleshey Castle in Essex, and was responsible, with his assistants, for the production of a group of at least ten luxury books for the family during this period. These survive in various European libraries, including the Bodleian, Cambridge University Library and the British Library.

The date of the psalter's acquisition meant that it just escaped loss or destruction during the dangerous years of the 1540s and 1550s, when various royal and government visitations relating to educational and religious reform proved deleterious to the safekeeping of college and university manuscripts. Unfortunately, as with many of the most beautiful and grand productions in Oxford and elsewhere, it did suffer vandalism with loss of major illuminated leaves in later years, possibly during the 18th century when many early manuscripts seem to have been carelessly managed by colleges. Despite this ill treatment, the manuscript remains an object of great beauty and has been enjoyed by many who have seen it while on loan to major exhibitions.

The absence of any early catalogues of Exeter's collections makes it impossible to estimate how many medieval manuscripts were owned before about 1600, but some 75 medieval manuscripts survive in today's Library, with only a handful acquired in the last 400 years. The earliest record of a library room in Exeter dates from 1374, a thatched building equipped, as was common practice, with chains for books not kept in chests. The Bohun Psalter, however, would have first been kept in the successor to that building, constructed in 1383 of stone with a lead roof on the east side of the current quadrangle. Three more libraries followed, including one that suffered a bad fire in 1709 to the detriment of many printed volumes. The last and present home to the psalter, Exeter's College Library, was constructed in the 19th century by George Gilbert Scott, in imitation of the Gothic style which defines the manuscript's own period of production.

who must have owned it before her divorce from Henry VIII in 1531, inscribing it 'This boke ys myn Katherina the qwene'. The psalter was presented to Exeter College, probably in 1567 along with a quantity of printed books, by its great Tudor benefactor, Sir William Petre, a courtier to Queen Elizabeth I from whom he possibly acquired it.

The large-format manuscript is preserved between original wooden boards covered in patterned damask of faded gold; it escaped the College's rebinding regime of the early 19th century. It comprises 125 parchment leaves decorated with calendar scenes, illuminated borders of great flair, rich frontispieces telling the Bible story and historiated (illustrated) initials which display, in their gilded complexity, the quality of jewels.

Christopher Fletcher, FSA
Fellow of the College and Keeper of
Special Collections at Bodleian Libraries

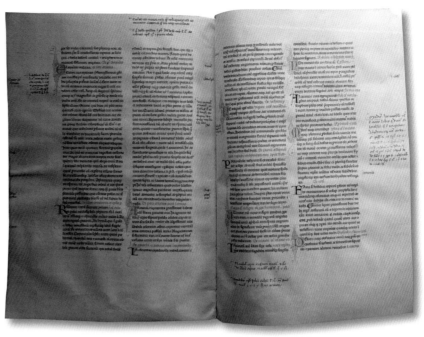

By 1624 the Library had moved into the old Chapel. Rector Prideaux's *Survey of College Buildings* (1631) describes it as 'having one room (some Time the Bachelors or Junior Common Room), and had two small Places, latterly used, the one for a Barber's Room and the other a Hole for Ashes.' In 1709, the 'hole for ashes' caused a fire which burned down the Library. Only one stall of books escaped the flames. Several benefactors now came forward with notable gifts of books and manuscripts: Richard Hutchins, Fellow, left his books to College in 1718 and in 1729 Edward Richard, Fellow commoner, gave his collection of Latin and Greek authors. In 1774 Joseph Sanford, another Fellow commoner, left his books and manuscripts to the Library. Sanford's collection, rich in 15th- and 16th-century works, includes a 1525 edition of Boethius's *De consolatione philosophiae*. These sizeable donations together with College's purchases meant that the Library became too small once again and a new building was erected in 1778. The new Library, like its predecessors, was open only to Fellows, but there was an acknowledgement that other members of College required access to the books and the following is inscribed in the College Orders, 1785: '… on the opening of the new College Library, that none have keys to it but actual Fellows: but that others apply to the Fellows for the use of their keys; or to the Bible Clerk, who is to have one as Sub-Librarian.' Junior members of College also had reading rooms scattered about the buildings.

By the mid-19th century, the College Library was again too small and also architecturally not to contemporary taste. So George Gilbert Scott was commissioned to build a library in Victorian Gothic-Revival style. Donations continued. Charles Boase, the historian who matriculated at Exeter in 1846, presented several Renaissance manuscripts, including Petrarch's annotated copy of Suetonius's *The Lives of the Twelve Caesars*. In 1889 the widow of the Biblical scholar Alfred Edersheim gave her late husband's library to Exeter College, consisting largely of Hebrew, Talmudic and early Christian literature.

In 1902 electric lighting was installed in the Gilbert Scott building and undergraduates were allowed to read there for the first time, although they had to enter by a back door and use a lower-ground floor reading room out of sight of senior members. Initially undergraduates could use the Library only in the mornings, but in 1904 they were granted permission to read in the afternoon upon application to the Librarian. Use increased steadily and borrowing figures went up year by year. Gradually undergraduates were allowed full access to the building and opening hours were extended until the 24-hour opening we have today.

The Library's stock also increased and in the 1920s new shelving was added in the Library annexe and upper reading room to accommodate it. In the 1950s, the annexe reading room was divided horizontally to provide a reading room above and extra storage in closed stacks beneath. Despite this extra space, the collection spilled outside the confines of the Library: the law collection was housed in the Quarrell Law Library

Above left: The first printed edition of the complete Hebrew Bible was published in Soncino in 1488. Exeter College owns one of the few existing copies of this work.

Above: This rare 14th-century manuscript of Suetonius's De vita caesarum (The Twelve Caesars) *was owned and annotated by Petrarch (1304–74).*

Above: Colour engraving and title page from Description de L'Egypte, *commissioned by Napoleon following his conquest of Egypt in 1798.*

Below: From the Library's copy of the magnificent 'Works of Geoffrey Chaucer', published by William Morris's Kelmscott Press in 1896. Its 87 illustrations are by Edward Burne-Jones.

under the Rector's Lodgings, many antiquarian science books were kept at the top of Palmer's Tower, and several collections of theological works were kept in the cellars of the Lodgings. Eventually, the installation of runs of compact storage shelving allowed these collections to be reunited within the Library. Access to some Library material has of necessity always been restricted, and in the 1970s many books freely available on the shelves were locked away after a spectacular series of thefts by a College porter.

The present College Library is divided between some 40,000 books on the open shelves which cover all subjects but which are chosen largely to support the curriculum and may be freely borrowed; and some 30,000 volumes locked in the closed stacks. In the stacks are the College manuscripts which range from a 12th-century Priscian to a typescript copy of a play by W. H. Auden. There are also many early printed books, including at least one printed by Caxton, Tyndale's translation of the New Testament, and several books apparently unique to the College. Worthy of special mention are *The Napoleonic Survey of Egypt* (*c*.1800) with its lavish colour plates, and a very large collection of tracts relating to the English Popish Plot of 1678. The College connection with the Pre-Raphaelite Movement is highlighted by the possession of two copies of the Kelmscott Chaucer, one belonging to William Morris and one to Burne-Jones, as well as various William Morris relics (his pen, spectacles, purse and pipes) presented by Nevill Coghill, Fellow in English.

The Library today retains plenty of neo-Gothic charm with its twisting stone turret staircase, vaulted upper reading room and bookcases elaborately carved with fruit and flowers. In term time, with over 450 junior members of College and only 65 reader seats, the reading rooms are often packed. Fortunate are those students who manage to 'bag' an individual desk in the nooks and crannies of the bookshelves upstairs where the windows look out on one side to the Fellows' Garden, 'one of the pleasantest gardens in Oxford', and on the other to the garden of the Rector's Lodgings.

Joanna Bowring
College Librarian

EXETER'S ART COLLECTION

Around the buildings of College there lies an interesting and varied collection of paintings that arc across the 700 years of the College's existence. Hanging modestly as they do, the paintings are part of the backdrop to so many shared experiences of College life over the centuries – watching over dinners in Hall, looking down on us in Chapel, catching our eye in the Library as we look up. Sometimes they become too familiar and do not receive the particular attention they deserve. Others are more tucked away and are less well-known to our eyes. Here are a few highlights from the collection, some old friends and perhaps some new acquaintances.

The earliest works in the collection are the two pairs of saints at the back of the Chapel. These were painted in egg tempera onto a gilded softwood panel at around the time of Exeter's foundation in 1314 but many miles away in a Tuscan workshop. They were almost certainly part of a much larger altarpiece by a follower of the Sienese artist Pietro Lorenzetti that at some point in its long history was carved up into sections and dispersed to different locations like so many of its kind. The panels came to Exeter thanks to a kind donation by Mr Gidley Robinson (Scholar, 1873–78). At the other

end of the collection, our most recent portrait is of the current Rector, Frances Cairncross, by Mark Roscoe, a lively and informal portrayal of our second female Head of House. Not only have the techniques of painting changed over 700 years from ground pigments bound in egg and gold leaf on wooden panel to manufactured oil or acrylic paints on canvas, but the subject matter has shifted too. No longer are artists limited to religious subjects. The anonymous 14th-century craftsmen who created our saints would have been more than a little surprised to find an artist boldly signing a commission of a University figure who was not only a woman but a layperson at that.

Exeter is very fortunate in having a number of memorable portraits of its Rectors, Fellows and benefactors. The oldest surviving portrait of a Fellow is of Sir William Peryam dating from 1599. Peryam, a cousin of Thomas Bodley, was born in the city of Exeter and later studied at Exeter for six months in 1551. He is shown here in the impressive robes of Chief Baron of the Exchequer, which office he attained in 1593. Exeter College was able to purchase this portrait on oak panel by an unknown artist in 1987 thanks to the J. L. Nevinson bequest and it is one of the few paintings to have been bought by the College rather than commissioned or given. Of a similar age but very different style and mood is the portrait of John Selden (1584–1654), an undergraduate at Hart Hall, Exeter's dependency, which later became Hertford College. Painted in oil on canvas rather than panel, Selden is the ▶

Above: *Section of altarpiece attributed to school of Pietro Lorenzetti, Siena c.1314.*

Above left: *Sir William Peryam, Fellow of Exeter, in the robes of Chief Baron of the Exchequer; unknown artist, dated 1599.*

THE PORTRAIT OF WALTER DE STAPELDON

The portrait that dominates Hall is that of the founder of Exeter, Walter de Stapeldon (1261–1326). Painted in 1780 by Matthew William Peters (1742–1814), and given to College by the artist, Stapeldon is depicted in a curiously romantic manner for a man whose calculating politics led to his swift rise and violent fall, his head hacked from his body by a London mob. Swathed in angelic white he looks down on the College he founded, the man who is said to have aided the rupture between Edward II and Queen Isabella and through his tax reforms filled not only the royal coffers but his own.

The frame around the portrait, which appears in its current position in the mid-19th-century pictures, is inscribed with the name of the founder of Exeter, Walter de Stapeldon. But Peters's painting resembles suspiciously closely a portrait of Jacques-Bénigne Bossuet (1627–1704), Court Preacher to Louis XIV of France and Tutor to the young Dauphin, which was painted by Hyacinthe Rigaud (1659–1743) and which has hung in the Louvre since 1821. Peters has an interesting history – a painter of some note and notoriety for his risqué paintings in his early career, he came up to Exeter in 1779 having decided to pursue ordination. He later combined his two passions by becoming Chaplain to the Royal Academy of Arts. Peters is known to have made copies of Old Masters on his many travels to Italy and France and it appears that this painting, which he gave to the College in 1780, may be an adaptation of one of his earlier copies. That would provide an explanation for the curiously baroque setting of this medieval bishop and politician.

Below: *Hyacinthe Rigaud's 1702 portrait of Jacques-Bénigne Bossuet (left) compared with Matthew William Peters's of Walter de Stapeldon painted in 1780.*

Far left: *Portrait of John Selden (1584–1654); unknown artist.*

Left: *Portrait of John Conant (1608–94); unknown artist.*

Below left: *Portrait of George Parker (1755–1842), 4th Earl of Macclesfield, by George Romney.*

melancholic counterpart to Peryam's sanguine pose and while Peryam boldly surveys Hall, Selden sits quietly in the SCR. A great scholar and prolific writer, Selden donated his considerable library to the Bodleian thanks in part to the intervention of the then Rector of Exeter, John Conant (1608–94) whose portrait also hangs in Hall. Conant became Rector in 1649 and found the College lacking in both discipline and funds. He set about remedying this with steady resolve as the steely look in his portrait would have us believe. The words 'Liturgy and Loyalty' are inscribed on the painting, a reference to the fact that when asked to take the mandatory oath of loyalty to the Parliamentary government in order to take up his post as Rector, Conant did so while declaring that he retained his liberty to declare allegiance to any future power God might wish him to follow.

The finest portrait from the 18th century is in fact not a Fellow or Rector but an undergraduate: George Parker, later 4th Earl of Macclesfield, by George Romney. A stunning example of this artist's work, the picture is unusual for our collection in that it is documented from its creation. Romney was paid 18 guineas for the portrait in 1776 by the sitter who then gave it to Rector Thomas Bray in 1777 and it has remained at Exeter ever since. Born in 1755, Parker came up to Exeter in 1773, going on to become MP for Woodstock and later Minehead and serving as Captain of the Yeoman of the Guard from 1804–30. Incidentally, a very handsome portrait of Bray with a view of College in the background hangs in Hall.

Moving on to the 19th century, the portraits of two Rectors, John Cole (Rector 1808–19), by his fellow Cornishman, John Opie, and Thomas Phillips's portrait of his successor, John Collier Jones (Rector

Above: *Portrait of John Collier Jones (1770–1838) by Thomas Phillips.*

Above right: *Portrait of Sir (Edwin) Ray Lankester (1847–1929) by John Collier, 1904.*

Right: *Portrait of John Mavrogordato (1882–1970) by Mark Gertler.*

Far right: *Portrait of Rector Eric Barber (1888–1965) by Pietro Annigoni.*

The 20th-century collection is no less full of interesting characters. From the early part of the century is the large portrait of Sir (Edwin) Ray Lankester (1847–1929) by John Collier, dated 1904. A talented invertebrate zoologist and evolutionary biologist, Lankester became a Fellow of Exeter in 1872. He went on to become the Director of the Natural History Museum in London where he fought for the Museum's independence from the supervision of the British Museum. But it is as a teacher that he is best known, so it seems fitting that he is portrayed here leaning on a copy of the *Quarterly Journal of Microscopial Science* of which he was editor, chalk in hand, a sketch on the board behind him, crustaceae in front of him (he founded the Marine Biological Association in 1884). It is equally fitting that he was painted by Collier, who had also portrayed his fellow zoologist, Charles Darwin (now in the National Portrait Gallery), and who was son-in-law to Thomas Henry Huxley, 'Darwin's Bulldog', one of the most influential scientists of the 19th century and a major influence on Lankester. It is no wonder it is such a personal portrait as painter and sitter were part of the same circle of friends.

until his death in 1838), stand out. The latter was a former naval chaplain on board HMS *Temeraire* (the ship immortalised in J. M. W. Turner's *Fighting Temeraire*) and here Jones holds a chart to remind us of his seafaring past.

Just as personal is Mark Gertler's small portrait
of John Mavrogordato (1882–1970). Mavrogordato
was an undergraduate at Exeter, returning in 1939
as Bywater and Sotheby Professor of Byzantine and
Modern Greek Language and Literature. Alongside his
academic life, Mavrogordato worked to foster political
understanding between Britain and Greece and was a
talented amateur artist. He was well known to many
galleries in London and through them got to know
members of the Bloomsbury and Camden Town groups,
some of whose works he purchased. He was close friends
with a number of these artists, among them the troubled
Mark Gertler (1891–1939), a part of the doomed love
triangle between Dora Carrington and Lytton Strachey,
who painted this very sympathetic portrait in 1926.

Another very fine example of 20th-century
portraiture is also of a Greek scholar, the 1954 portrait
of Eric Barber (Rector 1943–56). It is by Pietro Annigoni
(1910–88), most famous for his portrait of the young
Queen Elizabeth II. In its skill of execution, clarity of
detail and mood of still gravity this picture recalls early
Netherlandish portraiture while the strong chiaroscuro
gives the painting an almost sculptural quality.

The most well-known artists to have emerged
from the College itself are of course William Morris
(1834–96) and Edward Burne-Jones (1833–98),

founder members of the pre-Raphaelite brotherhood.
Although the College does not possess any paintings
by them, there is a small collection of beautiful
drawings by Burne-Jones in the Morris Room,
unmistakeably his with the softest *sfumato* shading.
These hang alongside tapestries by Morris of *Flora*
and *Pomona* and Kenneth Robinson's 1949 copy of

Above: *Dutch Interior,
attributed to Pieter Elinga
Janssens c.1660.*

Below left: *Pencil studies by
Edward Burne-Jones.*

G. F. Watts's portrait of William Morris (the original hangs in the National Portrait Gallery).

With such an array of styles of portraiture with subjects ranging from saints to scientists, one might be forgiven for forgetting that Exeter also has a couple of oil paintings that are *not* portraits. Both are Dutch and date from the 17th century but the similarities end there. Abraham Storck's *Harbour Scene* is a virtuoso caprice. Part Venice, part Amsterdam, it is a vehicle for Storck (1644–1708) to demonstrate his prodigious talents as a marine painter. While a dramatic gale howls across Storck's harbour, all is calm and still in

the *Dutch Interior* attributed to Pieter Elinga Janssens (1623– *c*.1682), a dedicated and detailed homage to the peaceful domestic interiors made so popular by Pieter de Hooch (1629–84).

Exeter's collection of paintings is by no means the largest or best known among the colleges of Oxford but it is not lacking in quality or depth. Rather like the College itself, it is outwardly modest but well worth taking a closer look at to discover the treasures within.

Georgina Dennis, *née Pelham*
(1988, Modern History)

Dutch Harbour Scene by Abraham Storck (1644–1708).

MUSIC

Unlike William of Wykeham's New College, where in 1379 provision was made for 16 choristers, Exeter does not appear to have had a choral foundation in the Middle Ages.

Music at medieval Exeter would surely have been the Fellows singing plainsong in the various Chapel offices and domestic music-making. The archives mention that a 'citola' (a stringed instrument that appears in much medieval iconography) was repaired in 1372, and in 1377 another stringed instrument – a 'fiola' – was bought for the Chapel. There must also at some point have been an organ (probably consisting of one rank of pipes) because in 1424 a bench was bought to support it and in 1475 a small sum was paid to repair it. It was dismantled in 1553 during the Edwardian years, but the 16th-century records give some clues about the nature of domestic music-making within the College. Two Fellows died in 1577 and in the inventory of their possessions, James Raynoldes is recorded as having 'a payre of virginalles' (a keyboard instrument) worth 20s. and a lute, worth 8s. (both worth a lot more than the organ, which had been dismantled and its pipes sold for 5s.); and John Symson possessed three lutes worth £3 and a book of music for lute worth 4s.

Records are scarce in the College's first 500 years, but from the mid-19th century they are plentiful. The first records of the Exeter College Music Society date from 1859, perhaps no coincidence since that year saw the consecration of the new Chapel. Concerts were, however, held in the Hall and a performance on Saturday 17 March 1859 consisted of choruses, solos and duets by such composers as Handel, Gluck, Rossini, Mendelssohn and Spohr. The 1861 minutes of the Society state 'that the direct object of ECMS be the encouragement and practice of Vocal Music'. This emphasis on vocal rather than instrumental music is intriguing, but playing an instrument, apart perhaps from the piano, was perhaps not an activity cultivated by Victorian Gentlemen.

A concert given in 1868 gives some idea of the content of the Society's early performances. Two things make this particular one special; first, it includes a piece by Exeter's most famous composer C. H. H. Parry, then an undergraduate; secondly, the conductor was Dr John Stainer, then Organist of Magdalen College, later to be Organist of St Paul's Cathedral, and Professor of Music at Oxford. Although Parry's work was well received by the local press, the minutes of the Honorary Secretary Heathcote Long recorded that 'the composition is clever but rather wants energy throughout it.'

The opening of the new Chapel in 1859 saw the appointment of the first organist: William Henry Bliss, later to be Vicar of Kew and Chaplain to the Queen. Boy trebles seem to have provided the top line for the choir from at least 1864 as the Music Society minutes read: 'No concert was given by the Society this term; for owing to the large importation into the Choir of boys who had little or no knowledge of music, it was deemed impracticable to give any concert whatsoever.'

Among 19th-century organists (or Organ Scholars – the terms seem to have been interchangeable), there were distinguished figures such as A. Herbert Brewer, later to be Organist of Gloucester Cathedral, and the composer Lawrence Collingwood, a friend of Elgar and a pioneering figure in the development of recording techniques. The Organ Scholarship seems to have been formalised in 1923 and until the late 1950s scholars were elected every four years. Among them were two future composers: Bernard Naylor, a pupil of Vaughan Williams and later conductor of the Winnipeg Symphony Orchestra, and John Gardner. The latter might now be known mainly for his light carols written for St Paul's Girls' School, but in the early 1950s Gardner was a force to be reckoned with. His First Symphony was premièred at the Cheltenham

Top Left: *Exeter Musical Society 1946.*

Above: The Rectoratorio, *written in 1949 to welcome the Rector back to his refurbished Lodgings.*

Below: *Recital programme, 1951, including John Gardner as accompanist.*

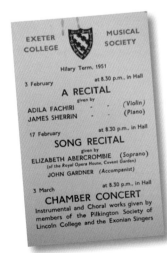

Above: *Organ Scholar George de Voil (2011, Music)).*

Below: *The College choir sings Matins on Ascension Day on the roof of the Lodge tower in 2012.*

Musicology as a discipline in England. His successor (as a Lecturer not as a Fellow – St Hugh's had snapped that up) was John Warrack in 1984. Warrack had been a prominent music critic, and helped to bring Alfred Brendel to give a piano recital in the Sheldonian Theatre, which successfully launched the appeal for the new organ. It was during his time that Exeter increased the number of music undergraduates it accepted to two a year. A larger and more vibrant musical community evolved, perhaps at its best in the Musical Evenings hosted by the Rector.

At some point during the 20th century the College started taking trebles from Christ Church Cathedral School to provide the top line for the choir which became a sort of Christ Church 2nd XI. With the admission of women, this became an anachronism, but it took ten years and heated controversy before the all-male choir gave way to a mixed one in 1996. With the advent of Choral Scholars from within the College, the choir now feels more part of the College – and has become one of the leading mixed-voice choirs in Oxford.

The old organ was an embarrassment by the late 1980s. The College took the bold decision to build a French-style Romantic instrument, a type of instrument not seen in Oxford before. The result, built by the firm of Walkers and inaugurated in 1993, was a triumphant success.

In the past 40 years, many Exeter Organ Scholars have had distinguished careers. They include some eminent choral directors, including Jared Armstrong (1948, Organ Scholar), Richard Tanner and Robert Sharpe at Blackburn Cathedral and York Minster respectively, Mark Sheppard who directed the Schola Cantorum of Oxford, Charles Cole, Director of the Schola Cantorum at the London Oratory School, and Jamie Henderson. They also number the internationally renowned cinema and classical organist Richard Hills. The absence of a senior member as Director of Music means that the running of the choir is entirely in the hands of the Organ Scholars. It is an advantage in attracting the best young musicians to have a remarkable organ, and to leave the choir in capable student hands.

Festival in 1951 by Barbirolli. During his time as Organ Scholar in the late 1930s he played piano duets with the émigré T. W. Adorno and there is something richly ironic about the composer of 'Tomorrow shall be my dancing day' sitting down with the foremost disciple of musical modernism (pupil of Alban Berg no less) and Marxist philosopher.

The Honours School of Music was established only after the Second World War. F. W. Sternfeld was elected Fellow in Music at Exeter in 1965. Universally known as Fred, he was a fine scholar and a true Oxford character. He had been brought up in Vienna: frequent was the tutorial when he was sidetracked into reminiscences of Richard Strauss.

Fred was a kindly man and a fine teacher who, through his supervision of a number of eminent young scholars, had a pivotal role in the cultivation of

David Trendell
(1983, Organ Scholar, Music); now College Organist and Lecturer in Music at King's College, London

SERVANTS AND SOCIOLOGY

In the Middle Ages the College employed few permanent servants. Then, from about 1550 to 1750, their numbers rose in line with the growing number of undergraduates and the general rise in the living standards of the Fellows. At the same time many of the undergraduates themselves provided service to the College in exchange for financial help. Finally, in the mid-18th century, undergraduate servants disappeared, to be replaced by men (never women) who would soon become known as 'scouts'. Living at first largely off sales to and tips from the wealthy young, rather than from College wages, they became by the late 19th century full-time paid employees of the College. These three phases were common to all colleges.

In the mid-14th century, Exeter employed only four servants: the manciple, paid £1 a year, the cook (8s.), the laundress (5s.) and the barber (4s.). These four continued to be the core servants until the early 17th century. The manciple who headed them was responsible for provisioning the College – a job open to many temptations. The reason for the barber was that ordained College members required weekly tonsuring.

But from about 1550 to 1750, the number of servants rose in line with the growing number of undergraduates and the College's growing prosperity. By the early 17th century, the number of Fellows had risen to 21, and that of undergraduates to 183. There was a corresponding increase in the number of servants. The Steward's Book of 1636 mentions weekly payment to a head butler and an under-butler, manciple, cook and undercook, trencher-scraper, gardener, porter and laundress.

An Undergraduate Hierarchy

By about 1620, the undergraduate hierarchy was based not on academic merit, but rather on money and social weight. At its head were the gentlemen-commoners – usually the sons of landed families in Devon and Cornwall. They shared a table in Hall with the Fellows, wore special gowns, often presented the College with much of its finest surviving silver, and equally often left without taking a degree. Below this elite came the most numerous class, the commoners, so-called because they took their

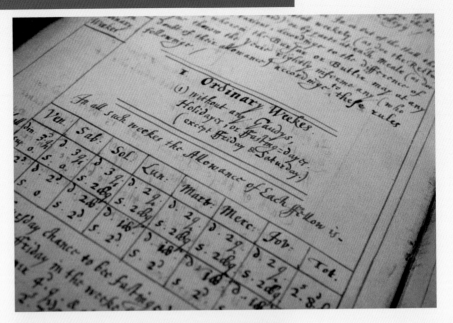

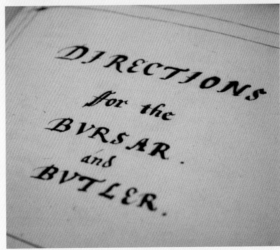

The College authorities exerted detailed control over non-academic staff. Liber Bursarius (above and left), *dated 1636, sets out directions for the Bursar and the Butler.*

commons, i.e. food and drink, from the College and were served it in Hall. Below them came the batelers, poorer men who purchased their own food more cheaply and waited on themselves. Last of all came the servitors, generally known at Exeter as 'poor scholars'. They received some tuition and maintenance in exchange for serving in Hall, helping in the kitchen and taking on other menial jobs around the College. Often the sons of tradesmen or of the poor country clergy, their heyday was the early 17th century: of the 183 undergraduates residing in 1612, 49 were poor scholars.

All four ranks were formal ones, officially registered at matriculation. Each faced a different scale of room rates and tuition and other fees and charges: In the 1630s, for example, library fees for a gentleman-commoner were four times those of a poor scholar. This fourfold division survived for more than two centuries. The last of the poor scholars was William Shepheard, son of the Reverend William Shepheard, Vicar of Ashreigney in the wilds of North Devon, who came up in June 1754 and left four years later without taking a degree. The batelers lasted rather longer. Numerous in the early 18th century, they disappeared completely after 1781. From then on the commoners and the former batelers were subsumed into a class henceforward known simply as 'commoners'. Last to go were the gentlemen-commoners, no doubt because their presence meant money. They flourished in the 18th century, when they included Viscount Parker, later Earl of Macclesfield, whose portrait by Romney still hangs in the SCR. But in the early 19th century they too disappeared. When the last of the line – J. C. W. Leslie, of Leslie Hall, Co. Antrim – graduated in 1832, the old hierarchy of undergraduates had gone for ever.

It was rare for a poor scholar to move far up the social and academic ladder, though Rector Prideaux, one of the most distinguished figures in the College's history, began his academic career by working in the College buttery. While it lasted, this route into the College provided for the talented sons of poor families on a much greater scale than the later scholarships and exhibitions which were competitive and open to the rich as well as poor. The social breadth of the College in the 17th century was much greater than it has been at any point in the last 100 years.

The Age of Scouts

The demise of the poor scholars and the batelers created the need for more bed-makers, waiters, kitchen hands and general servants. So, probably sometime towards the end of the 18th century, the 'age of the scout' began. Scouts initially made most of their money from the young and were regarded as a hazard of college life. One sign of the change may have been the construction in 1821 of a basement servants' hall beneath the present Old Bursary and Morris Room, in the area now occupied by the butler's pantry and the SCR lavatories.

Exeter College servants on the steps of the Hall, photographed in 1864.

From 1864 comes the first photograph of the College servants: 21 men, whose ages ranged, one guesses, from the 20s to the 60s, some with magnificent mutton-chop whiskers, most waistcoated, two holding stove-pipe hats, and at least one fob-watched.

During the 1860s, the College introduced new and elaborate rules of conduct, intended to curtail many of the servants' customary perquisites and to make them more fully the employees of the College. So in 1864, College servants were prohibited from taking any fees beyond the usual end-of-term staircase tips. Four years later, Governing Body set more systematic rules. Servants were no longer to supply milk and eggs; bedmakers' 'payments and perquisites' were to be bought out (though they were still to be allowed 'the remains of meals in their masters' rooms'); and in exchange for this payment they were to clean the windows of every room twice a term and take up the carpets once a year in each long vacation. One assumes that these jobs had previously been done only by private arrangement with the undergraduates. The College was to become a tighter and better managed ship.

College servants were now more fully integrated into College employment. Many continued in service for a remarkably long time. Tom Beesley, who entered the College in 1906, retired in 1961 after 55 years as a scout. Starting under Rector Jackson, well before the First World War, he ended under Rector Wheare. H. L. Stimpson retired about the same time after 38 years in College service, 31 of them as SCR butler. Jack Cantwell was a scout for 35 years, spanning four rectorships from Farnell to Wheare. Jack Waldron, who came to the College as a kitchen porter in 1921, became head porter in 1957 – 'the centre of the whole nervous system of [the] college', says Dacre Balsdon in his fine obituary in the 1966 issue of the *Register* – and survived into the 1960s. Many Old Members will remember these names. Their long careers testify to a second characteristic of College life: the strong esprit de corps of the servant body and the close identification of all its members with the College and its fortunes.

It was in recreation that the qualities of camaraderie and collegiality were most marked. Between the wars the servants played cricket against the dons, against servants' teams from other colleges and against conferences, put fours on the river (there

EXETER COLLEGE.

INSTRUCTIONS FOR THE COLLEGE SERVANTS.

SERVANTS are admitted into College at 6 a.m., but must be in before 7.15 in Michaelmas and Lent Terms, and before 6.45 in Easter Term, to call gentlemen for Chapel.

The servants are themselves expected to call gentlemen, and not to send their boys as substitutes.

Servants are expected to be in College from the time when they come in the morning till 12 on Weekdays, from 1 to 2.15, and to be on their Staircases from 5.30 till 9 p.m., except for the interval of the Hall-dinner.

On Sunday Mornings every servant must be out of College by 10.30, and not come in again before 12.30.

Servants are to report to the Sub-Rector next morning if a gentleman sleeps out: also if any one other than the proper occupant of the rooms sleeps in them.

Æger notes are to be delivered to the Sub-Rector before the bell for Morning Chapel has ceased ringing, and the names of Æger gentlemen are to be called on at the Buttery and Kitchen before they are closed.

Æger gentlemen may not take out commons for a friend, nor may they have a breakfast or wine-party.

Servants are not to lay the table for more than 12 at a breakfast, or 20 at a wine-party, nor for more than 8 for a cold luncheon.

No breakfasts or lunches can be supplied except from the College Kitchen.

These instructions for the College servants were signed by R. R. Marett (then Sub-Rector) in January 1896.

was a separate Servants' Boat Club from 1939), organised summer outings and held Christmas parties and dances, at which the health of the King, the Rector and the Fellows was drunk, and the Rector and Bursar responded. This small world had its own hierarchy, from head porter and SCR butler down to scouts' boys. It combined deference, paternalism, easy relationships across the social divide which separated servants from dons and undergraduates, and, on the part of the servants, a degree of independence and self-confidence and a strong sense of belonging.

But from the late 1940s all this began to change. The advent of gas fires and running water, the ending of private meals in rooms, and the transfer of College catering exclusively to the Hall, all greatly reduced the need for service; and Cowley could offer better wages than the colleges. The generation which died out in the 1960s was the last whose service spanned the decades. Nowadays, college employment for more than a few years is unusual. Four SCR butlers came and went in eight years in the 1990s and early 2000s. The College would be lost without workers from eastern Europe. The rooted world of all-male college service from adolescence to old age now seems almost as remote as the much more distant world of the manciple, the cook, the laundress and the barber. Not quite perhaps, but almost.

JM

BEHIND THE SCENES

Clockwise from top left: *Chris Probert, Head Porter; Carol Barker, Assistant Hall Supervisor; Lisa Thomas and Pauline Argyle, Scouts; Erica Sheppard, Rector's PA, and Lin Simmonds, Rector's Scout; Liberato Nigro, Mark Willoughby and Ian Cox, Chefs; Tom Coombes, Porter; Debbie Thurston, Gardener; Paul Heaton, Porter.*

THE MCR

The past century has seen a dramatic change in postgraduate studies: the growth in the number of postgraduate students, the broadening of their prior experience and background, and an explosion in the scope and diversity of their subjects of study.

In 1914, the D.Phil had just been invented, and few students took Masters degrees. Even by 1938, there were only 536 postgraduate students in the whole University: they made up 11 per cent of Oxford's student population. By the 1964–65 academic year the proportion of postgraduates had doubled and they accounted for 2,153 of Oxford University's students.[12] Exeter's own postgraduate population rose from 51 students in 1963–64 to 61 in 1964–65.

The relationship of postgraduates with their colleges differed from that of undergraduates: they were older, and their social lives and academic work were not focused mainly on their college. Their supervisors were generally elsewhere in Oxford. Colleges all too rarely could offer accommodation, even to students who were new to Oxford.[13] The first modern College 'Middle' Common Room, for postgraduate students, was established in 1958 at Lincoln College. Exeter followed suite only in 1965, celebrating with a dinner in Trinity Term and offering its postgraduates a room on Staircase 8 to provide them with a base in which they were not swamped by their undergraduate peers, and a society that functioned all year round and that

did not shut down at the end of Full Term. MCR membership was open to all students reading for advanced degrees and diplomas (which was deemed to include Part II Chemists, whose laboratory projects required them to stay up in the vacations).

Funding

Long before the MCR was founded, Exeter attracted a few graduate students funded by scholarships such as the Rhodes, or the Moody (later Donovan-Moody) awarded by Williams College in the United States. There has also long been a small portfolio of graduate scholarships endowed by the College: the Alan Coltart Scholarship in Anthropology; the Usher Cunningham Scholarships in Medical Sciences and in History; and the Senior Scholarship in Theology. The generosity and flexibility of the Amelia Jackson Senior Studentship has benefited successive generations of

Right: *The Exeter House campus consists of renovated early Victorian houses, a former convent building and new buildings to accommodate MCR students.*

outstanding Exonians. More recently, the College has supported research in Classics (through the Ratcliffe Scholarship), English (Wordsworth Scholarship), and in Law (Dr Mrs Ambriti Salve Scholarship). The Salve Scholarship, and scholarships funded by Peter Thompson and S. K. Pathak, have been combined with University funds to provide the finance for full scholarships covering both tuition fees and maintenance costs. However, a significant proportion of Exeter's postgraduates are funding all or part of their studies themselves.

Expansion – numbers and space

The 61 postgraduate students who became the first members of Exeter's Middle Common Room in Trinity Term 1965 were the precursors of much larger cohorts who were to follow them. When, in 1979, Exeter first admitted women students, it gained six women postgraduate students alongside 21 women undergraduates.[14] In 1992, the College admitted 45 postgraduates (of whom ten had already studied at Exeter) to begin higher degrees, to make a graduate population of 112. That number increased to 52 graduate freshers (including 18 who had been undergraduates at Exeter) the following year: there were thus more postgraduate freshers at Exeter in 1993 than there had been postgraduate students in the whole College exactly three decades earlier. This record intake in 1993 was welcomed into a fully renovated and expanded MCR which now enjoyed two sitting-rooms, a computer room, and a kitchenette. Membership continued to expand: by its 40th birthday, the MCR had more than doubled its membership to 134 postgraduate students.

Graduate courses were also changing. In the early 1990s, most Exeter graduate students were reading for a D.Phil, or for the two-year M.Phil programme. Only a few studied for one-year degrees such as the BCL. From the late 1990s, the prevalence of one-year courses started to rise, in part because of requirements for 'research training' Masters as a prelude to doctoral study, and in part because of the development of one-year stand-alone graduate programmes.

By 2011, the postgraduate population of Oxford University had expanded to 9,621 – 46 per cent of all students.[15] Exeter's postgraduate population had risen to 211 full-time students (38 per cent of all Exonians),

of whom 123 (58 per cent) were studying for research degrees. The College had the fifth largest ratio of postgraduates to undergraduates of any of the 'mixed' Colleges. A substantial change from earlier years at Exeter was the growth in the variety of courses in general – Exeter's postgraduate students could choose from 195 full-time degree programmes, or 17 part-time Masters courses – and of one-year courses in particular. In 2011–12, 55 of Exeter's full-time postgraduate students were on one-year Masters courses. These postgraduate students came from 44 countries.

Exeter House

Exeter's postgraduate students in the mid-1960s wanted more than a social club and an interdisciplinary community: they needed decent housing. College agreed, and at the same time as it was erecting a building for undergraduates on the corner of the Turl and Broad Street, the College was also seeking a suitable site for graduate accommodation. It succeeded, in early 1967, in purchasing at auction some accommodation in East Oxford, on the corner of the Iffley Road and Magdalen Road. St Basil's Home, a refuge for the

elderly run by nuns, was duly converted into Exeter House, a hostel for 26 mature and postgraduate students. It was handsomely equipped, with three common rooms, self-catering facilities, a resident caretaker, and a resident Fellow (a *custos* or 'warden', rather than a Junior Dean). The College obtained the site with an eye to the future: St Basil's sat on more than half an acre of land (which was quickly expanded with the purchase of an adjacent property in Stanley Road). Over time, the capacity of Exeter House was doubled. Eventually, as Exeter House reached its 40th anniversary, further land purchases, combined with philanthropy, finally enabled that vision to be achieved: by 2012, 112 students could be accommodated at the Exeter House site.

The facilities at Exeter House were part of a vision to create a community of postgraduate students, not just a far-flung hostel, disconnected from College life in Turl Street. By providing Exeter House, the College created a lively residential community of postgraduate students; by providing a congenial Middle Common Room in Staircase 8, the College ensured that this community was also seen fully in College.

By 1969, the College had further increased the links between its expanding postgraduate community and the rest of College with the creation of the office of Tutor for Graduates, to which Dr James Hiddleston, a young Tutor in French, was appointed. That office was later held by Rector Norman whose enthusiasm for the MCR encouraged its expansion, and embedded graduate students and their Common Room in the life of the College.[16]

Today's College

The College's community of postgraduate students has flourished into an intellectually and culturally diverse group. Earlier concerns that the student life of the College might become less coherent with the growth in postgraduate numbers, or with the creation of an alternative community at Exeter House, have both proved overstated. The College *Register* observed, on the opening of Exeter House in 1968: 'Perhaps in time ... the College to future generations will look increasingly "double-yoked"; but we shall always be very conscious of the fact that the double yokes lie inseparably within the same shell.' Wherever our postgraduates' energies are directed, their loyalty remains within the shell of the College.

Chris Ballinger
Academic Dean

Above: *Exeter House after its expansion in 2007–09.*

148

EXETER HOUSE AND THE TALE OF THE FLOATING BASEMENT

Building the basement.

Graduate students have been by far the fastest-growing part of the Exeter community in recent years, but for years, the College's graduate accommodation on the Iffley Road failed to keep pace with their numbers. Students lived in a ramshackle complex of ageing buildings, ten minutes' cycle from the city centre, which had grown up around a former Victorian Anglican convent and schoolhouse and two Regency villas.

So, in 2007, the College purchased 235 Iffley Road, a substantial Victorian-Gothic semi-detached house adjoining the existing corner site, and decided to undertake its most ambitious new building project since Staircase 9 was completed at Turl Street in 1988. Planning permission was granted later that year for a project designed by Anthony Pettorino of the Oxford-based firm of McLennan Architects. Over the following two years, the College undertook a substantial development of the 0.36 hectare site, putting up two new buildings and refurbishing most of the older ones on the site. The result is the creation of 112 en-suite rooms, increasing the number of bed spaces by 54. The rooms are arranged in flats of three to nine people, and each flat shares a communal cooking and dining area. The complex also includes a 'noisy' common room, and a 'quiet' common room, which appear interchangeable at points throughout the day.

The construction of the new site incorporated many new green technologies: the hot water is provided by photovoltaic cells on the roofs and the heating is generated from Ground Source Heat Pumps and Air Source Heat Pumps, the latter being a much tidier technology to install. I remember a wet November morning, attending the building site and seeing a bore hole machine spewing the earth's contents all across our site (and our neighbours), undoubtedly a messy clean up job for the new chap on site.

Building in mid-winter in Oxford provides other challenges and I am now proud to retell the story of the infamous floating basement.

Every building project looks to save money, and this is usually done by constructing in the most economical way. For the College this meant the large basement sat on top of impermeable Oxford clay. The design appeared logical – until the snow came in January, when the ground-floor concrete slab had just been poured. Returning to work one morning, I received a call from site asking me to come 'as quick as I can', at which my heart rate rose and the grey hairs grew. When I arrived I encountered a bemused site foreman whose first words were, 'That's not where I left the basement last night!'

It appears that, when snow melt meets Oxford clay, it can lift a basement as large as an Olympic swimming pool out of the ground by four inches.

With the help of some lateral thinking, the basement eventually sank back to its final resting place and the building project continued up and past the second floor so that HMS *Exeter* (as it became fondly named) could never set sail again. Today, the Exeter House complex has become a model by which other new graduate buildings are measured. The blocks, one named for benefactor Shri Krishna Pathak and the others for Rectors Barber, Wheare and Norman, now provide the graduate students of Exeter College with a place of identity in a development that feels like home.

Gerald Wells
Deputy Bursar

WILLIAMS COLLEGE AT EXETER

In 1793, almost 480 years after the founding of Exeter College – but a mere five years after the Commonwealth of Massachusetts ratified the new constitution of the United States – Williams College opened its doors in the far western reaches of Massachusetts. During the later 19th century, as Harvard College was transformed into Harvard University and other smaller academic institutions reinvented themselves as modern research universities, Williams began to articulate a vision for that alternative American institution, the modern liberal arts college. It was from that college, fast on its way to becoming one of the most eminent of its kind, that John Edmund Moody graduated in 1921. Subsequently, he moved to Oxford to study English Language and Literature at Exeter. On his way back from his holidays in North Africa in the spring of 1926, he died of typhoid in Messina. The following year his father, the American pioneer of bond ratings and founder of Moody's Investors Service, established a Fellowship in his son's memory (now the Donovan-Moody Fellowship), funding a recent Williams graduate to undertake two years of advanced study at Exeter. Institutional ties between Williams College and Exeter College were thus formally established, ties that are themselves now close to a century old.

The bonds between the two institutions were strengthened with the establishment of the Williams College Oxford Programme in the 1980s. One startling change in US higher education in recent decades has been the growth in the number of undergraduates spending all or part of their junior year (their third year of a four-year degree) away from their home institution. In 1979 roughly 5 per cent of Williams students studied abroad; that number had doubled five years later and it was in this context that Williams contemplated a programme in Oxford. On a tip from Exeter's Rector, Lord Crowther-Hunt, that a former language school in North Oxford would soon be up for sale, the President of Williams, John Chandler, purchased the school's four buildings on the southern edges of Summertown in the summer of 1984. A medieval historian at Williams, Francis Oakley, was destined to be the first director of the programme, although fate intervened and he instead became President of Williams. Born in Manchester,

Williams College students enjoying their academic year in Oxford.

he was an undergraduate at Corpus Christi College, Oxford. Oakley worked with various colleagues and with the Governing Body of Exeter to hammer out the academic structure of the programme. After renovation of the buildings, some two dozen Williams students moved to Oxford to begin their studies, inaugurating Williams in Oxford in Michaelmas Term 1985.

When the purchase of the Oxford buildings was announced, an editorial in the Williams newspaper urged that the 'College should hold up the principle of integration as they formulate the curriculum for the new program.' From the very beginning several Exeter students would live in the Williams buildings, helping to integrate Williams students into the life of Exeter. From the beginning, too, several Exeter Fellows took Williams students for their tutorials, although at first Williams students also studied in separate seminars that distanced them from Oxford academic life. Moreover, although Williams students were members of Exeter's Junior Common Room, their access to many other College resources was limited. Access to

University resources was also restricted, especially to the Bodleian Library. In the 1990s the proliferation of American students in Oxford – some attached to rather dubious programmes – initiated reforms that would eventually benefit both Williams and Exeter, furthering the 'principle of integration' that had been called for in 1984. Beginning in 2003, Williams students were formally admitted by Exeter to the University as 'Visiting Students', thereby entitled to the same access to instruction and facilities enjoyed by regular Oxford undergraduates. Reflecting these changes, the name of the programme was changed to the Williams-Exeter Programme at Oxford University.

When Williams and Exeter deepened their ties in the 1980s, the then Rector, Lord Crowther-Hunt – who had studied at Princeton and stressed the importance of transatlantic learning – observed that the creation of the new programme marked 'the most important development this century for our respective institutions'. At the time, this may have sounded a trifle hyperbolic. Nevertheless, the Williams that John Edmund Moody left in 1921 and the Exeter he entered soon thereafter have changed dramatically since then, in part as a result of the cooperation between the two institutions. Today the world is much smaller and we now stress the virtues of bringing together students from around the globe to learn from each other. Some

50 per cent of Williams undergraduates now study abroad and more than 700 of them have spent a year in Oxford, the most recent third as students *of* Exeter College, not just of Williams College *in* Oxford. Two of them have returned to Oxford as Rhodes Scholars. Many have rowed for Exeter and participated in numerous other College activities. Recognising their service to higher education and to society more generally, Williams has awarded honorary degrees to the two most recent Exeter Rectors, Marilyn Butler and Frances Cairncross (and Exeter has made Morty Schapiro, former President of Williams, an Honorary Fellow). New traditions have been established, such as Exeter's annual Thanksgiving Dinner. Exeter Fellows pay regular visits to Williams, while in 1988 Williams introduced tutorial instruction to its curriculum, now a hallmark of its own liberal arts education. Partly through the generosity of Bennett Boskey, an alumnus of Williams College and a family friend of Frances Cairncross, Williams has supported the appointment of College Fellows and Lecturers at Exeter who teach students from both institutions. The ties that bind continue to grow among these two institutions that can count between themselves almost a thousand years of history.

Chris Waters
Director of the Williams-Exeter Programme 2001–04

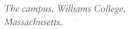

The campus, Williams College, Massachusetts.

WITS AND SASKATCHEWAN

In the course of the 20th century, a rapidly growing number of foreign graduate students passed through Exeter College. Often, they chose Exeter because one of their academic mentors had a link with the College.

So one of the most distinguished scientists and one of the most renowned lawyers the College ever produced came within five years of each other, advised by Humphrey Raikes, Principal of the University of the Witwatersrand from 1927 until 1954. Raikes had been a fine scholar at Balliol and a courageous soldier and airman during the First World War. After the War, he was elected a Fellow of Exeter College, where he was later appointed Sub-Rector. For a few years, he was also chief instructor to the Oxford University Air Squadron, earning the rank of wing commander – and in Johannesburg he set up the Witwatersrand University Flying Association and encouraged generations of students to fly.

Raikes persuaded a number of brilliant young South Africans to come to Exeter to study, including Sydney Brenner (who came in 1952 to do a D.Phil on bacteriophage resistance under Cyril Hinshelwood in the Department of Physical Chemistry, and was later a Nobel Prize winner), and Sydney Kentridge (1946, Jurisprudence), who became one of the world's most famous Human Rights lawyers. One advantage of Raikes's recommendation in those more informal days was that it was sufficient to guarantee a place.

At the University of Saskatchewan, Francis Leddy had a similar impact on generations of clever young Canadians. Leddy had held a Rhodes Scholarship at Exeter College where he studied Ancient History, graduating with a doctorate in 1938. Through the 1950s and 1960s, as Secretary of the Provincial committee responsible for selecting Rhodes Scholars, Leddy advised students who won a Rhodes to choose Exeter College.

Leddy felt that Exeter College suited Saskatchewanians. Some Oxford colleges, he warned them, had a reputation for treating Midwestern lads with a certain disdain. Exeter, Leddy used to say, was a 'middle of the road' college, and socially, they would be more comfortable there. And as with Raikes, Leddy's influence more or less guaranteed Saskatchewan scholars a place at Exeter. Among other distinguished figures, it brought the College Gordon Robertson, who became Secretary to the Cabinet, the top position in the Canadian public service.

Thanks to Leddy and the Rhodes Scholars he sent to Exeter, the College has its own lecture theatre, which the College named the Saskatchewan Room in 1985. Not only does this commemorate the Saskatchewan alumni – such as the lawyer Henry Kloppenburg, whose generosity made the room possible, and provided the photographs of the Canadian Midwest that decorate the walls – it has guaranteed that generations of young Exonians, almost uniquely in Oxford, can pronounce the name of one of the finest but least known provinces of Canada.

FAC

Above centre: Professor Sydney Brenner was awarded the Nobel Prize for Physiology or Medicine in 2002, shared with John E. Sulston and H. Robert Horvitz, for 'their discoveries about how genes regenerate tissue and organ development and programmed cell death'. Photograph by Steve Pyke.

Above: Sir Sydney Kentridge QC receiving his Knighthood in 2009. He played a leading part in some of the most significant political trials of the 20th century. He once said: 'I hope there's only one thing about my professional life of which I've boasted and which I think, as a lawyer, is unique on my part – I have acted as an advocate for three winners of the Nobel Peace Prize. I don't think anyone else has done that.'

DISTANT DAYS

FRANCES CAIRNCROSS

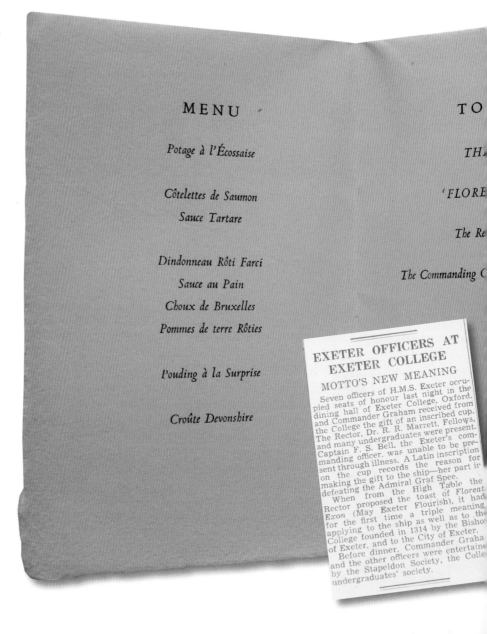

MENU

Potage à l'Écossaise

Côtelettes de Saumon
Sauce Tartare

Dindonneau Rôti Farci
Sauce au Pain
Choux de Bruxelles
Pommes de terre Rôties

Pouding à la Surprise

Croûte Devonshire

TO

TH

'FLORE

The Re

The Commanding C

EXETER OFFICERS AT
EXETER COLLEGE
MOTTO'S NEW MEANING
Seven officers of H.M.S. Exeter occupied seats of honour last night in the
dining hall of Exeter College, Oxford,
and Commander Graham received from
the College the gift of an inscribed cup.
The Rector, Dr. R. R. Marrett, Fellows,
and many undergraduates were present.
Captain F. S. Bell, the Exeter's commanding officer, was unable to be present through illness. A Latin inscription
on the cup records the reason for
making the gift to the ship—her part in
defeating the Admiral Graf Spee.
    When from the High Table the
Rector proposed the toast of Floreat
Exon (May Exeter Flourish), it had
for the first time a triple meaning,
applying to the ship as well as to the
College founded in 1314 by the Bishop
of Exeter, and to the City of Exeter.
    Before dinner, Commander Graha
and the other officers were entertained
by the Stapeldon Society, the Colle
undergraduates' society.

As barely two dozen pre-War Exonians survive, the period during and immediately after the Second World War is the earliest that is still in living memory. What follows is drawn from the recollections of many who responded to a request for their memories. The period saw attempts to retain and recreate the traditions of pre-war Exeter, many of them now gone for ever. And it was the twilight of the all-male Exeter of the previous six and a half centuries. The pranks, brutal, funny or merely inane, have largely disappeared.

Wartime Memories

Those who were at the College during the Second World War itself recall a largely empty college, shared by students from Exeter and Lincoln, and with the only Fellow on site the Sub-Rector, Nevill Coghill. Students were either on short courses or for some reason exempt from call-up. Chemistry students were in that latter category, and Dick Barlow who came up in 1943 recalled practising 'with the trailer-pump on Wednesday afternoons. I remember pushing it round to the Ashmolean to put out an imaginary fire – fortunately with imaginary water.'

Much time was spent on fire drills, using the static water-tank that had been sunk in the middle of the front quad (its outline can still sometimes be seen in dry weather). John McOmie who came up in 1939 took over the College Fire Squad and acted as assistant to Coghill, who was in charge of air raid precautions:

Previous pages: *Allied soldiers in Oxford, 1943.*

Right: *Exeter freshmen, 1947.*

Below: *Menu for the 1940 dinner for HMS Exeter in honour of the destroyer's role in defeating the Graf Spee. A replica of Exeter's 17th-century gold cup and cover (see page 27) was presented to the ship's Commander.*

There were twelve of us students in the Exeter Fire Squad and we had a Coventry Climax Trailer pump, nicknamed Lady Godiva. During the autumn and winter of 1940 there were air-raid alerts almost every night. As soon as the siren sounded, those of us on duty would put on our boiler suits and steel helmets and hurry to the pump. We then man-handled it across the lawn to the water-tank and ran the engine for a minute or two to make sure it worked but not to waste petrol unnecessarily. After we heard the planes pass overhead we waited in the Porters' Lodge until the planes returned and the all-clear sounded.

Ernest Roe, who also came up in 1939, spent much of his time, including vacations, living in College and fire-watching: 'So I spent many night hours on the College roof, and many daylight hours working in the Bodleian, with that strange feeling of unreality derived from almost total absence of sleep.'

The water tank survived the War, and Nicolas Banister, who came up in 1947, remembers watching the kitchen cat stalk and drown pigeons that stood on its buttresses to drink.

As the War ended, the College filled with a curious mix of battle-weary men and clever boys who had

been young enough to miss the fighting. Nicholas Thomas came up from Guernsey in October 1947 on a King Charles I Scholarship:

Half of us freshmen were straight from school and still teenagers. The other half, several years older, had been killing or avoiding being killed or imprisoned by our Axis enemies. At least one Exonian had been decorated for gallantry. Another had suffered severe facial injury. Some were married.

This mix of boys and men was our priceless introduction to the real world and its often puzzling language. I recall a pub crawl with some of these awe-inspiring grown-ups. One of them asked me what I would have. 'Half of bitter' was my harmless request. 'Chaser, old boy?' What on earth was a chaser? 'Thanks,' I replied in desperation. Whisky chased the beer down my innocent throat and I felt I had at last become a man.

For the ex-servicemen, too, there were anxieties. David McMaster, who arrived in 1948, was relieved to find that about 60 per cent of freshmen were ex-servicemen like himself. 'One felt sometimes that in those particular years it was those who had come up straight from school who had the more difficult time. In any case, ex-servicemen generally had more generous grants from public funds than school-leavers.' And the older freshers had a warm welcome from Rector Barber: 'You may be encouraged to know that we have found that a period in the military forces does not seriously or permanently damage the brain.'

Youngsters such as Harold Merskey, who matriculated in 1946, straight from school, were the butt of a certain amount of ragging. 'Rationing was still in place,' he remembers, 'and bananas were given only to children under 18. In the first day or two I read a notice in the Lodge that said, "Gentlemen wishing to obtain their banana ration should bring their green ration cards to the buttery." These were, of course, children's ration cards....'

Admissions

Securing a College place in those distant days was vastly less stressful than today. Derek Sawyer recalls how, in January 1947, he trudged through the snow in the coldest winter of the century, wearing the uniform of a Corporal in the RAF, to see Rector Barber. 'He asked me why I had chosen Exeter. I told him it was because I was a Devonian. Rector Barber and I had a pleasant chat and on the strength of that he agreed to accept me as a member of College in the autumn of 1948, by which time I expected my term of service with the RAF to be over. That was it! No entrance exam, no tricky interview questions.'

The tricky questions came for those who sat a scholarship examination. A few months after that cursory interview, Dennis Holman was sitting, 'cold and uncomfortable in the Hall scribbling furiously. I still have nightmares over the final three-hour paper – the General Essay. On the command, we turned over the sheet and one word – "Memory" – was revealed. What did I write, and were all those papers carefully read and assessed before the interview?'

Paul Atyeo records his post-war experience:

It was in the summer of 1947 that my mother received a letter from Rector Barber offering me a free place in College. I was the first, by quite a long way, of a group of boys who had lost their Exonian fathers as a result of enemy action during the War. The College's expectation was that this would apply to boys, with comparatively young fathers, who would not be interested for some years to come. My father was at Exeter at the beginning of the century. So here I was, ready and willing to come up forthwith, to some consternation on the part of the College.

I believe that some 14 boys came up under this scheme, which was eventually wound up in the middle of the 1960s.

Living Conditions

The overall impression of post-war Exeter, recalls Richard Coggins, is 'of how primitive things were: of loos (the 4th quad) that seemed miles away; of being awakened by the scout with a jug of hot(tish) water and told it was 7.30, sir.'

The cold pervades many memories. John Benton, arriving in 1945, recalled that his electric fire would go out each morning at 9 and would not come on again until the evening. Students crowded into the relative warmth of the Radcliffe Camera. His next-door neighbour was one of the very few undergraduates who had a coal fire in his room, and 'at his invitation many of us crowded in there for a morning's work, though in an atmosphere of pipe smoke and black coffee, it was inevitable that less work was done than should have been.'

Apart from the chill, there were mice to contend with: Brian Phillips lay in bed, listening to them galloping round his settee at night. And the plumbing was also antique. John Field Evans in 1949 shared rooms on the second floor of Staircase 6:

Chamber pots were emptied daily by the luckless scout. Hot water might be obtained with a jug from a 'Sadi' or similar heater on the landing. One washed using a bowl probably made by the Mason's Ironstone Pottery, which one emptied into a sink on the landing. To use a flushing lavatory one had to make one's way to a basement in the back quad. The wooden lavatory seats were on one occasion an adhesive trap, having been painted with clear varnish by invading undergraduates from Jesus early on the morning of St David's Day.

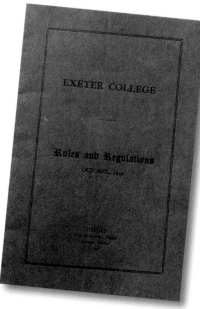

Red Book, 1949.

The subterranean water closets created lots of opportunities for japes. The JCR elected a Lord High Commissioner for Public Easement, recalls David Firth, whose post 'required the holder to report on the state of the College toilet arrangements and in doing so, relate stories from daily College life that had a little spice in them.'

Baths held similar perils. W. S. Beattie recalls in 1947 the 'series of catacombs that led down off the Back Quad. Within were alcoves, each containing a bath.' Because the baths were open plan, says John Barry (1948, Jurisprudence), 'if one went down during a busy period, the whole place was full of steam, and one had to find an empty one by groping about.'

Scouts

One of the oddest sensations for young men arriving in the late 1940s and early 1950s was the presence of scouts. The Head Scout, recalls Alan Russett who arrived in 1949, was 'bespectacled Bill, [who] was a strict disciplinarian and would bar the way if you tried

Details of College wartime rationing, issued by the Bursar on 4 October 1941.

CHOCOLATE.

Owing to the present shortage of chocolate, it is propsed to issue to undergraduates the total amount sent to the College in equal proportions on Monday next.   · Those not wishing to avail themselves of this offer, should notify the Office, No. 2 Staircase, before Saturday mid-day.

BISCUITS.

The Still Room will be open for the sale of biscuits at lunch-time when there are any available.

RATIONED   FOODS.

TEA & SUGAR have been issued for the whole term.

JAM has been issued for one month.

BUTTER & MARGARINE are issued each Saturday.

to scurry in late for breakfast improperly dressed – your pyjama jacket hopefully parading as a shirt collar over a crew-neck sweater.'

The main kingdom of the scouts was the Staircase. Michael Dryland came up in 1944 with a Choral exhibition:

> *My scout was old Fred who had been tempted out of retirement during the War. He had 'selective hearing'. I remember asking, 'Fred, when you next pass, will you please fill my kettle?' He vanished quickly with the reply, 'Arr, them kettles is very 'ard to find these days.' He managed to escape all jobs but the basics. However, to have a scout when I was aged 17 was an untold luxury.*

Frank King, a Rhodes Scholar in 1949, recalled: 'In January, when I had a bad cold, Simpson (if that was his name) said: "That's the trouble with Americans, sir. They take too many baths. Once a week is enough, unless he's out for sports." And in a sense he was right. Walking in the snow from one's room to the baths was inviting a severe cold or worse.' Peter Milton's (1945) scout 'for some very small sum sold me an umbrella – which in due course I mislaid, but next term he sold me another (which bore a remarkable likeness to its predecessor).'

Food

The other preoccupation was food. Rationing was still in full swing. John Saunders came up in 1947 and remembers that food was rationed until after he went down. 'I can still picture freshers from my staircase walking towards the Hall for breakfast clutching their minuscule packs of butter – butter was issued to each one of us at the beginning of the week and we had to look after our own ration very carefully.' Others remember the incongruity of terrible food in the splendour of the Hall.

The food may have been dire, but, as W. S. Beattie remembers, the scouts in the late 1940s insisted on proper dress: 'One morning, when I was in danger of missing breakfast in the hall because it was nearly 9 am, in my haste I omitted to put a tie on. Alas, the senior scout spotted it. I got my breakfast, but I also got a thorough ticking-off from him for unbelievably ungentlemanly behaviour.'

Sconcing

The peril of sconcing, for misdemeanours such as talking about work, returned after the War. David Firth in the first half of the 1950s remembers that 'the standard Sconce was a tankard holding three and a half pints of draught beer. The sconce would try to drink this in one go, without removing his lips from the tankard. If he paused too long, his colleagues at the table would start jeering and urging him to give up. If, however, he downed the sconce, he could sconce his accuser back for five pints – at the accuser's expense. Any sconce not consumed by the offender was offered round the table until it was finished.'

The Dons

Academic work plays a small part in people's memories, but the dons are vivid. There were few, by today's standards, and most were unmarried and living in College. Christopher Sheward (1949, Jurisprudence) describes a few of them:

> *Nevill Coghill – big, shambling. Pompous, snobbish Dacre (much imitated). Businesslike Herbert Nicholas. The shy Eric Kemp – he invited me to tea once, when conversation hardly scintillated. Derek Hall, the Law don, more interested in University politics and research than teaching. In addition there were old Professor Dawkins with a loud, cackling laugh and Professor Cyril Hinshelwood, FRS and Nobel Prize winner, another remote figure.*

For a young academic, this group was every bit as curious as for undergraduates. Sir James Gowans, then fresh from London University and a youthful Staines Medical Fellow (1955–60), remembers the agony of breakfast in Hall in the intimidating company of Cyril Hinshelwood, Nevill Coghill and Dacre Balsdon, 'the distinguished trio silent and hidden behind their newspapers'. Gowans recalled, on his first day at Exeter, sitting next to Balsdon at tea. 'Choosing my words carefully, I said, "This is a nice cup of tea, Dacre." "Yes, Gowans, it is, but I'm surprised to hear you say so." For a long time afterwards I agonised over how I had managed to put my foot in it so soon.'

PROFESSOR RICHARD DAWKINS

One of the great Exeter characters from between the wars was Professor R. M. Dawkins. Osbert Lancaster devoted a passage to him, and this drawing, in his second volume of memoirs, *With an Eye to the Future* (1967):

> *No eccentric professor of fiction could possibly hold a candle to the reality of Professor Dawkins whose behaviour and appearance placed him, even in an Oxford far richer in striking personalities than it is today, in a class by himself. Ginger-moustached, myopic, stooping, clad in one of a succession of very thick black suits which he ordered by postcard from the general store of a small village in Northern Ireland, he always betrayed his whereabouts by a cackling laugh of great carrying power. Once when passing alongside the high wall of Exeter, startled by this extraordinary sound, I looked up and saw the Professor happily perched in the higher branches of a large chestnut tree hooting like a demented macaw.*

Dacre Balsdon's presence dominated the College *(see pages 112–13)* but others seemed no less eccentric. James White remembers a tutorial with Eric Kemp, later Bishop of Chichester, in which Kemp fell fast asleep – 'and it was *my* essay that was being read! I remember mouthing, "What on earth do we do?" before noisily dropping a book.'

Rufus Churcher remembers Professor Dawkins, a renowned Homeric Greek scholar 'with rooms on the first floor of a staircase across the quad from the Porters' Lodge and famous for his fruit cake.'

At the height of the battle between Jesus and Exeter College students—undergraduates dressed in football kit and evening dress parade behind a piper in Jesus College.

Pigeons, birdseed and a battle at Jesus College

OXFORD police last night halted a "battle" between Jesus and Exeter Colleges—the traditional rivals that face each other across Turl Street.

Scores of on lookers watched from a safe distance during the 15-minute battle. While rockets were let off, bottles were thrown from windows and fire extinguishers played across the narrow street. At one stage three men ran along the Market Street front- age of Jesus spraying the college with a fire ex- tinguisher.

A pile of bicycles blocked the entrance to Jesus College, and afterwards the street was littered with broken glass.

Firemen called

The incident followed the dis- covery earlier in the day of a number of pigeons in Jesus College dining hall. Members of the college succeeded in getting some of the birds out through the windows, but seven of them settled on a high ledge and defied attempts to remove them.

The college contacted Senior Inspector John Ambrose, of the R.S.P.C.A., who arrived at about 9.30 p.m., after the pigeons had gone to roost to- gether with Oxford firemen, who had been asked to pro- vide a ladder long enough to reach them.

With the help of the firemen and working with a torch, he captured the birds and took them away in a basket in the hope of finding out from their rings where they had come from.

Cycle barricade

When the college gate was opened for him to leave a pile of bicycles was found at the entrance.

'As I came out of the college I was met with a barricade of bicycles, and bottles were be- ing thrown and fireworks let off. I have never seen any-

thing like it,' said Mr. Am- brose.

Earlier in the evening members of Jesus Soccer Club held a dinner at the hotel watched by the seven ninety-nine house. While firemen struggled to get their ladders into the hall they had first to remove one of the doors—celebrating un- dergraduates, some of them in evening dress, paraded past in the narrow passageway be- hind one of their number who was playing bagpipes.

At one stage during the evening a white flag flew above Jesus College, but it was soon re- moved.

At about the time the pigeons were discovered a packet of bird seed arrived at the col- lege, addressed to the Prin- cipal.

No arrests were made.

Long feud

There has long been a feud be- tween Exeter and Jesus, which has a number of Welsh connections, and in the past there have been incidents on March 1—the day of Wales's patron saint, St. David. It is believed that yesterday's in- cident with the pigeons was a reprisal for last St. David's Day, when damage was done to lawns at Exeter.

The traditional rivalry between Exeter and Jesus made the headlines of the Oxford Mail *on 19 May, 1962.*

To be taught by a figure of brilliance, then as now, could be life-changing. Stansfield Turner, an American Rhodes Scholar who read PPE 1947–50 and went on to become a US Admiral and Head of the Central Intelligence Agency, was taught by the distinguished philosopher, William Kneale: 'Whatever position I took in our discussion, he inevitably took the opposite view,' Turner remembers:

He drove home the point that there are almost always two sides to any issue. This was particularly valuable to me in my later years in the Navy. So much of what you do in a military career is either right or wrong. If you shoot the gun the right way, you are likely to hit the target. Yet, when you reach the higher echelons in the military, the issues with which you grapple do not have right or wrong answers. Years after I left Oxford, I had come to appreciate that there are very few just right or wrong answers in life.

History tutorials with C. T. Atkinson at the top of Palmer's Tower were less cerebral, and his pupils recall a succession of fearsome dogs.

Richard Yeo in the early 1940s recalls him cycling in from North Oxford with his faithful cocker spaniel, Jumbo, running beside him:

He was a sartorial eccentric: heavy brown army boots, baggy creased grey flannels, a cardigan partially buttoned, since buttons and respective button-holes failed to synchronise: all this finished off with a navy blue striped suit jacket. As he stood with his back to the gas fire, you were invited to sit down … 'No, not in that one – that's Jumbo's!'

Peter Marsh recalls Atters scooping leftover meat from his plate to save for the dog.

The dog sometimes played a more active part in tutorials. Colin Hunter was there with another undergraduate 'who read out his essay in which he described the Duke of Wellington as "an ass". Atters was a great fan of the Duke's, and said to the dog, "Bite him!" The creature tried to attack, but fortunately I managed to restrain him.'

Greig Barr, later to be Rector, was a popular and effective Sub-Rector in the post-war years, admired for his distinguished war record and love of rugby. Colin Hunter recalls a St David's Day invasion in 1947 by Jesus men, who:

broke into one of the ground-floor rooms on the Turl. A big fight ensued. In the middle of it, Greig Barr entered. He asked one combatant, 'Which college are you?' 'Trinity, Sir,' was the reply. Greig seized him by the ear and said, 'Get out! This is a historic Exeter v Jesus fight.' He ejected him through the front gate and went to bed.

Michael Green remembers buying, with a friend, an illicit and utterly broken down Austin 7 for a few pounds:

It subsequently collapsed and resided partly in my friend's room and partly in mine. I was brought before the Proctors, one of whom was Greig. I somewhat cheekily argued that it was not a car at all, but bits of a car in different places. He smiled and let me off.

Two Rectors span this era of the College's history. John McOmie recalls that Ranulf Marett, Rector at the outbreak of War, used to entertain small groups of freshers to tea in his Lodgings:

I was invited in my first term. That day his daughter was acting as hostess. During a lull in the conversation, Marett suddenly said very loudly, 'Have you seen my daughter's bust?' Most of us were shy young men and felt embarrassed. After a pause of shocked silence he said, 'It's over there, in the corner. You know my daughter is a sculptress.' Indeed the bust of himself was there and we all admired it.

165

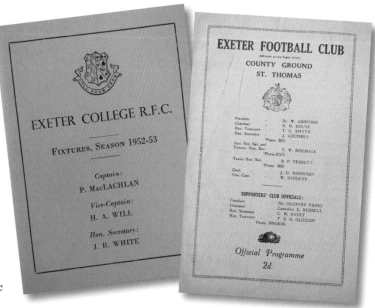

Eric Barber, a classical scholar whose stern portrait by Annigoni stares down on High Table, 'gave decorous sherry parties from time to time,' recalls John Field Evans (1949–52), 'at which we had a glass or two of South African sherry, about all you could get in the immediate postwar years: "Landdrost", I think it was called. The invitation specified the hours at which the party would start and finish. The decanters were peremptorily withdrawn to indicate the close of play.'

Peter Milton, coming up at the end of the War, describes Mrs Barber as 'utterly charming; she gained enormous popularity at the Rector's sherry party for freshers when she accidentally picked up the wrong decanter and filled our glasses with whisky.' Robin Wallace, in the late 1950s, remembers that a journalist interviewed Rector Barber after a particularly awful modern music recital in Hall. Mrs Barber broke in to say, 'Of course the Rector enjoyed the concert but I'm afraid Mr Barber does not have an ear for that sort of music.'

Barber could be alarming. John Drewett (1949) remembers his first Collections in Michaelmas 1949. Derek Hall, his Law Tutor, complained that, although he appeared to do a lot of work, in reality he did very little. Rector Barber responded, 'Well, Mr Drewett, I do not know quite how you will achieve this result, but I wish you to do a lot more work even if in doing so you succeed in giving the impression of doing much less.'

Another Law student, recently out of the army, relied on little volumes known as 'The Nutshells' which contained the bare bones of a given subject: 'The Law of Tort in a Nutshell', 'Criminal Law in a Nutshell', etc. At Collections, his Tutor furnished a dismal report of his term's work. John Field Evans remembers this exchange:

> Rector: 'Well, Mr XXX, *that is not very satisfactory, is it?*'
> Student: 'No, Rector.'
> Rector: 'What do you propose to do about it?'
> Student: 'I suppose I shall have to buy some thicker books.'

Sport

More than work and dons, though, it is the sport, the social life and the pranks that linger in the memory 60 years on. As Stanley Walker who came up in 1947 points out, the late 1940s were one of the high points for Exeter's sport. Exeter's rowing was at a high level, as was rugby and cricket. John Kendall-Carpenter, who subsequently captained England and won 23 caps, captained the University rugby side while Chris Winn captained the University cricket. Both were Exeter men.

Even more remarkable was the Exeter Athletic Club, blessed at the end of the War with a good number of enthusiastic ex-Servicemen. John Saunders (1947, Modern History) recalls that four members of the Club were members of Achilles in 1948, the year of the London Olympics. One hurdler, Ray Barkway, took part in the Olympic Games. Saunders recalls going to the Athletic Club just a few days after arriving in College in January 1947:

> *The track was covered in deep snow, though a very narrow track had been made in the circumference. There was only one person there. Trudging round the track in the bitter weather was Roger Bannister. I remember thinking, 'This young man will make a name for himself as an athlete.'*

The river in this era also attracted people of future distinction – though not always for their rowing prowess. Among Captains of Boats were the future ambassador, Sir Martin Le Quesne, and Peter Crill, subsequently Bailiff of Jersey. Other rowers in 3rd or 4th VIIIs or Torpids included Sydney Kentridge,

College photograph, June 1950, with Roger Bannister in the front row.

later one of South Africa's most distinguished lawyers; Stan Turner, subsequently US Admiral and Head of the CIA; and Sid Newman, a South African rugby full back and a man of immense strength, who famously managed while rowing to break an oar.

David Firth in the first half of the 1950s spent so much time rowing that he 'failed some of my medical exams not once but twice and had to repeat at least a year of Physiology lectures. Today I would be asked to leave, but then, taking part in a sport was regarded favourably.' He remembers being invited to stroke the Schools VIII in 1954:

Seven of my friends from previous years rowing together joined me. All of us were sitting Schools. The boat seemed to run on rails and we made five bumps in four nights. We earned our oars and mine still hangs in my living room to this day. We also burnt a boat in Broad Street (not our eight but an old one given to us by Salters, the Boat Yard). The Fire Service arrived and put it out. The Proctors also arrived and cautioned any of us still hanging about to 'Report to your College'.

One year, recalls Henry Will (1950, PPE), the Rugby Club crewed the Exeter IV boat for Eights Week:

Few of us had any rowing experience but we trained with enthusiasm. On the Saturday, we had actually managed nearly to catch the boat in front but instead of overlapping it, our over-exuberant cox (and scrum half), Paddy Malone, rammed it. The bow of our shell crumpled and the boat rapidly filled with water. On Tuesday disaster struck again. We were bumped by Jesus IV. The sharp prong of their bow caught one of our rudder lines, and we were driven straight into the bank. Nothing could take away the shame of the Oxford Mail's *memorable headline: 'Exeter Sinks Again!'*

In those days, Exeter had a barge, a real one, moored on the Christ Church Meadows bank. It was used as a changing room. In Eights Week it also entertained the Boat Club guests. Tea and sandwiches were served on the upper deck. Eights Week, recalls Peter Milton, was a week of six nights racing – Thursday to Wednesday with a break on the Sunday – and:

the top deck of the College Barge became a
high-class social venue. Unfortunately our finery
was restricted by post-war conditions – we could
get 1st VIII ties, caps and scarves, but the only
blazers available were one or two donated by
Old Members. Our cox always wore a blazer
and sported the Order of the Chrysanthemum
presented pre-war by Crown Prince Hirohito. The
boat always carried a fine bunch of red peonies,
grown and donated by the Rector's wife, attached
to the flag at the bow.

Drama

This was also the start of a golden era for College
drama, thanks to the influence of Nevill Coghill. In the
mid-1940s, Exeter had two of its greatest actors ever, in
Richard Burton and Martin Starkie. Stanley Walker was
one of the lucky ones who recalls Coghill's production
of *'Tis Pity She's a Whore* by the College's now defunct
John Ford Society, and his OUDS production of *The
Tempest* in Worcester College, performed by the lake. 'It
was sheer magic. Ariel flew over the water as dusk fell.
That will be remembered forever.'

Social Life

Fellows played a considerable part in College social
life. Encouraged by Dacre Balsdon, the Adelphi Club
was revived after the War. Peter Milton who came up
in 1945 remembers that 'The Adelphi blue and gold
waistcoats and bow ties were unavailable except for one
or two donated by Old Members, but we dined in white
tie and tails to the amazement of other members of the
College.' At one of these dinners, he heard a member tell
Balsdon, 'Dacre, you are the only man I know who can
strut sitting down.'

In this era, the College still held a Commemoration
Ball every three years. Stanley Walker recalls:

*The ticket for you and your partner was five
guineas, and this was exchanged for a bottle of
champagne. Dinner was held in the Hall whereas
the dancing took place in a huge marquee which
swallowed the main quad. Two bands from
London kept festivities alive till 6 am. At that
point, you both retired to a punt on the Cherwell,
had a picnic breakfast and drifted away the rest of
the morning.*

John Saunders remembers the thrill of the Commem
Ball of 1949:

*We had a truly famous band, and we danced to
the best-known songs of the best-known American
musicals. The setting was wonderful and the
decorations in the marquee quite magical. I have
treasured one souvenir: the card you were given
on which to record the names of the partners you
would be dancing with, by agreement beforehand,
during the evening. Very few couples would have
used them, but the cards were a subtle suggestion
that our Ball was a high-class event to match pre-
war events of equivalent status.*

He adds, 'My partner of the 1949 Ball and I were
married four years later. We have now passed our
60th wedding anniversary.'

There were, of course, no women in College. In
1952, Denis Vandervelde had:

*a delightful blonde girlfriend, very slim – which
was just as well as I used to bring her into and
out of College by way of a ground-floor set of
rooms with a window which could be only partly
closed. The occupant, a freshman, was a devout
Christian and thus doubly unhappy that the
College regulations were regularly violated.*

Pranks

For many students, a social life involved some skill in
getting back into College after hours. One option was
to climb in. In 1944, the easiest illegal entrance was up
the drainpipe in Brasenose Lane and over the wall into
the garden. Colin Hunter discovered that this meant
climbing the wall immediately under Nevill Coghill's
window (he was then Sub-Rector):

*At 3 am, I was sitting on the wall when the
window opened, and there was Nevill two feet
away. 'What are you doing there, Mr
Hunter?' he asked. 'Birds-nesting, Sir,'
I replied. 'There's a robin's nest
in the Rector's Garden.'
'Good night,' he
said – then shut the
window!*

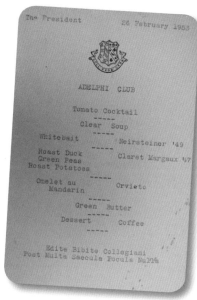

Top: *1958 Commem Ball menu.*

Above: *Adelphi Club menu,
February 1953.*

Below: *Adelphi Club bow tie.*

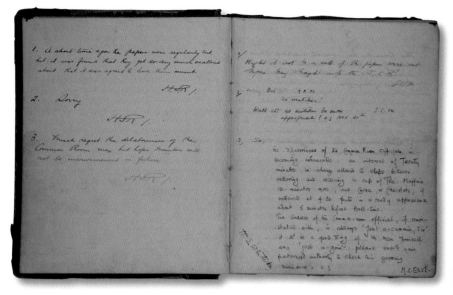

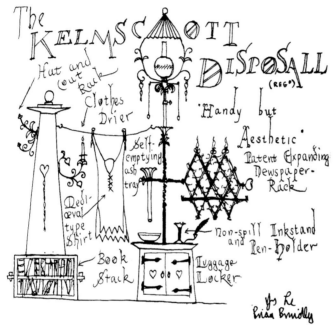

Rufus Churcher, arriving from South Africa in 1950 with a spell in the services behind him, was given rooms above Parker's Bookshop at the corner of the Turl and the Broad. Once the main College gates were shut, it was impossible to get into College to see his friends. Noticing that a key to the outside door was displayed in a red box in case of fire, and that the door had an old-fashioned heavy mortice lock, he bought a blank at an ironmongers in Abingdon, borrowed a vice and did all the filing by eye. 'It was a piece of cake. Over a number of week-ends, I managed to make a key that let me in and out!'

Other pranks were more elaborate and less practical. There were several tales of rugby balls lobbed over or onto the roof of the Chapel. Roy Somerset remembers that Alan Helm, an Amateur Golf champion, managed to chip a golf ball over the Chapel with a niblick.

And there were endless fights with Jesus College, including regular invasions on St David's Day. In 1950 Terence John Harvey was one of a gang of three (which also included Roger Bannister) who constructed an effigy of St David dressed in an old pair of grey flannel trousers and a Jesus rugby jersey, stuffed him with paper and straw and added a tall conical black hat, a golden harp and a leek. With accomplices from the College bar, they invaded Jesus and marched around the inner quadrangle singing 'Lloyd George knew my father. Father knew Lloyd George' to the tune of 'Onward Christian Soldiers'.

When the Jesus men began pouring out of Hall, the Exonians set fire to Dewi Sant and headed for the main gate. Finding that the Porter had locked it, John Kendall-Carpenter held out his massive hand and said, 'The keys, if you please.' The Porter handed them over immediately. The next morning, Exeter escaped retribution only because a blind Law student always put his hand to the toilet seat to locate it. 'He was able to raise the alarm early the next morning when our seats had been painted with glue.'

Finals

Eventually there was the ordeal of Finals. And when those ended, Derek Sawyer says, 'The drill was to leave ten bob with the College Porter, who would notify you of your result by telegram. Initially the telegram came in the form of a phone message. I was so overcome that I could not believe it until the typed confirmation arrived: CLASS TWO. What could be more laconic than that? I was overjoyed.'

OTHER VOICES
Qian Zhongshu

In this excerpt from her memoir We Three, *the newly married Yang Jiang describes her time at Oxford while her husband, Qian Zhongshu, was studying for a B.Litt at Exeter College (1935–37). Formidably erudite, Qian was an outstanding scholar, a brilliant novelist and critic.* Fortress Besieged, *his famous satiric novel, was published in 1947. Yang became a successful playwright, author and translator.*

In the July of 1935, Zhongshu was less than 25 years old, and I was several days to 24. We got married and sailed to Oxford to study. We were both awkward and nervous, for we were far away and no longer under the wings of our parents. But we had joined our lives together and could be each other's support.

Upon his arrival in Oxford, Zhongshu 'kissed the Oxonian ground' [i.e. fell over] – and lost half an incisor.

Zhongshu entered Exeter College as a B.Litt candidate. However, I had to arrange all my academic matters by myself. I attended several classes, and studied in the Bodleian Library the rest of the time. The library was a quiet place with very few students – and I set for myself a reading list, and carefully consumed one book after another from the frontispiece to the back cover. How could I ever feel unsatisfied?

As term began, Zhongshu received a gown with two black stripes on the back. In China, he had a scholarship, because of the Boxer Indemnity, but at Oxford he was a 'Commoner' and every Commoner, male and female, wore this style of gown. All through the streets of Oxford were these well-dressed students, and just like a pupil who has dropped out of school, I was so jealous of their gowns.

Zhongshu's classes at Exeter were held in the College dining hall. For him, the most important classes were the one-to-one tutorials. As for me, every day I put on my Cheong-sam and sat on the auditing benches at the side of the classrooms with a feeling of inferiority. Zhongshu, however, said he would gain more if he were given a larger freedom of reading.

There were plenty of vacations at Oxford, and Zhongshu spent all his time in the libraries. The classics in the Bodleian were restricted to the 18th century or earlier, so about every two weeks we would visit the City Library to borrow the 19th- and

Qian Zhongshu and his wife, Yang Jiang, in 1935.

20th-century masterpieces. In a word, we have never worried about lacking books.

In the tranquil and cosy little town of Oxford, each day we took a walk or 'adventure' together after breakfast, and another one before dinner. We strolled slowly through the grand avenues and narrow lanes, through the gates of every college and through every field in the countryside. Passing through the flow of people in the streets, we would speculate on their identities and find a match for each person in the literary works we had read. Oxford has a beautiful human touch. If we happened to meet the postman, he would warmly hand us our family letters. When we returned home, we lowered the curtains and then quietly enjoyed reading face to face.

During term time, our teachers would invite us to tea in their houses, and our classmates in the dormitories. They taught Zhongshu and me how to make tea: first warming up the teapot, then everyone prepared a full spoonful of tea leaves: one spoon for you, one for me, one for him and one for the teapot ...

This academic year was the most cheerful in my entire life, and also my most hard-working year.

Correlli Barnett CBE
(1948, Modern History)

Three years in Exeter provided me and many of my contemporaries with a ladder from the lower-middle-class to the professional upper-middle class. And yet I doubt whether, in the strictly teaching sense, either the University or the College offered a first-rate service to those undergraduates reading the humanities.

We who came up in 1948 were for the most part ex-servicemen on what was called the Further Education and Training Scheme, a scheme funded by the taxpayer and intended to make good the wartime shortfall in output of graduates in various disciplines. We swelled university numbers by about a third over pre-war. In normal times, only a fraction of our age-group would have got into Oxford, and very probably not myself.

We were therefore as green in Oxford terms as new recruits turning up at an army depot. Yet there was no kind of induction course; no clear guidelines about methods of study, use of sources or the proper technique of writing essays. You were left to sort yourself out.

As for the tutorial system, no one explained how it was to work or what was expected of us. I thought that it was an absurd waste of time to read an essay during the tutorial itself, rather than submit it in advance. And what was the point of university lecturers, who simply droned through summaries of their books and articles? To me, the bread-and-butter lecture remains a positively medieval method of transmitting knowledge and understanding.

In 1948, 'Modern History' signified AD 410 to AD 1914, after which no further history had apparently taken place. It has to be asked: in what ways did this subject, as then defined, prepare us for a career in the post-war world? The whole syllabus was dominated by political and constitutional development, starting with Church, Crown and Parliament in the Middle Ages. Economic history came a long way second in importance to political history. The history of technology and industrial change, and the crucial influence of these factors on the shaping of society, were almost entirely left out.

C. T. Atkinson (Atters), famous in College for his smelly, snappy little dogs, his food-stained cardigans and his grey flannel trousers secured by bicycle clips, was the judge of the entries for the Murray Naval History Prize. When I submitted an essay on the

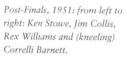

Post-Finals, 1951: from left to right: Ken Stowe, Jim Collis, Rex Williams and (kneeling) Correlli Barnett.

development of carrier aviation, Atters wished to disqualify it on the grounds that a twentieth-century topic could not be history. In the end, I shared the prize with Laurie Le Quesne, who had written a properly historical essay on the royalist navy during the Civil War.

Let me emphasise that I am talking about Oxford in the immediate post-war era. It was a time of austerity and universal rationing. And we were students on an education scheme funded by the taxpayer. Yet Oxford seemed to take absolutely no notice of such realities. We were actually required to bring dinner-jackets as part of our kit, so there we all were at college dinners wearing secondhand pre-war dinner jackets with the moth-holes darned. We had scouts to make our beds and empty our chamber pots, just as if we were real gentlemen used to personal servants.

It was a kind of cut price 'Brideshead' life, all tremendously enjoyable – but surely, in the national circumstances of the time, an escapist fantasy.

Post-war Oxford was not at all a realistic preparation for a career within a struggling industrial economy in urgent need of capable technocratic leadership. Quite the contrary – the whole sub-Brideshead culture made us positively despise industrial and commercial life. When chaps who had gone down the year before came back and told us about their experiences as 'graduate trainee' with Proctor and Gamble stacking Daz cartons in village shops, we all fell about screaming with laughter.

Oxbridge's academic values have perversely harmed Britain as a technological society competing in a world market. The British elite today still prizes academic attainment above practical capability; still prizes the humanities above science; still prizes 'pure' science above technology; and still esteems technological pioneering for its own sake above eventual market success.

The long-term answer to the problem of Britain's incompetent governance must be to change the basic thrust of our education from cleverness on paper to personal capability in solving real-life problems; from emphasis on the critical faculties to emphasis on the creative and constructive – problem-solvers, instead of problem-raisers.

Is our own College meeting the challenge?

Roger Bannister
(1946, Physiological Sciences)

The Porters' Lodge directed me to my room on the top floor of Staircase 11. I had a large sitting room with a small bedroom adjoining it. There I met my scout, Dennis. I had no understanding of the relation between a student and a scout. Certainly no one had ever called me 'Sir' before.

The College in 1946 was a strange mixture of students: 80 per cent were ex-servicemen who had been accepted by the College from school before being called up for wartime service. The oldest had been in the War since 1939, and so were vastly experienced in life and war. Not surprisingly, many of them found it difficult to settle down to study in Oxford. In the first term some spent most of their evenings after dinner drinking in the bar and emerged singing army songs when the bar closed.

In my first week among a mass of notices in the Lodge, I found a notice about the Oxford University Athletic Club, but decided to practise first on the Exeter College ground with a friend, Alan Eddy. After a while, the groundsman came up to talk to us, saying how well he remembered Jack Lovelock, a Rhodes Scholar at Exeter who won the Olympic 1500 metres in Berlin in 1936. He then praised Alan Eddy's style but was rather dismissive of mine, as he perceived a gangling 17-year-old who was over-striding.

The Secretary of the Oxford University Athletic Club, Russell Grice, was much kinder and more helpful to me. I duly came second in the freshman's mile race in November 1946 with the very modest time of 4 minutes and 52 seconds. But I was on my way.

After four years studying medicine at Exeter, I was awarded a Harmsworth Senior Scholarship at Merton College. But it was Exeter which changed me, mainly because I was given considerable responsibility for administration at an early age, which has always been possible at Oxford. In 1948 I was President of Exeter College JCR and at the same time President of the Oxford University Athletic Club and also President of Vincent's Club, Oxford's major sporting club.

The Presidency of the JCR was the most enjoyable of these responsibilities. The proceedings were hilarious, including the usual complaints about the lavatories and the food. One of the duties of the President of the JCR was to compose answers to

all manner of contributions to the leather-bound 'Suggestion Book'. In my time, one of the most scholarly and frequent contributors was Correlli Barnett, whose books later led to a revision of views about the role of the First World War generals.

My four years at Exeter were some of the most interesting in my life. I made friendships which have endured and learnt a great deal, especially from the ex-servicemen. The strange interaction between those of us who came up straight from school with those who had fought in the Second World War will never be repeated.

Sir Roger Bannister went on to become a distinguished neurologist, and Master of Pembroke College, Oxford.

Stansfield Turner
(1947, Rhodes Scholar, PPE)

May 26, 1949

Dear Mom and Dad

I'm afraid it's been some time since my last letter, but the first race of Eights week was a week ago today....

We lined up for the first race rather confident we'd catch the boat ahead of us, St Catherine's III, as we'd heard they were pretty bad. Well, we started rowing and didn't seem to catch them at all, and about a third of the way down we noticed that St Cath's had bumped the boat in front of them and had dropped by the side of the river as you have to when you bump. We went merrily onward, but lo and behold, Corpus II was hot on our tail....

As we went along, the boat gradually dropped back, but the people kept cheering us on very much and I suddenly realised that we were catching up with the boat that had started three ahead on us. By the time we started down the home stretch I was about exhausted. The home stretch is lined with the barges of various colleges, magnificent old houseboat sort of things with gay paintings, flags and all sorts of people sitting atop having tea, and cheering. I watched each barge go by. I kept praying for the end to come but it seemed like it never would.

Suddenly we 'got a gun' which meant that somebody on the bank shot a gun indicating that we were catching up to the boat ahead to within half a length, soon we got two guns meaning a quarter length. I then knew I'd better pull with all I had left as there wasn't much distance to go, and suddenly we hit them, ten yards from the finish in a mile course!

We all collapsed, but with great joy as this 'over bump' is quite a rare feat and meant that we had moved up the river three places in one fell swoop. I was extremely elated and really think it is one of the most exhilarating moments of my Oxford career....

[after further races, on Saturday]… We all had tea and watched the rest of the races until 6.30. I then stepped in to the role for which Mother had prepared me when she sent over all that china, glassware, etc, after reading of the days of good old Oxford dinner parties.

We all came back to the room for cocktails, and appetisers including Mother's pheasant pate on Ritz…. Dennis [his scout] had arranged that we could use the room across the hall for dinner and had set up the table magnificently with borrowed solid silver candlesticks, flowers in the aisle, my fine china, navy glasses, wine glasses, doilies, my napkins, and wooden handled cutlery. It was really something … There were eight altogether. The chef did us up a fine meal too, starting with Eggs Portuguese for the first course, chicken, asparagus, and new potatoes for the main entree, and a wonderful dessert very similar to a baked Alaska! It was all well cooked and we had claret wine to go with it all.

After dinner Dennis served coffee back in my room, and then liqueurs and we all sat around and chatted until about 10.30 when everybody left after what had been a very delightful day. The weather had been perfect and the river was beautiful and the dinner had been a grand success.

Love,
Stan

Stansfield Turner, who became a US Admiral and Head of the CIA, relaxing in his College rooms.

Alan Bennett
(1954, Modern History)

It was at Oxford that I first had a room of my own …
and having a room that I could do up and arrange as
I wanted was what made me look forward to Oxford.
University had less to do with broadening the mind
than finding a place I could call my own. I had never
had a room to myself; at home I had shared with my
brother, and during my two years' National Service
had been in various barrack rooms.

It was not until my second year that I achieved
the sole occupancy of a set of rooms, under the eaves
of the front quad and, looking out at the back over
Exeter garden and the walls of the Divinity School,
I could see the towers of All Souls and the spire of
St Mary's. Still, it was less the view than the interior
I was interested in. I put my wallpaper up on the
chimney breast and at the windows I hung long
grey curtains of some shiny material which were
purely for decoration because, since I was on the top
floor, nobody could see in anyway. To the left of the
fireplace I hung a plain gilded nineteenth-century
mirror, which was falling to pieces then and is falling
to pieces now where it hangs at the top of my kitchen
stairs. Below it in the photograph is a small black-
and-white portrait of myself in profile. Though I
am no artist, I was immensely pleased with it and

*Drawings from the mid-1950s
JCR Suggestion Book.*

Left: Alan Bennett, award-winning playwright and author, seen here on the far left in the JCR Smoker, 1957.

Below: Bennett's set of rooms were 'under the eaves of the front quad'.

mortified when it was later lost, the linen on which it was painted recycled, I've always thought, by a young painter for one of his less distinctive efforts. I had painted a coloured portrait at the same time and this has survived. However, since I was the only subject I seemed able to tackle, I thought it was best, or at any rate healthiest, to cease production.

Also in the photograph is a red lacquer tea caddy, spotted in a junk-shop window as I was coming into Lancaster on the bus when I was about fifteen. I got off, ran back and bought it for five shillings and this, too, I still have, some dusty leaves of fifty-year-old tea a relic of that time. Next to it is a grey-and-blue mocha mug, also extant, and a Staffordshire dog which got the elbow sometime in the sixties. I note, too, that even I had succumbed to the lure of record sleeves – one of them, I believe, with a photograph of Prague, at that time an unvisitable place.

From Untold Stories, *by Alan Bennett, first published by Profile Books, London, in 2005: extract and photographs by kind permission of the author.*

Joseph Nye
(1958, Rhodes Scholar, PPE)

I was a rather naive young American when I arrived at Oxford, but I learned a lot there. I learned some basic economics: for example, the difference between a capital-intensive and a labour-intensive economy. At Princeton, I had to buy my own milk, but I had a refrigerator to store it in. At Oxford, my scout brought the milk to my room, but there was no refrigerator to store it in. Of course it didn't matter much, because the room was like a refrigerator anyway.

Indeed, the words 'cold' and 'Oxford' are firmly linked in my memories. My wonderful high-ceilinged 18th-century rooms were heated by a small electric coil. I studied by pulling a chair and blanket as close to the coil as I could without setting the blanket on fire.

One night I was reading in my room when I realised that I was late to Hall. I threw on my gown, rushed across the quad, and found that there was only one seat left in the Hall, and it was not on the long benches, but was a chair by the blazing fire. I could not believe my luck – and I was right.

It turns out that the chair is reserved for the senior scholar, and the price of my usurpation was that I was 'sconced': ordered to purchase a pint of cold beer. A waiter brought a cold silver tankard. If I finished it without taking it from my lips, I had the right to sconce back the other student who had sconced me. For the sake of deterrence, I did that, and a two-pint tankard was delivered to my antagonist. Alas, he downed it and returned the obligation, but when a three-pint tankard of cold beer was delivered to me, I surrendered. I learned that deterrence does not always prevent escalation – something that served me well in my later work with nuclear strategy.

And finally, I learned never to underestimate the British – something that has also served me in good stead when I later worked closely with British colleagues in Intelligence, diplomacy and defence. At the time, however, I learned this lesson the hard way.

At some point in history, an American Rhodes Scholar had obtained a key to the back gate of Exeter College. The key was passed from one Rhodes Scholar to another, but since there were two American Rhodes Scholars in the year I inherited the key, and being an equalitarian American, I thought I should share it. So I took the key to be duplicated in a shop a good distance from college.

A week later, there was a knock on my door and the Senior Tutor entered with the key in his hand. 'Is this yours?' 'It was,' I said. From this I learned, first, never underestimate British intelligence, and second, don't get carried away with American equalitarianism.

From a speech on 'The Universities and the Future' delivered at the annual Washington, D.C. Oxford– Cambridge Boat Race Dinner, 2011; reprinted in The American Oxonian, *Vol XCVIII Number 2.*

Joseph Nye in his student days. He was later head of Harvard's Kennedy School and Assistant Secretary of Defense.

The gargoyle depicting Rector Wheare overlooks the Fellows' Garden. The kangaroo and emu carved on either side represent his Australian origins.

RECTOR WHEARE RECALLED

In my second year at Exeter, I had rooms (yes – a bedroom and main room) in Palmer's Tower, which at that time (1965) was covered in scaffolding due to deteriorating stonework. I had a party one night on the roof for a few friends, one of whom (rather later on in the evening) managed to produce a passable rendition of 'God Save the Queen' by blowing down a scaffolding pipe like an Alpine horn. So pleased was he with the result that he repeated it at frequent and regular intervals. Eventually, the tower door onto the roof creaked open and Jack the Porter stuck his head round.

'Excuse me, sirs,' he wheezed, 'Rector's tired of getting out of bed and standing to attention. Will you please desist.'

Paul Gittins
(1964, English)

Michael Preston
(1964, Literae Humaniores)

Early in Michaelmas 1966, the JCR Committee appointed me Chairman of the Eights Week Ball Committee. By early November, I had come up with two bands, both relatively unknown – Pink Floyd and Cream. While Pink Floyd were visually more striking, I plumped for the superior musical abilities of Cream. At least Eric Clapton had a reputation from his time with the Yardbirds. And at £400, Cream were just within our budget. The tickets went on sale, but by the time we went down for Christmas, we had sold only a tiny portion of what we needed to break even.

Then in January 1967, Cream had their first Top-Ten hit. Tickets were sold out by February. But the history of Oxford balls is littered with no-shows and price increases. So there began a four-month agony of suspense.

However, on the evening of the Ball, a van arrived in the back quad. I recognised Eric Clapton, Ginger Baker and Jack Bruce under their shoulder-length hair. Their equipment was set up in the marquee, and they gave a performance which was striking for both its quality and its length. Booked for two 45-minute sessions, Cream gave us 60 minutes of uninterrupted

playing in their first session, and nearly 75 in their second.

At one point, I went to chat with the band in their room. They were surprisingly pleasant, if a little removed from planet Earth, but there was a smell in the room that wasn't quite incense but was clearly not after-shave. The room had been booked in my name, and this was something that had to be dealt with then and there. I went to the Rector's Lodgings and asked to see Sir Kenneth Wheare.

The Rector greeted me affably: 'How is it going, my boy?' I reminded him that we had a very famous pop-group in the College. 'Rector, I should consider it a great personal favour if you would come and see them.' He was obviously reluctant, but he followed me across the quad and up Staircase 14.

The encounter was surreal. The world's leading constitutional lawyer talking to three stoned rockers. I do not know whether either side understood a word of what the other was saying, but courtesies were observed and the Rector said his goodbyes.

As we reached the open air, Sir Kenneth looked at me kindly. 'I understand, Preston. All is well.'

At that point, the cloud lifted and I could enjoy what remained of the evening.

Philip Pullman
(1965, English)

I came up to Exeter in 1965 callow, boastful and ignorant. I left three years later in much the same state. That was entirely my fault. The College supplied me with everything needed to make me modest and knowledgeable (the callowness would take a few years more to rub off) but I took little notice of it. If I could go back and do it all again …

Well, if I could, I don't suppose the outcome would be any different. But if I could come to Exeter now, I know it would. The greatest difference between then and now is, of course, the presence of women. The place feels more civilised, more courteous and friendly altogether, simply nicer. And then there is the world outside. Students nowadays leave university burdened with debt and with little prospect of finding work; in 1968 tuition was free, we had grants to live on, and there was work to be found quite easily. No wonder I stayed callow for so long.

One of the first things I did after entering the College in that autumn of 1965 was to change the name I was known by. I had never liked Philip; a silly sort of name it seemed to me, so I told everyone I was called by my second name, Nicholas. Friends I made at Oxford still call me Nick. Not long ago I met a man who'd known me as Nick and whom I'd never seen since. He had read Philip Pullman's books and had no idea I was the same person.

Anyway, armed with a new name, clad in my scholar's gown, I set about my first tutorial. I was reading English, and my Tutor was Jonathan Wordsworth, whose rooms were at the top of the tower over the Lodge. I toiled all the way up those steps and read him an essay on something or other. It must have taken him about five minutes to realise that he'd made a mistake in giving me a scholarship. I don't remember anything that he told me about literature during my three years in that comfortable room. He seems, in my memory, to have spoken much more about painting. He was particularly fond of Andrew Wyeth, I recall. And I remember his expression when looking at me: a sort of amicable puzzlement, as if he was too polite to say 'What are you doing here?' while certainly wondering it.

Nick Pullman, later author of the best-selling His Dark Materials, *in the 1960s.*

English Language and Literature took what I considered an unnecessarily broad and inclusive view of itself, and began with Anglo-Saxon. To make up for that, it stopped at 1900. I couldn't get on with Anglo-Saxon; I was never going to write in it, and all the stuff worth reading was in translation; but to make up for that, our Anglo-Saxon Tutor was a blonde goddess called Mrs Longrigg. Every year she seemed to give birth to another little Longrigg, and I remember tutorials taking place in her house in north Oxford, which was filled with drying nappies, distant wailing, and the smell of baby powder. Consequently I could never really separate those impressions from the Anglo-Saxon language itself. The association still remains.

Apparently there were lectures at frequent intervals. When I found out where they were going on, I went to one. It consisted of an elderly don reading slowly and indistinctly out of a book of his own, which I thought I could read rather more quickly myself, if I could find it in the library. I knew I could deal with the Radcliffe Camera: you just had to take a book from the shelf and leave a slip there before sitting down at one of the long tables, getting out your pencil and paper, and deciding that it was time for a coffee at the Cadena Café.

The main Bodleian was a bit more difficult. First you had to remember which door to go in, and then how to look up what books you wanted, and then how to order them, and then, hardest of all, remember to go back the following day when they'd be waiting for you. I never mastered any of that till many years later, when I was properly grown up and had nothing to do with the University any more, and the Cadena was long gone from the Cornmarket. I certainly spent more time at the Cadena than in the Bodleian. There was a long dark cafeteria downstairs where the coffee was so-so but the currant buns were excellent, and a posher part upstairs, where you were waited on by elderly waitresses in black dresses and white aprons. I used to go upstairs to celebrate with sardines on toast whenever I had a win on the horses (the depravity). The Cadena was such an agreeably old-fashioned place that it was bound to be torn down and destroyed. I'm glad I knew it.

The chap who showed me how to win on the horses was called Dave Harding. He read History

Filming Pullman's The Golden Compass *(2007) in College.*

at Exeter, and he was delighted to be told one day by his Tutor that he led the life of an 18th-century gentleman, doing not a scrap of academic work and devoting all his time to playing cards and betting on horses. I think that was all he learned about the 18th century. I was sorry to lose touch with him, and with other friends such as Jim Taylor, whose roof-climbing exploits were legendary. Years later I stole Jim Taylor's name for a character in some of my books.

But other friends remain. On my first day I met an impressively mature, sophisticated, and dynamic young man called Caradoc King. He is still all of those things but one, and has been my literary agent for most of my professional life. Caradoc was a man of mystery: how could someone so young be so, somehow, grown-up? Graham Chainey was another man of mystery. His conversation consisted of long silences interrupted by pauses, but he was good at music. I remember listening astounded to his LP of Messiaen's *Et Exspecto Resurrectionem Mortuorum*. Graham went on to be an expert on the literary history of Cambridge, and wrote a longer book on that subject than you might think possible.

In the third year, Caradoc and I shared a cottage at Garsington with another friend, Richard Eeles. At that time you weren't allowed to live in unapproved digs, but Caradoc put the case to the Rector that we were victims of unhappy family circumstances, and persuaded him to let us live there. We lived in a sort of mock old club man's style. We pretended to be old buffers sitting in our club, had sherry before dinner and took turns to cook.

Sir Kenneth Wheare, the Rector in those days, once invited the three of us to dinner. The guest of honour was J. R. R. Tolkien, then at the height of his fame. Tolkien turned to Richard and said 'Now tell me, young man, how are they pronouncing Anglo-Saxon these days?' Richard hadn't a clue and could only open and close his mouth like a fish. Not entirely pleased, Tolkien tried Caradoc instead. 'And did you enjoy *The Lord of the Rings*?' Caradoc said 'I'm awfully sorry, I haven't read it.' That was the end of Tolkien's conversation for the dinner.

I was very happy at Exeter, and much of that happiness is due to laughter. I hope those nice undergraduates today still find things as funny as we did.

179

Martin Amis

(1968, English)

Nobody can be forced to work at Oxford, but things are made easy, pleasant and stimulating for those who want to work. And just as there is the time for pleasure, there is the time for boredom and neurosis, which only work can fill. At the beginning of my third year, owing to an impetuous scheme to share a house in the country with unstable and profligate friends, work was fatally eased out by pleasure, most of it pleasureless, and for my last two terms I radically readjusted.... I moved into the Annexe of my college, a grim bastion ... on the unattractive Iffley Road. It was a large flat house that smelled of locker rooms and lavatory spray, a suspended echoic warren of shuffling caretakers, winded cats and dozens of progeriac postgraduates.... It suited me perfectly.

Here I went again: I rose at 6 am, drank a great deal of coffee (real coffee by now), worked until 8, went into college for breakfast, took my seat in the college library by 8.45, worked until 1, had lunch in college, took my seat in the college library by 1.45, worked until 7, returned to the Iffley Road, worked until 9, prepared for myself a Vesta Beef Curry or a Vesta Chicken Supreme or – best – a Vesta Paella (not a single item of genuine nutriment, I can safely say, passed down my throat at Exeter House), returned to my desk and worked until 1 am. I rose at 6 am ... at this rate, I was going to look a bit of a bloody fool if I didn't do very well indeed. The nine three-hour papers came in a heroic blur. I got a formal First, coming third in that year.

The unique freedom of Oxford – now more than ever, probably – is that you don't have to account for more than, say, 90 minutes a week for 18 weeks a year. That's about three days out of three years of your life. Conventional ways for filling that time are gone; it is all yours now. It doesn't happen to you before and it never happens to you again. Perhaps once is enough – but not more than enough.

Extract from My Oxford, *ed: Ann Thwaite, Robson Books, 1977, by kind permission of the author.*

Martin Amis and his mother, Hilary, in 1968.

Imogen Stubbs (left) as Irina in the OUDS production of Chekhov's Three Sisters *at the Oxford Playhouse, 1980.*

Imogen Stubbs
(1979, English)

I had an odd time at the College because I was in the first minuscule intake of girls (I had already been part of a tiny minority of girls at Westminster and have four brothers) and I was the only girl for whom lots of boys was not a novelty and more importantly who wasn't in the rowing team.

I was a bit of a rebellious tom-boy and wore grungy clothes before they were in any way fashionable, and I think my tutors – who were already struggling with having to teach girls for the first time – found me wearisome, feminine-impaired and borderline offensive. And many of my peer group did too. Which perhaps I was.

In my last year I lived in a ruined cottage in a wood with no electricity, no bathroom facilities and all water pulled up in a bucket from a well. I got there (Begbroke) by motorbike and then walked for a mile through cow fields. It was a totally wonderful life in the summer but unfortunately we hit one of the coldest winters of the last century and I don't know how we survived. We revised by candlelight wrapped up in duvets – but at least we had no technology to distract us. I also worked in Browns as a waitress because my grant had failed to materialise – and I was in the Oxford revue at the Playhouse and various other painfully under-rehearsed shows. All during my Finals term. Mad.

Patric Dickinson
(1969, Modern History)

The Exeter Machine

Over a period of nine terms (Hilary 1971 to Michaelmas 1973) Exeter provided four Presidents of the Union (Michael House, Christopher Tookey, myself and David Warren), one Treasurer (Philip Vander Elst) and two members of Standing Committee (Michael Lee and John Quelch). All seven of us appear in the photograph, taken on 15 June 1972 immediately before that term's Farewell Debate at the Union, along with Rector and Lady Wheare, just before Rector Wheare's retirement.

We regarded the Exeter Machine as rather a joke. On the other hand, we did do a lot to create and nurture the myth. And I suppose it had some reality. I always regarded its zenith as the summer of 1971 when Tookey was Editor of *Isis* and Quelch was Editor of *Cherwell* and we therefore controlled the student press. The only arena in which we fared badly was the Exeter JCR election in 1971 when we all signally failed to achieve office!

There were so many references to the Exeter Machine in Union debates during Mike House's Presidency (Hilary 1970) that on 25 February, in the course of a debate on social services, Judith Hart (Overseas Development Minister in Harold Wilson's government) felt obliged to apologise for not being a member of Exeter College.

David Warren's Presidency marked the final flowering of the Machine. At his Farewell Debate in December 1973 I made wistful reference to its passing:

... which leads me on to another farewell we are witnessing tonight – the final demise of a rather unusual, semi-mythical institution, commonly known as the Exeter Machine. The Machine, if I may borrow the happy turn of phrase employed last term by the ex-Librarian from Corpus – the Machine stops here. The retirement of yourself, Sir, the fourth Exeter President in three years, makes this possibly the saddest day in the history of the College since Walter de Stapeldon, Bishop of Exeter, our popular and much-beloved founder, was murdered by a London mob outside St Paul's Cathedral in October 1326.

Editor's note: *David Warren went on to become British Ambassador to Japan, Michael House to be a barrister, Michael Lee to be chief executive of Ithmaar Bank in Bahrain, Chris Tookey to be film critic of the* Daily Mail, *Patric Dickinson to be Clarenceux King of Arms, John Quelch to be Dean of the China Europe International Business School (CEIBS) and Philip Vander Elst to stand for the European Parliament as a candidate for the UK Independence Party.*

The Exeter Machine, 1972.

Reeta Chakrabarti
(1984, English and French)

Wham! and the miners' strike. Band Aid and a famine in Africa. The mid-1980s at Exeter College were a whirl of good times punctured by events that reminded us we were a fortunate few. Ours was a world that preceded tuition fees – and preceded internet and social media too.

The tatty newspapers in the JCR and the sole TV in the chocolate vending-machine room next door were our one connection with the outside world, and the place where intractable geo-political issues were fought over and resolved. Some of that happened in the Undercroft too, usually after several pints or Pimms, depending on your poison and the season. Pimms it had to be in the summer, during Eights Week and for the Exeter Ball – although one year (1986?) the ball was a wash-out, we cowered inside, and our compere, the late John Peel, berated us from the sodden marquee for being so miserable.

Being at the epicentre of town made us horribly lazy, and we stuck to the Radcliffe Camera for Mods, and to the river for Eights Week. Although in general a sports refusenik, I found rowing a joy, and waxed lyrical with the best of them about the calm of the dawn, and the crisp snap of the blades. Steak dinners to build us rowers up were the dining hall's finest hour, although they also did a mean Eggs Florentine, and the puddings weren't bad.

We learnt a new lexicon to boost our sense of belonging – coming up, and going down, battels and scouts. Our scout Antonia was long-suffering, and patience itself, turning a blind eye to bottles, binges, and illegal guests. Our rooms – shared in the first and second-years – were, with her efforts, cleaner than we deserved. My view over the quad was lovely, but the furniture was functional and the décor had a whiff of The Office about it. There was one communal bath at the top of the stairs, which made coming down clad in a bathrobe more exciting than it should have been. I had my miserable moments, but overall my time was one big gloriously happy whirlwind. And I realise, reading this, that I've made no mention of the work …

Reeta Chakrabarti is now education correspondent at BBC News.

A Student Blogs

'A wonder happened on the wave'
– From Riddle 66, the *Exeter Book*

The wonder being that I got on the wave and didn't immediately tip the boat over, aka, I went rowing Wednesday morning (having somehow, miraculously, gotten onto the women's B team). I am, of course, irredeemably rubbish, but it's probably good to be humiliated a little bit, and I'd never get out of bed otherwise. A caveat: waking at 5:45 am is no fun. But being on the river at 7:00, gazing out at the pale October sun as it burns the mist off Christ Church Meadows and glances off the golden spires of Merton College chapel…. that makes up for a whole lot.

Oh – happy news – I've got housemates for next year! We will be living together (hopefully in Cowley, an area of Oxford where a lot of students live and which I'm already rather fond of). I'm absurdly excited about this. One of the hardest things about living in College, for me, is the lack of a kitchen in which to cook and sing and hang out. I really love to put music on and sing while I make dinner, and although it's nice to just go into Hall and be served hot food, it also means I can't do what I love to do. There is a kitchen in the JCR that undergraduates can use, but it's more industrial – it's not really the kind of kitchen you hang out in. Anyway, the point is that I already have people to live with. Which is great. Assuming that we don't all fall out, which I can't really see happening; we're all far too sensible.

I really hate the fact that I need sleep – I would much prefer to function without it – but unfortunately I am the sort of person who needs it, and I keep getting too little of it. Tomorrow is going to be absurdly busy, and I suspect that I will (yet again) have to postpone doing my laundry…

Academia is, of course, marvellous. All the lectures are, if not enjoyable, at least valuable (except for one last week, which was ostensibly in a series about Victorian fiction, but which instead comprised a lady standing there reading a paper about auto/biography at us. Utter nonsense).

Meanwhile, there is the strangeness of awaking each morning in a town that you are trying to claim for your own, and not quite recognizing yourself. I see myself sometimes in the mirror and know that I am who I am. Other times I wonder what I am, where I'm

from, what I'm becoming. There are very few anchors from the life before. I've put up pictures on the board in my room, and the people in them look out at me as though I knew them once, ever so long ago. I wanted this – I think most 18-year-olds do – but it is strange and new.

And yet things are so beautiful here. Leaves are turning red; skies are blue (or grey, sometimes, but even the grey is pretty damn picturesque); light is gold; whenever I think there's no one around, there's a wave or a smile in the quad, sometimes even an invitation to get coffee. It's the bluebird of happiness: you go looking for it only to find that it was right there all along.

Eleanor Franzen
(2010, English)
exeterelle.word.press.com

A Day in the Life of a JCR President

The following is the amalgamation of two real days in Hilary Term 2012

7:30 am: Woken up by a missed phone call from the Junior Dean. She texts me to say that the JCR is in a mess and I need to organise a clear-up.

7:45 am: I've cleaned a bit up myself and so have some helpful Freshers. I text the JD to tell her it's clear and she texts back thanking me. I even get a kiss at the end of the text. Score.

8 am: I've cycled back to Cowley to shower and deconstruct what happened to my friends the night before after I failed to come back and watch TV in bed.

9 am: I have liaison meeting. It's with various representatives from College and I brief them on some of the things the JCR is doing. We're greeted with the usual mix of strong support and a couple of more conservative 'ooh that's not been agreed fifteen years in advance.' It's productive though and our plans for a Finalists' Ball and Williams Dinner are coming to fruition slowly.

10 am: I've cycled to the Social Sciences Library to get some work done before lectures but it quickly becomes clear that I won't.

A big story is breaking about a conference Exeter is holding in the Easter vac. Those hosting it look like they might have some offensive views. I have three emails from the student papers and a couple of missed phone calls. College is being slow to understand the potential communication risk on this one so I send a couple of emails to the Rector and others explaining the situation.

10:30 am: It becomes clear that this is going to be tricky. There's an amalgamation of legal and practical issues on top of the need to support JCR members. ▶

THE REMORSEFUL DAY

I was standing by the window of my College rooms, looking over the western side of the Front Quad. I must have been on the telephone, which sat on the ledge there. Outside Staircase 8 there seemed to be a

commotion. Trouble? – no. Television? – probably; I knew that a crew was in College that week. A grey-suited man was collapsing on to the quad grass. Of course! Inspector Morse was once again in town, and the story going about had been that he was due to die.

It turned out that his death was not to be on Exeter's premises, but after an ambulance drive to a nameless hospital. Exeter was nameless too, used to simulate a performance of Fauré's *Requiem*. The finished and broadcast episode shows part of that performance inside the newly smartened Chapel: a sickly looking Morse (in the Sub-Rector's pew), a soloist, the organist (doubtless Exeter's Organ Scholar, heard but not seen) and the chorus (definitely a Chapel choir contingent although it was second week of the vacation). For myself, I saw only what happened later, outside, but on seeing I reasoned, 'They don't do these things only once; there'll be a repeat or two.' So to my camera. So to a snap of the third 'death' of Inspector Morse, photographed through window glass on 22 March 2000.

Christopher Kirwan

I've given a couple of quotes to the student papers making a clear statement.

It turns out my exec are being called too so I remind them of our policy about not talking to the press without liaising with me so that we can keep a clear message.

11 am: Lecture.

Midday: The situation has worsened. A small but important contingent of the JCR are upset about what's going on and I spend the next half hour explaining it to some of them.

12:30 pm: Lunch.

1 pm: Work.

2 pm: Governing Body meeting. This is a meeting of all of the Fellows from College and I sit in on it. I decide it's important to have input on the conference problem and so explain the views amongst the JCR and suggest some communication improvements. The Fellows are fortunately very receptive and agree to send out some emails and reconsider their commenting policy to the student papers.

3 pm – 5 pm: Work.

5 pm: I get a call from a JCR President friend at another college. They're having some problems dealing with their exec and want some advice. We speak about that for about five minutes, and then chat for another 15. It's been good to get to know all the other Presidents very well.

5:30 pm: My Politics Tutor has invited me for a chat in his study. I'm hoping there will be coffee and biscuits. Fortunately there is. We chat about various things going on in College and he gives me some excellent advice. He also lets me know about an event in Trinity where I'll get to meet Aung San Suu Kyi. Fantastic!

6 pm: Meet with the entz reps to talk about our plans for the Finalists' Ball and work out what needs to be done. I'm lucky to have a great team.

6:30 pm: I get an email from the Chaplain inviting me to coffee in his room the next day. Praise the Lord for Stephen!

7 pm: I get a call from a friend in the student papers who warns me that the conference story is going national in one of the weekend papers. I'm not that bothered because I'm happy with what we've said as a JCR and the advice we've given to College. I get an email from College agreeing that a body to consider conference approvals in the future has been set up, and I manage to get the JCR a seat on it.

7:15 pm: Half-way-hall. Friends and wine. Perfect.

8 pm: Dana informs me I'm making a speech. This is a total surprise. Oh well, it'll be fun.

10 pm: Junction – Oxford's premier nightlife venue, even equipped with a foam machine.

Benjamin Clayton *(2010, PPE) was elected President of the JCR in Hilary Term 2012.*

Benjamin Clayton with Aung San Suu Kyi, on the day she finally received her honorary degree from the University of Oxford, 20 June 2012.

I Remember

I remember nerves outside my entrance interview. Jeri Johnson dragged a rubbish bag from the room and drawled, 'The body of the last guy.'

I remember admitting I'd referenced, 'Moby Dick' without having read it. 'Wise coming clean,' she said.

I remember walking into college on my first day and the big smile of welcome on a second-year's face. I had a hip-flask in my pocket. I never drink out of a hip-flask.

I remember pogoing to The Mules in the Undercroft Bar. I was sure they'd go all the way.

I remember the legendary James W downing a pint of cider-and-black at my first college bop – and immediately vomiting it up all over me.

I remember Jeri's stern sympathy when a friend died. Steady in the face of panic.

I remember the siren-call of the Fellows' Garden at sunset. And sunrise. And in the middle of the night.

I remember Rector's Collections, being told to have more patience with my Old English Tutor.

I remember seeing a girl across the quad and just knowing.

I remember the trudge to Sainsbury's that began every essay crisis. Three Red-Bulls and a carrot cake.

I remember whiskey gulps with my tutorial partner at five in the morning.

I remember the text from his girlfriend: 'What have you done to him?'

I remember Brin, the 'Big Issue' seller, beneath my window. His voice was a nasal knife but he was good at his job.

I remember the wafts of Hassan's kebab van. He's renamed it, 'Chez Hassan'.

I remember tumbling into the sun at nine-forty-five to drag my tutorial partner across the quad.

I remember Jeri supporting me when he attacked me for 'semantics'. 'That's what we're in the business of.'

I remember her ledger as she pulled the legs from my arguments. Repeatedly.

I remember lunch in the Dining Hall. Pie.

I remember salads in the Covered Market. Lunch.

I remember midnight fire drills and stained glass.

I remember a third-year crying as she looked out of my college window. 'I've been so happy here.'

I remember a rugby-shirted type elbowing me out the way at the last Mules gig. 'The best band in the world!'

I remember the run-up to Finals. Keeping it together.

I remember the nocturnal solace of the college library. The only person still in there, Milton, revellers muted and inarticulate outside.

I remember answering my phone in there. Whispering, though no-one else was around.

I remember sobriety in a tux at the last college ball. A girl with a flower in her hair actually talked to me.

I remember Jeri's good-luck card acquiring a talismanic significance.

I remember Finals dinner and realising I hadn't made enough effort to know these people. A real pit-of-the-stomach regret.

I remember packing up, wondering if I'd ever see my college mates again.

I remember one of those mates giving me my results. Stuttering away relief.

I remember James W's new opera last year.

I remember making my tutorial partner's best man speech in the Dining Hall this summer. It was the first time I'd felt like an adult in that room, which scared me.

I remember sitting alone in the Fellows' Garden as his wedding dance played. Missing the place I was sitting in.

Michael Lesslie
(2003, English)

FLOREAT EXON

TODAY AND TOMORROW

FRANCES CAIRNCROSS

Simply to survive for 700 years is a remarkable achievement. But this book has demonstrated how different today's College is from what has gone before. True, we are on the same site – my office is probably on the very spot to which we moved from Hart Hall in 1315. But even in the past half century, the College has undergone dramatic change.

Some of those changes are superficial: the evolution of the custom for Finalists to wear white, pink or red carnations with their sub-fusc to mark their progress through Finals, say, or the excitement of 'trashing' – showering returning Finalists in buckets of cold water to resounding cheers. Some are profound: the retreat of religion from College life, the admission of women, the growth in the numbers of international

students and graduates and in the importance of the sciences and of academic research. To get a place at Exeter is vastly more competitive today than in the past, and the pressures on students are greater than ever before. No wonder the College now devotes to pastoral care time and resources unimagined in the days of 'moral tutors'.

Other changes are still unrolling. Gone are the days when an academic ran the College finances: the College now has a full-time Bursar, with a deputy and an accountant. The burden of managing the endowment, coping with the ceaseless flow of legislation, and handling the building first of Exeter House and now of Walton Street could not be undertaken by a part-timer. The office of Senior Tutor, for years managed part-time by an academic, is now increasingly complex and demanding. Exeter has been experimenting with a full-time Academic Dean instead.

Our Library, still the intellectual heart of the College, is now full of the tapping of keyboards. How long will its books be needed? The scientists have already largely abandoned them. Others may follow. The laptop and the tablet, once rare luxuries, are now the universal tools of learning and of teaching. Students prop them on their knees in the Front Quad; Fellows bring them into Governing Body to read their papers on screen. The Presidents of the MCR and JCR send out notices from their phones.

And then, ahead, there is Walton Street. The creation of a third quad – only seven minutes' walk from Turl Street – will give the College a 50 per cent

Previous pages: *View from the Sheldonian looking west over Exeter rooftops.*

Left: *Antique bookstand and page marker in Exeter College Library.*

Opposite: *The Rector's Garden.*

190

increase in its usable space in central Oxford. When students move in, they will find a building that tries to reimagine the traditional Oxford quadrangle, with interwoven spaces in which to read and to teach and to meet and to drink a cup of coffee with a friend. One of the key tests for this development will be whether it enhances student life on both central sites, or whether one exerts a greater pull than the other, to the detriment of both.

In spite of all these changes, some important things endure. The tutorial method of teaching survives against all the odds: hugely expensive and demanding but also a powerful way to develop the minds of the young. The emphasis on learning to present an argument and then to defend it remains one of Oxford's tremendous strengths. Oxford undergraduates in the humanities and social sciences still spend far more time working alone, and produce far more written work, than their opposite numbers in other universities.

One of Oxford's other strengths is the fostering of friendships. The 100 or so undergraduates who arrive at Exeter each year quickly form a large and ramshackle family group. The architecture of the College, with its large Front Quad through which everyone walks, gives endless opportunities for making and meeting friends. Exeter House, with its warren of small flats, brings together graduates from around the world into new networks that create international friendships. And many of these friendships then last longer, and mean more, than those our students make in later life.

Most indestructible of all is Exeter's fundamental role down seven centuries: that of educating and mentoring young people in order to improve the society they live in. That was one of Stapeldon's main reasons for founding the College in the first place. For centuries, most Exonians went back to play their part – initially in the West Country and then, after William Petre's reforms, throughout the country. Today – and tomorrow – Exonians make their mark not just in one region or one country, but across the world. *Floreat Exon*!

Left: *Graduation day.*

Opposite: *Leaving Exeter.*

FOOTNOTES

1 The History of the University of Oxford, Vol. I: *The Early Oxford Schools*, ed. by J. I. Catto (Oxford: Clarendon Press, 1984).

2 *Art and Industry in the Fourteenth Century*, in *The Collected Works of William Morris*, ed. by M. Morris (London: Longmans, 1910–15), Vol. XII, p. 388.

3 Geoffrey Tyack, 'Gilbert Scott and the Chapel of Exeter College, Oxford', *Architectural History* 50, p. 130.

4 George Gilbert Scott, *Personal and Professional Recollections* (London: Sampson Low, Marston, Searle and Rivington, 1879), pp. 214–15.

5 Scott, *Recollections*, pp. 214–15; cf. Tyack, 'Gilbert Scott and the Chapel of Exeter College, Oxford', p. 143.

6 Scott, *Recollections*, p. 216.

7 Tyack, 'Gilbert Scott and the Chapel of Exeter College, Oxford', p. 143.

8 Scott, *Recollections*, pp. 217–18.

9 Such drinking songs were popular in the 18th and 19th centuries in the student bars in Germany. The full refrain appears to have been 'Edite, bibite collegiales, post *multa saecula pocula nulla*' ('Eat and drink colleagues, in the distant future there won't be any cups [i.e., carousing]').

10 William John Francis Keatley Stride, *Exeter College* (London: F. E. Robinson & Co., 1900).

11 Charles William Boase, *Register of the Rectors, Fellows and Other Members on the Foundation of Exeter College, Oxford* (Oxford: Clarendon Press, for the Oxford Historical Society, 1894), p. xxix.

12 Franks Report, Vol. II: 1,829 of these (1,048 in arts and 861 in science) were men; 12 of the 22 other men's undergraduate colleges had a higher ratio of postgraduates to undergraduates than Exeter in 1964–65.

13 In 1964–65, 50.4 per cent of men were accommodated in college-owned accommodation, though since many colleges gave preference to undergraduates, and because married quarters were scarce, it is likely that the proportion of postgraduates who were offered accommodation was much lower than this figure. Half of undergraduate colleges tried to give unmarried postgraduates a year in college if they were new to Oxford (Franks Report, Vol. II, 33, 35).

14 These 27 women, with one or two imports from next-door, made up the 24 members of the three women's VIIIs, which raced on the river in May 1980, its first Eights Week as a mixed College (the contribution of women to its prowess on the river was not an issue foreseen in the Governing Body's earlier analysis of the pros and cons of 'co-residence', as going mixed was then known).

15 5,371 students (25 per cent) were pursuing research degrees; 4,250 (19 per cent) were reading for taught Masters degrees.

16 The College's ethos, however, remained predominantly that of an undergraduate community: despite their rising number, the achievements of postgraduates in obtaining their degrees were recorded in the College's *Register* only from 1970, and even then they quickly disappeared, only to become a regular item after an absence of 20 years. Graduate Freshers were listed in the *Register* as their own category from 1992. MCR Presidents published their own reports in the *Register* alongside their JCR counterparts only from 1993.

SELECT BIBLIOGRAPHY

Betjeman, John, *An Oxford University Chest*, John Miles, London, 1938

Boase, Charles William, *Register of the Rectors, Fellows and Other Members on the Foundation of Exeter College, Oxford*, Clarendon Press, Oxford, for the Oxford Historical Society, 1894

Buck, Mark, *Politics, Finance and the Church in the Reign of Edward II: Walter de Stapeldon, Treasurer of England*, Cambridge University Press, Cambridge, 1983

Catto, J. I. (ed.), *The History of the University of Oxford*, Vol. I: *The Early Oxford Schools*, Clarendon Press, Oxford, 1984

Davies, E. W. L., *The Out-door-life of the Rev. John Russell, A Memoir*, Richard Bentley & Son, London, 1883

Dickinson, P. L. *'The College Arms'*, Exeter College Association Register 2006

Emmison, F. G., *Tudor Secretary: Sir William Petre at Court and Home*, Longmans, London, 1961

Exeter College Association Register

Farnell, Lewis. R., *An Oxonian Looks Back*, Martin Hopkinson, London, 1934

Garth, John, *Tolkien and the Great War: The Threshold of Middle-earth*, HarperCollins, London, 2011

Lodel, M. D. and Salter, H. E. (eds), *The Victoria History of the County of Oxfordshire*, Vol. III (chapter on 'Exeter College' by R. W. Southern, pp. 107–18), Oxford University Press, Oxford, for the Institute of Historical Research, 1954

Maddicott, John, lecture on Walter de Stapeldon given in Hong Kong in November 2009. Dr Maddicott expands on Stapeldon's career in his forthcoming book: *Founders and Fellowship: The Early Years of Exeter College, Oxford 1314–1592*, to be published in 2014 by Oxford University Press

Oxford Dictionary of National Biography, Oxford University Press, Oxford, 2004–13

Preston, Matthew, 'The Undergraduate Body of Exeter College, Oxford: 1801–1900', Final Honours school thesis in Ancient and Modern History, 1994 (in the College Library)

The Proceedings of the British Academy 65, pp. 573–86 (obituary of Dacre Balsdon by Peter Brunt, British Academy, London, 1979)

Rowlands, Guy, 'Scholarship and Sleaze', Exeter College Association Register 1997, pp. 58–9

Scott, George Gilbert, *Personal and Professional Recollections*, Sampson Low, Marston, Searle and Rivington, London, 1879

The Stapeldon Magazine

Stride, William John Francis Keatley, *Exeter College, Oxford* (University of Oxford College Histories), F. E. Robinson & Co., London, 1900

Topliffe, Lorise, *Exeter College Library*, Exeter College Association Register 2000, pp. 46–54

Tyack, Geoffrey, 'Gilbert Scott and the Chapel of Exeter College, Oxford', *Architectural History 50*
Oxford: An Architectural Guide, Oxford University Press, Oxford, 1998

Watson, Andrew G. A., *A Descriptive Catalogue of the Medieval Manuscripts of Exeter College, Oxford*, Oxford University Press, Oxford, 2000

ACKNOWLEDGEMENTS

The Rector is indebted to her co-editor, Hannah Parham, and
to John Maddicott and Christopher Kirwan for their invaluable
editorial support and contributions to this book. She would also like
to thank the other main contributors: Chris Ballinger, Joanna Bowring,
Georgina Dennis (née Pelham), Christopher Fletcher, John Garth,
Katrina Hancock, Stephen Hearn, Oswyn Murray, David Trendell,
David Vaisey, Chris Waters, Gerald Wells; and Lucy Freeman Sandler,
for sharing her recent research on the Bohun Psalter.

The Rector would like to record her thanks to the following
alumni and students, who were generous in providing articles,
memories, photographs and ephemera, and who supported the
project in a variety of ways. Unfortunately, for reasons of space
not all submissions could be included.

Martin Amis (1968, English)

Carol Amos (née Stainton) (1980, Physiological Sciences)

Leopold J. Antelme (1948, Jurisprudence)

Jared Armstrong (1948, Music)

John Ashworth (1956, Chemistry)

Paul Atyeo (1947, Literae Humaniores)

Nicolas Banister (1947, Forestry)

Sir Roger Bannister (1946, Physiological Sciences)

Lisa Barber (Daughter-in-law of Rector Barber, 1943–56)

Dick Barlow (1943, Chemistry)

Correlli Barnett CBE (1948, Modern History)

John Barry (1948, Jurisprudence)

Jim Baynard-Smith (1949, PPE)

William S. Beattie (1947, Modern History)

Alan Bennett (1954, Modern History)

The Revd John Benton (1945, Theology)

Rodney Bligh (1964, Geology)

Paul Bolitho (1948, Modern History)

John Bury (1948, Jurisprudence)

David Carey (1938, PPE)

Reeta Chakrabarti (1984, English and French)

Rufus Churcher (1950, Forestry)

Benjamin Clayton (2010, PPE)

Richard Coggins (1947, Modern History)

Gerald Coombe (1943, Jurisprudence)

Neil Cooper (1955, Literae Humaniores)

John Creighton (1950, Agri-Economics)

Geoffrey Dawe (1950, Modern History)

George de Voil (2011, Music)

Douglas (Bobby) Dennis (1930, PPE)

Patric Dickinson (1969, Modern History)

Christopher Doidge (1966, Modern Languages)

Ian Downing (1955, PPE)

John Drewett (1949, Jurisprudence)

Michael Dryland (1944, Jurisprudence)

Harry Eccles (1954, Modern Languages)

Bedrick Eisler (1946, Chemistry)

John Field Evans (1949, Jurisprudence)

Graham Falconer (1950, Modern Languages)

Keith Ferris (1948, Medicine)

David R. Firth (1950, Medicine)

Michael Frankl (1972, Modern Languages)

Eleanor Franzen (2010, English)

Paul Gittins (1964, English)

Sir James Gowans (Staines Medical Research Fellow 1955–60)

Michael Green (1949, Literae Humaniores)

Terence John Harvey (1944, Jurisprudence)

Roy Holden (1943, Modern History)

Dennis Holman (1949, Modern History)

Michael Horniman (1943, Modern History)

John Hughes (1950, PPP)

Colin Hunter (1944, Modern History)

Frank H. H. King (1949, Rhodes Scholar, PPE)

John Laity MBE (1943, English)

Michael Lesslie (2003, English)

Siran Li (2011, Mathematics)

Raymond Lloyd (1935, Engineering Science)

Peter Marsh (1949, Modern History)

David McMaster (1948, Geography)

John F. W. McOmie (1939, Chemistry)

Harold Merskey (1946, Psychology and Physiology)

Ian Michaelson-Yeates (1948, PPE)

Peter Milton (1945, Literae Humaniores)

Michael Nassim (1961, Physiological Sciences)

Joseph Nye (1958, Rhodes Scholar, PPE)

Norman Oliver (1950, Physics)

Brian L. D. Phillips (1948, Physiological Sciences)

John Pollard (1946, Greek Religion)

Michael Preston (1964, Literae Humaniores)

Philip Pullman (1965, English)

James Riddiough (1981, Modern Languages)

Ernest Roe (1939, Literae Humaniores)

John Roper (1953, PPE)

Alan Russett (1949, Modern History)

Peter Ryan (1951, Modern History)

Nigel Salmon OBE (1960, Physics)

John Saunders (1947, Modern History)

Derek Sawyer (1948, Modern Languages)

Robert Shaw (1951, Agriculture)

Christopher Sheward (1949, Jurisprudence)

John Shobbrook (1956, Geography)

David Shorney (1951, Modern History)

Robert Smith (1948, Modern History)

Roy Somerset (1945, Modern History)

Nick Stokes (1966, Modern History)

Imogen Stubbs (1979, English)

Robin Taylor (1967, English)

Murray Tobias (1961, Jurisprudence)

Nicholas Thomas (1947, Modern History)

Stansfield Turner (1947, Rhodes Scholar, PPE)

Denis Vandervelde (1952, Jurisprudence)

Stanley Walker (1947, Chemistry)

Robin Wallace (1955, Medicine)

Ken Waller (1957, PPE)

George Weld-Blundell, father of Joe (2011, Engineering Science)

Jan Weryho (1952, Persian)

Thomas Weston (1945, Literae Humaniores)

Richard Wheway (1950, PPE)

James White (1962, Modern History)

Henry Will (1950, PPE)

Rex Williams (1948, PPE)

Richard E. Yeo (1942, Modern History)

LIST OF SUBSCRIBERS

This book has been made possible through the generosity of the following subscribers

AM = Associate Member
DFO = Distinguished Friend of Oxford
EF = Emeritus Fellow
F = Fellow
Fr = Friend
FF = Former Fellow
FL = Former Lecturer
FS = Former Staff
HF = Honorary Fellow
L = Lecturer
S = Staff
VS = Visiting Student
W = Williams-Exeter Programme
(Year) = Non-matriculating entry year

Felicity Abbott	2009
Ben Abdoo	2010
Stephen Adam	1965
A. K. Addison	1964
Peter Agius	1971
Ivor Agyeman-Duah DFO	Fr
Sajid Ajmeri	1990
Chris Albiston	1972
Richard Alderson	1964
James G. Aldige IV	2003
Professor Gursel Alici	1990
Christopher Allen	1964
Miranda Allen	1994
Norman G. Allen	1957
Brittany Allesandro	2012
Andrew Allner	1972
Christopher Allner	1979
Leonie Amarasekara	2010
Dr Phil Ambler	1981
Carol Amos (née Stainton)	1980
Uday Raj Anand	2009
Keith Anderson	1963
Stewart Anderson	1958
Dr Malcolm J. Andrews	1977
Andy Anson	1983
Leopold Antelme	1948
Dr James Appleyard	1954
Christopher Archer-Lock	1982
Philip Archer-Lock	1984

Dr Simon Ardeman	1949
Professor David M. Armstrong	
	1952 HF
J. R. Armstrong	1962
Jared Armstrong	1948
Christopher Arnold	2003
Dr Richard Arnold	1956
James Arthur	2003
Georges D. L. Ascione	1974
Frank C. Ashby	1943
John Ashdown	1986
Stewart Ashurst	1964
Sir John Ashworth	1956 HF
Georgia Aspinall	2009
Richard Astle	1983
Daniel Robert Edward Atkin	2001
Nicolas Atkins	1993
The Very Revd James E. Atwell	1965
Paul Atyeo	1947
Nick Avery	1980
David Badcock	1964
John Badcock	1958
Chris Bailey	1979
Robin Bailey	1964
George Bainbridge	2008
Alexandra Baker	2009
Walter Baker	1949
Joy P. Baker Griffin	1996
John Baldock	2010
Emily Ball	2005
Dr C. Ballinger	F
Mark Ballman	1976
Nicolas Banister	1947
Dr Lisa Barber, in honour of her late husband, Giles Barber, son of Rector Barber	
Igor N. Barilik	2011
Aarif Barma	1978
Matthew J. C. Barnes	1979
Correlli Barnett	1948
Greig Barr	1936 Rector, HF
Alex Barrett	2009
Hugh Barrett	1956
Renny Barrett	1988
Samuel Barrow	2010
Luke Bartlett	1994

Graham Bartram	1964
Marcus John Bartram	2002
Christopher Bates	2008
Adam Baxter	2011
The Revd Dr Anthony Baxter	1962
Jim Baynard-Smith	1949
Canon John Bearpark	1956
William Beattie	1947
John Beck and Lucy Baker	
	1983, 1985
Stephen J. Bedford	2007
Robin M. Beechey	1956
Professor John L. Bell	1962
Jonathan B. Bengtson	1992
Bill Bentley	1952
Eric Bergbusch	1957
Professor Ed Berman MBE	1962
Sally Berris (née Willers)	1994
Dr Dominic Berry	1983
D. J. Best	1958
Michael Bevington	1972
Shom Bhattacharya	1971
J. M. Bickerdike	1953
Rachel Billinge	1981
Roger Billings	1955
Andrew John Bissette	2010
Theodor Björkmo	2012
Ole Black	1972
Christina Blacklaws	1985
Robin Blades	1983
Neil Blair	1986
Rebecca Bland	1997
R. C. Blayney	
Alexandra Bleasdale	2011
Russ Blenkinsop	1976
Thomas M. Bloomfield	2008
Joseph Bluck	2011
Margaret Blunden	
Ian Kenneth Boardman	1984
Owen R. Boger	2000
Paul Bolitho	1948
Natalie Bollinger	1998
David H. W. Bolton	1953
Hugh Bostock	1962
John Boulter	1954
Godfrey Bowles	1955

Martyn Bracewell	FL
Ian Bradbury	1979
Reg H. Braddon	1948
Michael Bradley	1964
Anthony Brailsford	1965
Ian Brammer	1956
Dr Mario Brandhorst	1997
Bill Branson	1963
Linda Bray	1989
Georgina Brittain	1987
Nigel Brotherton	1972
Dr C. P. Brough	2001
Adrian Brown	1949
Henry Brown	1967
Michael Brown	1990
Patrick Brown	1960
Craig Bruce	2006
Anton Buckoke	1956
Michael K. Budd	1954
Larry Donald Budge	1961
Rip Bulkeley	1961
Ian Bunting	1954
Andrew Bunting	2012
Dr Mark T. Burchell	1982
Professor R. A. Burchell	1960
Emily R. R. Burdett	2008
Eleanor Burnett	S
Dr and Mrs James A. Burns	
Xandra Burns	2010
Kenelm O. L. Burridge	1946
Dr Richard Burton	1957
John Edward Bury	1948
Robert Lester Bush	2011
Nick Butland	1974
Edward Butler	2006
Sarah Butler	2006
Edward Bygott	1953
Xiao Yun Cai	2006
Frances Cairncross Rector (2004–14)
Emma Callanan	2011
Fiona Cameron	1992
Stephen Cameron	1977
Joseph Camm	2008
D. J. Camp	1973
Hugh Campbell QC	1962
Peter James Campion	1944

Nick Campsie	1993	Ian Cooper	1968	Douglas Charles Dennis	1933	Peter J. Farmer	1999
David Cannon	1973	John Cooper	1940	Georgina Dennis	1988	Patricio Farrell	2010
Sebastian Carballo	2002	Martin Cooper	1978	Jon Devaney	1997	John Fassnidge	1968
Bruce Carnegie-Brown	1978	Neil Cooper	1955	Rohan Dey	2011	Bernabe Francis Feria	1971
Professor John Carrick	1969	Marshall Corwin	1972	Abigail Dickens	2007	Michelle Fernandes	2008
M. G. Carter	1959	Professor Peter Coss	EF	Patric Dickinson	1969	Paola Ferrari	2009
Daniel Cashman	2008	Charles Cotton	1965	Chris Digby	1982	Ian Field	1985
Kate Cashman	2008	Helen Cottrell	1997	Alison Dight	2002	Robert Field	1973
Keith Cassidy	1958	Martin Couchman OBE FRSA	1966	Eve Dimery	2012	Stephanie Fielding	1995
Kate Cato	1983	Peter R. Coulling	1967	In memory of Ashley James Dixon		Sandie Fillingham	1983
Tim Cato	1980	Pete Coulson	1972		1949	Jonathan Finn	1985
Susanna R. Cerasuolo	2012	Robert Coulson	1966	Benjamin Joseph Dobson	2012	Michael L. Firth	2006
Simon Chadwick	1974	Andrew Coulton	1979	Nicholas and Jennifer Dobson		Peter Fisher	1952
Simon Chadwick	1982	Emma Cousin	2004	Christopher Doidge	1966	H. N. W. Fletcher	1942
Graham Chainey	1965	Clive Cousins	1967	Emily Dolmans	2011	William Flett	1962
James Champness	2002	Michael Cousins	1965	Jennifer Donnellan	2005	Peter Flippant	1980
Dr Sumit Chanda	1976	Henry G. Coutanche	1955	Gareth Downing	2010	Karen Fogden (née Broadbent)	1990
Kai Yue Charm	2009	Sophie Cowen	2009	Ian Downing	1955	Ben Fox	1997
Emeritus Professor J. A. Chartres		Matthew Adam Cox	2004	Christopher Drake	1975	Keith R. Fox	1973
	1963	Tom Coy	2011	John Drewett	1949	Jeremy Fox-Geen	1992
Mark S. Chatterton	1976	Simon John Craig	1992	Cornelia Drutu Badea	F	Michael Frankl	1972
Alan X. Chen	2010	James E. Craven	2010	M. H. Dryland	1944	Eleanor Franzen	2010
Christopher Cheung	2012	Dr S. M. Cretney	EF	Richard du Parcq	1961	Joseph Fraser	2005
Serene Chew	2005	Katherine Croft	2008	Richard Dudley	1989	Andrew Freedman	2004
Tiffany Chezum	2010	The Honourable Thomas		Elizabeth A. Duffey	1992	Myriam Frenkel	2009
David Ching	2005	A. Cromwell	1976 HF	David J. V. Dumas	1977	John Frood	1963
Christopher Chinn	1985	Roger Croucher	1956	Michael L. Dumelie	2006	Benjamin Frost	
Dr Mudasser Chowdhury		A. D. B. Crumpton-Taylor	2006	Alex Dundas	1994	Rachel Frost	
Roman Cizdyn	1972	Brian Cunningham	1957	Peter Dunkley	1953	Ianthe Fry	2010
Donna M. Clark	1994	Clark E. Cunningham	1957	Cai Durbin	2007	Eddie Fu	2010
Amy Clarke	2000	Graham G. Curtis	1967	Peter Dutton	1953	Sarah Fuller (née Ibbotson)	1990
Dr Chris Clarke	1983	Sir Richard Curtis QC	1954	Raymond Dwek	EF	John Fulton	1968
Dr Simon J. Clarke	F	Megan Daffern	1998	Andrew Dyson	1975	Professor Michael Furmston	1953
Colin Clowes	1951	Chris Danilewicz	1977	George Eason	2012	Elizaveta Futerman	2012
Emma Cochrane	2003	Karen Darnton (née Thackery)	1992	Dr Rodney Edrich JP	1969	Mark Gadsden	1975
Tom Cochrane	2001	Santosh Das	2012	Gareth Edwards	1976	Stephen Gale-Batten	1972
William Kenward Cochrane	2004	Sandrey Date	1962	Lorna Edwards (née Shaddick)	2004	Lindsay A. Gallagher	2000
Joseph R. Coelho	1995	Gemma Davey	2001	Claire Eeles	1988	Clive Gallier	AM
Alan Cogbill	1970	Russell M. Davidson	1978	Bedrick Eisler	1946	Penny Gammage	
Andrew M. Coggins	1964	Christopher Davies	1981	Guy Elliott	1974	Russell Gammon	2005
Richard Coggins	1947	Colin Davies	1967	Liz Elmhirst	1995	John W. Gann	1952
Sir Ronald Cohen	1964 HF	Huw Alban Davies	1966	Stefan Elrington	(2007) W	Ralph Garbett	1963
Emmet Coldrick	2002	Rowland Davies	1945	Dr Walter Eltis	1953 EF	Rowan Gardner	1986
Tony Cole	1960	Sian N. Davies	2012	Jonathan Emerson	1972	Russell St John Gardner	1976
M. J. Coleman	1979	Timothy Davies	2010	Chloe Feldman Emison	2010	Kristian J. Garner	1994
Nicholas Coleman	1953	Gabriella C. Davis	2009	Dr Karsten Engelberg	1976	Ian Gatenby	1961
Richard Collett-White	2011	Phil Davis	1991	Eric Engler	2004	Jason Georgatos	2001
William Collier	2001	Stephen Dawson	1973	R. A. F. Eustace	1961	Jonathan Harry George	1997
Jackson Collins	1988	Professor Robert J. Day	1952	His Honour J. F. Evans QC	1949	Andras Gergely	1996
James Collins	2012	Charles de Bourcy	2008	Kate Evans (née Redfern)	1993	Philip Alexander Gerken	2007
Peter Collins	1970	George R. F. de Voil	2011	Olivia Evans (née Crowther)	1997	Nicholas Paul Gerrard	1976
Cliff Collis	1983	Mrs Paul de Voil		Peter N. Evans	1954	The Revd Roger Gilbert	1966
Richard Condon	1962	Estelle A. Dehon	2001	Mark Evens	1972	Oliver James Gillespie	1990
Matthew Ryan Conroy	2009	David Delameillieure	2003	Chloe Evenson	2010	Cosima Clara Gillhammer	(2010) VS
Sarah Victoria Cook	2009	The Revd S. B. H. Delves Broughton		Professor Graham Falconer	1950	Charles Gillott	1978
His Honour Gerald Coombe	1943		1953	R. A. Falle	1959	Richard Gilman	1947
David Cooper	2003	Nick Denman	1978	Dr A. J. Farmer	F	Jon Gisby	1987

M. R. H. Gittins	1956	Richard Harrison	1973
Paul Gittins	1964	Robert Harrison	1982
Ian A. Glen	1991	Stephen Harrison	1965
L. Glye Hodson	1950	The Revd Mark Hatcher	1974
John Gold	1957	Alan Hatwell	1956
David S. Goldbloom	1975	John Hawkes	1964
Julian Goldsmith	Fr	The Hon Justice K. M. Hayne	
Andrew Goldsworthy	1980		1969 HF
Andrea Gomes da Silva	1990	Bob Haynes	1980
Dr David Gooch	1969	Beverley Head	1979
Tom Goode	1961	Christopher Paul Headdon	1975
Glen Skiles Goodman	2004	Alan Heald	1982
P. Gopalan	1996	Dr Matthew Hedges	1994
Reginald Gorczynski	1966	Philippe Hein	1959
Dr Bill Gordon	1959	Timothy Hele	2007
John Goslin	1956	Maggie Henderson-Tew	2012
Professor Hugh Gough	1962	Ray Hennessy	1956
Jonathan Gough	1986	Bryony Henry	2011
Jeremy C. W. Gould	2001	The Revd John Henstridge	1952
Sir James Gowans	1947 HF	J. J. Herbert	1981
Sarah A. Graham	2001	Jenny Herbert	1979
James Grant	2000	Benjamin Herd	2012
Professor John M. Gray	1967	Roman Herman	(2004) W
J. W. Grayson	1971	Christopher Herrick	1961
Anthony Green	1979	William Hesselmann	2011
E. M. B. Green	1949	Gerald Hewertson-Tisdall	1959
David Greenwood	1972	Phillip Hewett	1943
Huw Griffiths	1988	Philip Heycock	1960
Dr Mike Griffiths	1969	George Heywood	1999
Bruce Gripton	1978	Martin Hibbert	1987
David Groom	1969	Ian Higgins	1960
David Grosser	2012	Katherine Higgins	2007
Kate Grove	S	Steve Higgins	1979
The Rt Revd George Hacker	1949	Mark Higgs	1998
Richard Hackett	1969	Marc-Xavier Chivot Highton	AM
Ursula Hackett	2006	Samuel Hillman	2012
David Hadden	1965	Dr Brian Hillyard	1967
C. I. Hall	1993	Alan Hing	1965
Geoff Hall	1971	Michael Hinman	1968
Gordon Halliday	1956	Malcolm Hitchings	1968
Peter Halliwell	1966	Sam Hitchings	2007
Stewart Hamilton	1972	Janet W. Y. Ho	2003
Catriona and Mike Hammer	1985	Peter Hobbs	1959
Chris Hancock	1986	Philip Hobday	1999
David Hancock	1998	Emma Hodgson	2011
Katrina Hancock (née Beadle)	1998 F	Adam Hogg	1962
Sarah Hand	2007	Patrick Bart Holaday	
Dave Handley	1991	David Holgate QC	1974
Richard Hannah	1975	A. J. Holland	1965
Alistair Hanson	2007	Ian Hollands	1953
W. J. Hare	1982	Sir James Holman	1965
Ian Harmer	1965	Jorn Holmgren	
Graham Harper	1986	Chris Holroyd	1964
Anthony Harpur	1974	Jeremy Holt	1974
Peter Harris	1964	Alex Homan	1992
Colin Harrison	1957	Simon Hooker	1983
David Harrison	1986	Barry Hooks	1965

The Earl of Hopetoun	1987	Colin Joseph	1965
Peter Hopkins	1956	Helen Kaltegartner	2011
Toby Hopkins	2003	Alexei Kalveks	2009
John W. Horn OBE	1952	Pritam Kamat	1989
Dale Rosanne Horne		Paul Kane	1976
Michael Horniman	1943	Nivedita Karthik	2012
M. A. Hoskins	1965	Grigoris Katsiolides	2009
Bradley C. Hosmer	1959	Nikita Kaushal	2012
Ben Houghton	2009	Merata Kawharu	1994
Elizabeth Houghton	2012	James Kay	1988
Mark Houghton-Berry	1976 HF	C. A. M. Keefe (née Wooding)	1979
Christopher House	1999	Graham Keeley	1955
Graham Howell	1972	Andrew Kelion	1985
Brad Hoylman	1989	Sally Kelion	1986
May Huang	2008	Neil Kelleher	2004
Gideon Hudson	1963	Peter J. Kelly	1974
Martin Hughes	1958	Raymond Edward Kendall	1953
Robert Hughes	1961	Dorothy Kennedy	1997
Ronald Alfred Herbert Hunkin	1936	Dr and Mrs Ian Kennedy	
Lady Diana Hunt	Fr	Alison Kent	1984
Colin A. Hunter	1944	Kathryn R. Kent	(1986) W,
David Hunter QC	1966	Director, WEPO (2012–14)	
Sami William Husain	2008	Sir Sydney Kentridge	1946 HF
Oliver Hutchings	2010	O. Kerfoot	1951
Giles Hutchinson	1991	Alasdair G. Kergon	1989
Marguerite Hutchinson	1993	D. Brian Kethero	1953
Frank Hutton-Williams	2011	Teng Lip Khoo	1996
Adam Alexander Hymes	1989	Tanja Khosrawi	1996
Michael Imison	1956	Sanghon Kim	2010
Robert Ingram	1967	B. B. H. King	1962
Grace Jackson	2009	Frank H. H. King	1949
Natasha Jackson	2010	Mark King	1974
Philip Jackson	2007	Ronny and Diana King, who	
Richard Jackson	1971	made my education possible	
William Jackson	1983	Toby King	1986
Jake Jacobs	2011	Brian Kingshott	1959
Professor Michael Jacobs	1960	Nicholas Kirk	1972
Philip Richard James	2007	Andrew Kirkman	1990
David Japes	1952	Henry R. Kloppenburg	1968
Richard Jarvest	1974	Dr Gregory Erland Klyve	1980
Derek Jenkin	1949	B. A. G. Knight	1957
Tim Jenkins	1994	Sang In Know	2011
William P. J. Jensen	Bursar, F	Peter Knowlson	1969
Jolyon Jesty	1964	Rachel J. Knubley	1990
Runqian Jiang	2012	Michael Krantz	1967
Jeri Johnson	F	Sarah Kroloff	2012
Oliver Johnson	2010	Tomasz Krzyzewski	1993
Dr Peter Johnson	F	Professor Roger Kuin	1962
R. W. Johnson	1957	Ruslan Kuzamysh	2012
Stanley Johnson	1959	Dr David Kuzan	1997
Dr Richard H. Johnston	1967	Esther Kwan	2012
Sophie Jolliffe	2012	John Laity MBE	1943
Simon Jolly	2000	The Revd W. Colin Lake	1952
David Jones	1957	Yan Ting Lam	2011
Gwynne Jones	1988	Noel Lamb	1975
Joseph Jones	2009	Richard Lamb	1976
Peter Jones	1978	Zoe Lambourne	2004

Alan J. Lammin	1974	Felicity Mary Jacob Long	2003
Bo Lan	2011	Hannah Long	2009
Richard Landon	1967	Geoff Lovell	1990
Peter Lane	1944	John Lovell	1955
Sarah Lane (née Tringham)	2000	Dominic Low	1958
Aidan Langley	1977	Richard Lowman	1969
Emma Langley	1986	Colin Luke	1964
John Laslett	1954	Dali Ma	2005
Richard Latham	1956	Conall Mac Niocaill	L
John Launchbury	1982	Lara Macdonald	2009
Richard Law	1971	Roger MacNicol	1977
David Lawley	1975	Richard Madden	1976
Ian Lawrie	1970	Anthony Magauran	1964
Philip Le Brocq	1957	Sarah Maggs (née Milliams)	1991
K. J. Le Page	1972	Simon Maggs	1992
Anthony Leach	1962	Yassir Mahmood	1994
Felix Leach	2005	Mark Mahoney	2009
John Leach	1976	Richard Mahoney	HF
John Leadley	1980	Rhys Maliphant	2010
Martyn Leaver	1979	Neil W. Malloy	2007
Peter Lederman QC	1977	Stephen Malone	1958
Georgina Lee	2012	Lina Man	2010
Joyce Lee and Sheung Kai Yung		Alison Manaker (née Ehrlich)	1985
	1986, 1983	Michaela Manning (née Liddle)	1983
Robert J. Lee	2009	Stephen Marfleet	1965
Martin Leech	1981	Jonathan Marks	FS
David Leeks	1985	Alice Marques	2003
John Leighfield CBE	1958	Nico Marsh	2012
Jasmine Leng	2011	Peter Marsh	1949
Rowan Lennox	2012	Arthur F. J. Marshall	1947
John R. Lenton	1966	Dr Andrew C. Martin	1992
Kok Choong Leong	1988	G. P. Martindale	1940
Alex Leuba	2004	Anthony Maton	1985
T. G. D. Levinson	1965	Hannah Matthews	2003
G. Brandon Levy	2005	Benedict May	2011
Alan Lewis	1994	Gordon Harold May	1946
David Lewis	1949	Michael Mayo	2010
Matthew Lewis	2001	Naomi McAllister (née Tasker)	1993
Sally Lewis-Szekely	1979	Rachael McCabe	1995
Paul C. Leyland	1975	Dr James McCaffrey	2001
Michael Lightfoot	1957	Christopher McCallum	2004
Dr Gregory B. S. Lim	2003	Ryan McCarthy	2003
Joanna Lim and Peter Warne		Ardis McClean	1971
	2000, 2000	Sarah McCowie	S
Min Lim	1991	Ian McDonald	1984
Shuyu Lin	2012	Tessa McDonald	1982
David Ll. Lindsay	1968	Gregory McGann	2012
Duncan D. Lindsay	1934	Kate McGibbon	2012
Ian Llewelyn	1976	Ian McGowan	1964
Dr Matt Lloyd	1985	I. M. McGregor	1974
Raymond F. Lloyd	1935	Alasdair McKeane	1971
Susan Lochner	EF	Andrew McLeod	2012
Michael H. Lockton	1953	David McMaster	1948
Hannah Logan	1995	E. C. Meade-King	1969
Daniel Loh	2010	Richard Meddings	1977
Adrian Robin Long	1976	Edward Meinert	2001
Arthur John Long	1938	Kathrine Meloni	1990

John Melotte	1976	Adrian Neil	1961
Gregory Mercier	2008	Katharina Neill	2010
Patrick and Nadya Mercier		Cheriel Hui Yu Neo	2011
Professor Peter Meredith	1953	William Neville	1963
Tom Merren	1958	Peter Newborne	1974
Lt Col (Retd) Charles Messenger		A. Menai Newbould (née West)	1993
	1962	Jeffrey Newman	1960
Ian Michaelson-Yeates	1948	Robert Newman	1967
Lee Mickus	(1988) W	Robert Newnes	2008
Mark Simon Middleton	1989	Roger Newport	1963
James Midwinter	1951	Alan Newton	1975
Birgit Mikus	2009	Hannah K. J. Nicholson	2011
Paul Mildred	1964	Edward Nickell	2011
Andrew Joseph Miles	2008	David Nickoll	(1991) W
John Miller	1975	Edward Nicol	1972
Jonathan Miller	1982	C. B. Nixon	1949
Paul Miller	1957	Philip Nokes	1971
Christine Milligan		Keith Norman	1962
Joe Mills and Family	2011	Lady Norman	
Robert David Milnes	1959	Colin Nunn	1976
Andrew Milton	1980	R. Scott Nycum Jr	1971
Nigel Milton	1990	Paul O'Brien	1974
Peter Milton	1945	Tim O'Brien	1971
Challenger Mishra	2011	Jack O'Mahoney	2011
Mahima Mitra	2008	Rachel O'Neill	2002
Peter Moffatt	1961	Sean O'Sullivan	1992
Dr Vik Mohan	1991	Norman Oliver	1950
William J. Moir	2006	Heston Orchard	1998
Lachlan Molesworth	2012	Canon Richard Orchard	1959
Dr J. M. H. Moll	1960	Alice Osborne	2012
Neil C. A. Monnery	1980	John Oxford	1954
Peter Hills Monroe	1965	Turner Anthony Ozturk	1979
Annabel Monteiro	2012	Barry Packham	1966
George E. Moody	1955	Kenneth Padley	1997
Edward Moores	2006	C. J. F. Painter	1972
Tristan Mora	2012	Jessica Palmarozza	2010
Alexander More	1964	Paul Pamment	2007
Anthony Moreton	1952	W. Eric Pankhurst	1952
Christopher Morgan	2010	Dr A. Parchami	FL
Stephen Moriarty	FF	Brian Park	1953
Yves-Marie Morissette	1973	Adrian Parker	1971
Mark Moroney	1965	Susan Parker (née Wolowacz)	1981
Fred L. Morrison	1961	David Parkin	1967
Dr Benjamin Wilson Mountford		Robert Parkinson	1975
	2008	Mr and Mrs M. Parnell	
Maximilian Mulvany	2009	Timothy Parritt	1982
Philip Munday	S	Imogen Parry	2007
Catherine R. Mundell	1986	J. R. Parsons	1959
Roger Munnings	1969	John Partridge	1954
Kathleen Elizabeth Murphy	2007	Dr Girish D. Patel	1972
Kovthaman Murugaratnam	2009	Andrew Paton	1976
Rebecca Anne Musgrove	2011	Alonso Patron-Perez	2006
Hannah Mycock	2004	Lesley Pattinson	2000
Sajeel Nasar	1997	David G. Pattison	1960
David Nash	1963	Jo Payne	1990
Jerrold Nathan	1952	Paul Paynter	1981
Dr Plamen Natzkoff	1995	Arthur Peacocke	1942 HF

Name	Year	Name	Year	Name	Year	Name	Year
Davina Pearce	2011	Robert Randell	2010	Hugh Rowlinson FCIC	EF	Matthew Sheppee	1990
N. W. G. Pearson	1949	John Ratcliffe	1971	Guy Rowston	1961	C. J. Sheward	1949
Richard S. L. Penn	1957	Philip Ratcliffe	1967	Simon Ruckert	1979	Clare Louisa Shobbrook	1997
James Percival	1985 FL	Jim Rathbone	1972	Sam Rudgard	2006	John Shobbrook	1956
Sam Perkins	2011	Richard J. Rathbone	1964	Roman Rudkowskyj	1976	Dr David Shorney	1951
Dr C. W. Perrett	1974	Jonno Raveney	1990	Professor Carlos Ruiz	EF	David Short	1965
The Revd J. W. B. Perry	1961	Jonathan Rayers	2004	Marie Ruiz		Douglas Shugar	1978
Terry Pethick	1953	Mgr Gordon Read	1967	Mike Runnalls	1962	Stephen Siddall	1961
Trevor Pethick	1979	T. P. Reed	1972	Alan Russett	1949	Dr Robert D. Sider	1956
Professor Philip H. Pettit	1942	Andrew Reekes	1970	John Ryan	2009	Amrit Sidhu-Brar	2012
Ian G. Philip	1956	William J. Reeve	1974	Nicola Sadie	2011	Colin Silk	1958
Dr Brian L. D. Phillips	1948	Brian L. Regan	1952	Elisabeth Sadler	2012	Andrew Sillito	1956
James Phillips	2010	Roger Rehahn	1956	Dr Ned T. Sahin	(1996) W	Alan Simcock	1961
Charles Philpin	1961	Alistair Reid	2007	Aamir Saifuddin	2005	John Simons	EF
Imogen Pierce	2010	Anthony Reid	1995	Adrian Sainsbury	1986	Dr Chris Simpson	1959
Gloria Chung Pilz	1991	Robert Reid	1974	Nigel E. Salmon OBE	1960	Millie Simpson	2011
Andrew Pirie	1959	Aaron Resch	1998	Christopher Salt	1987	Paul Slack	EF
E. R. M. Pitkin	1950	Abi Reynolds (née Bradfield)	2001	Geoff Salt	1975	Christopher Charles Slater	1969
Stephen James Pix	1961	Hugh Reynolds	1977	Richard Salter	1970	Philip Slayton	1965
Simon Pleydell	1976	Tom Reynolds	2001	Herman Tutehau Salton	2007	Professor Peter Sleight	EF
Hee Kim Poh	1981	James Reynoldson	2008	Prajakt Samant	1992	Andrew Martin Smith	1971
Jane Pollard	1984	Alistair Rice	2011	David Sarre	1945	Barry Smith	1974
Anthony Pollington	1954	Candace Rice	2006	Jessica Saul	2008	Charles Smith	1978
Michael Alexander Pontikos	2010	Dr Colin Richards	1951	John Saunders	1947	Ian D. Smith	1974
Adam Popat	2000	Dr David Richards	1962	Derek John Sawyer	1948	J. G. Smith and Mrs H. V. Smith	
David Pope	2006	Ella Richards	2012	Edwin Saxton	1945		1962
Andrew Popham	1974	Guy Richardson	2011	Steffen Schaper	2005	Jeremy Smith	1979
Nigel Portwood	F	James Riddiough	1981	Michael Schofield	1959	Joanna Elizabeth Smith	2004
Charles D. Postles	1985	Richard Riddle	1989	The Revd Nicholas Schofield	1994	Dr Martin Smith	1972
Ian Potts	1962	John Ridley	1984	Joe Schork	1955	Paul Smith	1974
Adrian Powell	1986	Alexandre Rigolet	2012	Peter Schweizer	1977	R. W. Smith	
Andy Powell	1990	Brian Rimmer	1979	Andrew Scott	1998	Robert E. G. Smith	1948
David Powell	2000	Mr and Mrs Leo Ringer	2006	F. A. Scott	1978	T. C. Smith	1971
Graham Powell	1956	Edward Ritchie	1990	Dr Laura Scott-Brown	2006	Thomas Joseph Smyth	2005
Richard Powell Jones	1965	William Rivers	1979	Alan Seager	1955	J. M. Snell	1964
The Revd Dr Brian Powley	1959	D. J. Roaf	EF	Dr David Seamark	1973	Winky Wing So	2009
Dr Terry Powley	1964	Dr Jane Roberts	1984	David Seconde	1959	Jorn Soerink	2007
Costas Prapopulos	1955	Katherine Elizabeth Roberts	2009	Dr David J. Seddon	1974	Adam Solomon	1989
Margaret Elan Preston-Whyte	2011	Carol Robertson	1986	Henry Selby (Inselberg)	1956	Dani Solomon	1989
Eric Pride	1953	Matthew Robinson	1995	Andrew Semple	1991	Robert C. Sopwith	1963
John S. Probert	1948	Janet Becker Rodgers	2012	David and Brenda Semple		Peter Southgate	1951
Ashley Pugh	1951	Raul Rodriguez	2000	Artem Serebrennikov	2011	Robert Sowler	1990
Tom Pugh	2001	David Rodway	1957	Stephen Serpell	1971	Richard Sparks	1970
Lisa Pugh (née O'Shea)	2000	Ernest Roe	1939	J. C. Servan-Schreiber	1934	Dr G. S. (Memo) Spathis	1954
Philip Nicholas Pullman	1965 HF	Dr John H. Rogers	1955	Ian Shackleton	1975	Laura Alice Spence	2012
Roger Pyne	1956	David Rolfe	1949	Peter Shadbolt	1975	Peter Spriddell	1948
Christopher John Pyrah	2011	Arianne Allaire Romney	2006	Mark Shaddick	1975	Dr Brian S. Sproat	1971
Geoff Quest	1957	Giles Rooke	1951	Neeraj Shah	1991	Andrew and Kit Stables	
Thomas Quin	1979	Michael Rose	1953	Eleanor K. Shallow	2012	Rachel Stables	2011
Holly Quinlan	2011	Howard Rosen	1974	J. C. L. Sharp	1960	The Revd Dr Ole Martin Stamnestro	
Mari Rabie	2012	Angus Ross	1960	The Revd David Sharpe	1952		2001
The Revd Patrick Fabian Radcliffe		Arabella Ross-Michaelides	2011	John Shaw	1972	Tessa Stanley-Price	S
	1948	James Rous	1991	Stephen Shea	2004	Violetta Rae Steeples	2010
Anya Radford (née Liversedge)	1994	David Rowe	1959	Neville Sheard	1955	Douglas Stembridge	1975
Michael Ramsbotham	1957	John Rowe	1960	Gareth Shellard	2008	Lydia Stephens	2011
J. D. Ramsbottom	1974	Christopher Rowell	2009	Deepak Kumar Shenoy	1991	Dr Glenn A. Steppler	1979
Jonathan Ramsden	1983	Sir Richard Rowley BT	1978	Erica Sheppard	S	David Stewart	1979

Nicholas J. Stokes 1966
Fr Peter Stone 1953
Sir Kenneth Stowe 1948 HF
Ian Stoyle 1957
Robert Strachan 2009
David Stranger-Jones 2001
Hannah Stranger-Jones (née Green) 2001
David Strudwick 2010
Hal Stuart 1959
John Stuart 2003
Chris Sturdee 1975
Glen Suarez 1981
Jonny Sultoon 1997
Roger Surcombe 1964
Keith Sussemilch 1984
Jenny Sofia Svanberg 2002
Maria Sveidahl 2012
Tristan Swain 1995
Geoffrey W. M. Sweet 1946
Hugh Sweet 1959
Tony Sweet 1973
Richard Swinburne 1954
Andrzej Szkuta 1968
Tse Wen Tai 2001
Rajiv S. Tanna 2003
Cora Tanner
Professor Jared Tanner F
John Tayler 1952
Andrew Taylor 1968
Dr John Taylor 1974
Robin Taylor 1967
Philip Terzian 1976
Professor Adrian L. R. Thomas 1981
E. J. (Jim) Thomas FF
Frank Thomas 1950
Nicholas Thomas 1947
Peter Thomas 1953
Victoria Thomas 2005
Peter M. Thompson 1965
Emma J. Thompson 2001
Peter Thompson Fr
Tony Thomson 1965
Peter Thorley 1964
Arnold Thornton 1961
Simon Thornton 1979
Ian Thrussell 1973
Ronald Tidmarsh 1947
Stephen J. Till 1988
Murray Tobias 1961
H. F. Tolkien 2007
R. I. Tolkien 1974
Nigel Tonkin 1961
Alison Tooth 1989
Lorise C. Topliffe FS
Philip Towler 1987
David Townshend 1988

David Travers 1968
C. N. B. Trigg 1957
Peter William Trinder 1954
Martyn J. Truman
Paul J. Truman 2001
David Tucker 1970
Admiral Stansfield Turner 1947 HF
Michael Turner 2007
Matthew Tye 2009
Abigail Tyer 2011
Lord (Paul) Tyler 1960
Jeremy Tyrer 1981
Andreas C. Uhl 2011
Weng Kuan Un (Josephine Un) Fr
Matt Urhammer 2005
The Revd John Urquhart 1985
Costanza Uslenghi 2010
Philippe G. Vallerand AM
Wilma M. A. van der Slot (1993) VS
Madeleine van Oss 2011
Dr Chris van Zyl 1953
Timothy A. Vanderver Jr 1965
Graham van't Hoff 1980
Dimitris Vayenas 2012
Alfie Vibert 1976
Gabriel Viesca 1995
Erin Wadden 2007
Patrick Wadden 2006
Dr Robert H. Wagstaff 2002
John Wainwright 1962
Jerry Wales 1973
Alice Walker 2007
Andrew Walker 1963
David Walker 1987
George Walker 1960
Peter Walker 1961
Professor Stanley Walker 1947
Dr A. R. G. Wallace 1955
Ken Waller 1957
Toby Wallis 1978
Carly Walsh 2005
Stephen Walsh 1976
Andrew G. N. Walter 1971
Clive N. Walter 1987
Derek E. P. Walter 1966
Julian M. S. Walter 1963
Dr Martin Walter 1964
Peter R. Walters 1963
Adam Ward 2011
Brian Ward 1964
Christopher Ward 1964
Jennifer Ward 1998
Robert Ward 1969
John M. Warden 1982
Dr Eric Warner 1974
Helen Watanabe-O'Kelly FBA EF

Chris Waters
Director, WEPO (2001–04)
Dr R. E. Watkins 1943
Professor Andrew G. Watson 1947
David Watson 1967
Emily Watson 2002
F. A. H. Watson 1949
Helen Watson 1988 F
P. P. Watson 1949
The Revd D. H. Watts 1948
Benjamin Way 1998
Jeffery Wear 1957
Oliver H. Wearing 2009
W. M. Wearne 1948
David M. Webb 1983
Ian Webb 1972
Paul J. Webb 1961
Zander Wedderburn 1955
Robin Weekes 1968
Dr Jamieson Weetman 1999
Alexander Ross Weiss 2012
Krystina Weiss 2011
Barry John Welch 1973
George M. Welch 1953
Jo Welch 1953
Hans Wells-Furby 1953
Laura Beth Welsh 2008
David Welti 1948
Murray Wesson 2001
Ewan West 1978
James West 2011
Imogen West-Knights 2010
Emma Westley (née Molyneaux) 1998
Martin Weston 1965
Thomas Weston 1945
Kate Westwater (née Werran) 1991
Sandy Westwater 1989
Mark Westwood 2008
Henry Wheare
Rector's Lodgings 1956–72
Joan Wheare
Rector's Lodgings 1956–72
Katie Wheare
Rector's Lodgings 1956–72
Philippa Wheare
Rector's Lodgings 1956–72
Tom Wheare
Rector's Lodgings 1956–72
Derek Wheeler 1978
F. H. (Bill) Wheeler 1951
Paul Wheeler 1955
Richard Wheway 1950
Dr J. C. P. White 1983
James A. White 1962
John White 1951
Kathryn V. White 1986

Dr D. A. Whitelock 1954
Dr Kelley Wilder 1997
Dr Brian R. Wilkey 1952
Karim Wilkins 1989
Chris Wilkinson 1985
D. H. Wilkinson
Eric Wilkinson 1954
Simon A. Willbourn 1969
Mark Willder 1989
Professor Peter Willett 1971
Alun Williams 1963
Cat Williams 2005
Claire Williams 1986
Cristyn Williams 1984
Rhidian Williams 1986
Rhodri Williams 1981
Tony Williams 1960
Professor Edwin Williamson F
Lord (David) Williamson 1952 HF
Harry Willis 2009
Stephen Charles Willmott 1968
David Wilson 1963
Michael Wilson 2009
Stephen L. Wilson 1970
Richard Wiltison VS
C. E. Winn 1948
Richard Winn 1950
The Revd Henry Hoyte Winwood 1849
Thomas Henry Ricketts Winwood 1870
Thomas Roger Winwood 1960
Till Wirth 2011
Richard V. Wolfenden 1956
Christopher Wolstenholme 2010
Queenie Kwan-Yee Woo 1997
David Wood 1963
Heather Wood 1991
John R. Wood 1955
Peter Woodbridge 1978
Jane Woodley S
Nicholas Worskett 1982
The Revd Geoffrey J. Wrayford 1958
The Revd Canon Hugh Wybrew FS
Roni Yadlin 2009
Nikki Yeatman S
Jade Yee 2001
Allen Yeh 2002
L. J. Yeo 1974
Matthew Yeowart 2005
John Hardin Young 1975
Justin Young 1972
Dr Carl U. Zachrisson 1965
Marta Zarzecka 2009
Dr Harald Zeller
T. Price Zimmermann 1956
Kenneth Zucker 1955

INDEX